MW00415702

ESPECIALLY FOR

....

FROM

....

DATE

....

DAILY
WISDOM
FOR MEN

2024
• DEVOTIONAL COLLECTION •

BARBOUR
PUBLISHING

Print ISBN 978-1-63609-618-6; 978-1-63609-854-8
Adobe Digital Edition (.epub) 978-1-63609-619-3

Cover Design: Greg Jackson, Thinkpen Design

Published by Barbour Publishing, Inc., 1810 Barbour Drive, Uhrichsville, Ohio 44683, www.barbourbooks.com

Our mission is to inspire the world with the life-changing message of the Bible.

 Member of the
Evangelical Christian
Publishers Association

Printed in China.

WELCOME *to the* 2024 *edition of* DAILY WISDOM FOR MEN!

The theme for this year's *Daily Wisdom for Men* is *take heart.* The word *heart* appears more than one thousand times in the Bible, usually in reference to a person's spiritual, emotional, moral, and intellectual center.

The heart of a man is very important to God, simply because it is the most essential part of our inner being. That is why the Bible says, "Above all else, guard your heart, for everything you do flows from it" (Proverbs 4:23 NIV), and why God commanded His people to "love the LORD your God with all your heart and with all your soul and with all your strength" (Deuteronomy 6:5 NIV).

The inspiration for this year's daily devotionals is taken from each day's scripture readings in our popular "Read through the Bible in a Year Plan," which you can find at the end of this book. It will give you a full context for the verse or verses on which each day's devotional is based.

God wants to grow you into a man whose heart is 100 percent committed to Him and His Word. It is the hope of the men who wrote this year's *Daily Wisdom for Men* devotionals, as well as the people at Barbour Publishing, that God will use your daily Bible reading, as well as the writings in this book, to help make you a man who follows, loves, and obeys God with all his heart.

The Editors

A NEW YEAR'S COMMITMENT

Blessed is the one who does not walk in step with the
wicked or stand in the way that sinners take or sit in the
company of mockers, but whose delight is in the law of
the LORD, and who meditates on his law day and night.

PSALM 1:1–2 NIV

Today is New Year's Day, a day when a man of God can reflect on the good things the Lord has done for him over the past 365 days—and think about what God has taught him through His written Word, the Bible, during that same time period.

January 1 is a day when many well-meaning folks make New Year's *resolutions*, personal promises and goals meant to improve themselves or their station in life. But God calls us Christian men to something much higher—a *commitment* to daily time in the scripture He's given to teach us, encourage us, and admonish us.

Why not purpose in your heart to start your year-long journey of scripture reading today, New Year's Day, by reading today's reading in the "Read through the Bible in a Year Plan", found at the end of this devotional book?

. . . .

Lord God, You have promised that I can find great blessing by
purposefully taking joy and encouragement in Your written
Word. On this, the first day of 2024, I commit myself to spending
daily quality time with You, both in the Word and in prayer.

A PROMISE OF RENEWAL

Then the LORD God said to the serpent, "Because you have done this, you are cursed more than all animals, domestic and wild. You will crawl on your belly, groveling in the dust as long as you live. And I will cause hostility between you and the woman, and between your offspring and her offspring. He will strike your head, and you will strike his heel."

GENESIS 3:14–15 NLT

The devil fired the first shot in his war against this world and against humanity—and he scored a direct hit when Adam and Eve sinned, bringing death, suffering, and destruction into the human experience.

Since that terrible day, Satan has enjoyed his heyday on this earth, and he's still mostly having his way in this world. But his time is short—he knows it, we who search the scriptures know it, and, best of all, God knows it.

Jesus, the one referred to as a woman's "offspring," came to earth to die the horrific death of a common criminal so that our sins could be forgiven so that we could be reconciled to our all-holy Creator. And one day, He will return and make all things new (Revelation 21:5).

Lord Jesus, it can be disheartening to look around me and see the horrible effects of sin on this world. But You promised back in the garden that Jesus would one day destroy the works of the devil. I take comfort and encouragement in that promise.

WHEN GOD BECAME ONE OF US

*Then Jesus went from Galilee to the Jordan River to be baptized
by John. But John tried to talk him out of it. "I am the one who
needs to be baptized by you," he said, "so why are you coming
to me?" But Jesus said, "It should be done, for we must carry
out all that God requires." So John agreed to baptize him.*

MATTHEW 3:13–15 NLT

From the moment the angel Gabriel announced to Mary that she,
a young virgin girl, would miraculously give birth to the Messiah,
everything about Jesus fulfilled God's perfect will for the Savior.
That included His baptism by John in the Jordan River.

Jesus was the one and only perfect man to walk the earth, and yet
He insisted that He undergo baptism, an outward act symbolizing
inward repentance. Jesus wasn't baptized as a symbol of repentance
from sin—this perfect man never sinned in any way (Hebrews 4:15).
Rather, He was baptized so that He could fully identify Himself with
sinners. In a very real way, Jesus became one of us that day.

*Lord Jesus, I am encouraged and overwhelmed at the thought
that You came to earth to live as a man and as God's only Son.
You did both perfectly, down to the very last detail, so that You
could present Yourself as God's perfect sacrifice for the sins
of all humanity. Thank You for all You've done for me.*

TRUE SATISFACTION

Why is everyone hungry for more? "More, more," they say. "More, more." I have God's more-than-enough, more joy in one ordinary day than they get in all their shopping sprees.

PSALM 4:6–7 MSG

Since the moment the devil-in-snake's-clothing spewed out to Eve the words "Did God really say. . ." (Genesis 3:1 NIV), he's been working at double and triple time, trying to persuade men to look to anything and everything for true satisfaction in this life. Since that terrible day, men have consistently looked to the pleasures of this world to find what only God can give them.

From the very beginning, God never intended for us humans to look to anything but Him for purpose, fulfillment, and satisfaction. Nothing—not all the wealth, power, or personal recognition—should come even close to replacing God's "more-than-enough."

Do you ever find yourself desiring or fantasizing about "more"? If so, then take those desires to your heavenly Father, repent if needed, and ask Him to show you in real and tangible ways how He truly is your source of true satisfaction.

. . . .

Heavenly Father, while most men seek satisfaction and fulfillment in the pleasures and comforts of this world, I choose to seek You and love You above all things life here on earth has to offer. You are and will always be my more-than-enough. Thank You for who You are and all You do for me.

BEING LIGHT IN A DARK WORLD

"You are the light of the world. A town built on a hill cannot be hidden. Neither do people light a lamp and put it under a bowl. Instead they put it on its stand, and it gives light to everyone in the house. In the same way, let your light shine before others, that they may see your good deeds and glorify your Father in heaven."

MATTHEW 5:14–16 NIV

It's not difficult to see that this world is covered in spiritual darkness. We see the darkness in news reports, in entertainment media, and in countless other places. If we're not careful, this world's darkness can leave us feeling discouraged, even overwhelmed.

Jesus didn't take us to heaven at the very moment we were saved. Instead, He allowed us to stay in this dark, hurting world, giving us this special assignment: *you* be the light this world needs to see.

You needn't spend all your time lamenting this world's darkness and the effect it has on all of humanity. Instead, you can choose to let your light shine so that others can see the power of Jesus to save and transform.

*Lord Jesus, the world I live in is shrouded in darkness.
I see its terrible effects every day. Encourage and empower
me to let Your light shine from within me every day.*

A GOD OF MERCY

*Lord, do not rebuke me in your anger or discipline
me in your wrath. Have mercy on me, Lord, for I am
faint; heal me, Lord, for my bones are in agony.*
PSALM 6:1–2 NIV

Psalm 6 is a somewhat mysterious plea for God's mercy, mysterious because it's not clear why David feels as though he's under God's heavy hand of discipline. What is clear is that David was miserable and desperately needed to hear from his God.

Perhaps you can relate. Perhaps you've had that sense of inner turmoil, that feeling that something isn't quite right between you and the Lord. When you're in that place, it's good to do as David did: cry out to God for mercy.

By the end of Psalm 6, David feels the deep sense of inner joy of a man who is assured that his gracious, forgiving God has heard and acted on his prayer for mercy: "The Lord has heard my cry for mercy; the Lord accepts my prayer. All my enemies will be overwhelmed with shame and anguish; they will turn back and suddenly be put to shame" (vv. 9–10 NIV).

. . . .

Lord, thank You for Your love and mercy. I need both every day. I never want to take this part of Your character for granted. Instead, I will thank You for it each and every day, for without Your desire to reach down and extend Your hand of mercy, I would be forever sunk.

PRAYING TO A LOVING HEAVENLY FATHER

*"When you pray, don't babble on and on as the Gentiles do.
They think their prayers are answered merely by repeating their
words again and again. Don't be like them, for your Father
knows exactly what you need even before you ask him!"*

MATTHEW 6:7–8 NLT

What does the word *prayer* mean to you? In today's scripture passage, Jesus taught His followers what prayer should be by first telling them how *not* to pray. Much like today, nonbelievers thought that if they simply repeated their prayers over and over, their pagan gods would hear them and answer.

Jesus warned against that kind of praying for those who followed Him and therefore knew God as their heavenly Father.

God is your Creator, your Lord, and your source of all good things, including your eternal salvation. He's all those wonderful things, but He's so much more. He's your tender, loving Father in heaven who has adopted you into His eternal family and made you the object of His love and kindness. As such, He wants you to connect heart-to-heart with Him every day as you speak with Him in a real and intimate way.

. . . .

*Thank You, Father, both for hearing my prayers and for knowing
better than I do what I need. May my prayers always be from my heart
to Yours and never formal repetition. You are my loving Father, and
I want to communicate with You in a very real, very personal way.*

OUR AMAZING CREATOR FATHER

*When I look at the night sky and see the work of your
fingers—the moon and the stars you set in place—
what are mere mortals that you should think about
them, human beings that you should care for them?*

PSALM 8:3–4 NLT

If you want to feel very small and insignificant, go far from city lights
on a clear, moonless night and look up and observe the incredible
multitude of heavenly bodies—then consider that what you can see
represents a tiny fraction of what's "out there."

When David looked up into the night sky, he was amazed at what
he could see—though he had no idea what else God had created and
placed beyond what appeared to him. But when he considered that
the same God who created those things simply by speaking them
into existence loved him, cared for him, and thought about him, he
was *in awe*.

God's creation is so vast that even the most brilliant minds can't fully
comprehend its size. But God's love—His love *for you*—is even bigger.

*Father in heaven, I am astounded at the thought of the vast,
complex universe You created—just by speaking it into existence.
Your creation is far beyond my ability to comprehend. Even more
amazing to me is that a God who has the power to create such things
so deeply loves an insignificant man like me. Thank You for Your love.*

GOD KEEPS HIS PROMISES

God visited Sarah exactly as he said he would; God did to Sarah what he promised: Sarah became pregnant and gave Abraham a son in his old age, and at the very time God had set. Abraham named him Isaac. When his son was eight days old, Abraham circumcised him just as God had commanded.

GENESIS 21:1–4 MSG

God had made Abraham and Sarah—the eventual father and mother of the Hebrew nation—an incredible promise: they would have a son who would be a great blessing, to them and to the entire world.

God didn't fulfill His promise exactly nine months after He first made it. Abraham and Sarah had to wait some time before He gave them Isaac. But "at the very time God had set"—when Abraham was an old man—God miraculously kept His promise.

God keeps 100 percent of His promises, 100 percent of the time. Always has, always will. He may not do it when you think He will—or when you think He should. But you can count on Him to come through for you at what He knows is the perfect time and in the perfect way.

Loving Father, I take great encouragement in knowing that You are a God that can be trusted to keep every promise You've made—even ones that seem impossible. When my sense of trust in You wanes, remind me through Your Word just how trustworthy You really are.

HEARING AND DOING

"Therefore everyone who hears these words of mine and puts them into practice is like a wise man who built his house on the rock. The rain came down, the streams rose, and the winds blew and beat against that house; yet it did not fall, because it had its foundation on the rock."

MATTHEW 7:24–25 NIV

The apostle James enjoined followers of Jesus, "Do not merely listen to the word, and so deceive yourselves. Do what it says" (James 1:22 NIV). James went on to warn that those who hear but fail to obey God's Word are "like someone who looks at his face in a mirror and, after looking at himself, goes away and immediately forgets what he looks like" (1:23–24 NIV).

Jesus' words for the disobedient were more dire: "Everyone who hears these words of mine and does not put them into practice is like a foolish man who built his house on sand" (Matthew 7:26 NIV). That house, He said, would come crashing down and be swept away when life's storms hit.

God's Word is faithful and true. So make sure to not just hear it but obediently put it into practice every day.

. . . .

Lord Jesus, You stated that You spoke only the words Your Father in heaven gave You to speak and did only the deeds He commanded You to do. For that reason, I can trust every word You spoke and apply everything You said to my daily walk with You.

HE'S ALWAYS THERE FOR YOU

*Why do You stand afar off, O Lord? Why do
You hide Yourself in times of trouble?*

PSALM 10:1 SKJV

Even the most devoted followers of Christ have gone through seasons when they can identify with the sentiments in today's scripture verse. Whether their feelings of distress are the result of severe medical issues, crushing financial issues, or the heartbreak over a damaged or broken relationship, things can feel lonely when we're stressed out and suffering.

But we believers can take heart in the truth that God is faithful and that He loves us and will stick by us, even when we're not at our best spiritually or emotionally.

When you're enduring difficulties in this life—and Jesus promised that you will (John 16:33)—you may feel as though God has hidden Himself, as though He's not paying attention. That's when you should cling with all your might to this amazing promise: "Never will I leave you; never will I forsake you" (Hebrews 13:5 NIV; also see Deuteronomy 31:6).

. . . .

Faithful God, when I'm going through difficulties, I find it easy to relate to the psalmist's words in today's scripture verse. You know when I feel as though You're far off, as though You are hiding Yourself from me. In those times, quietly remind me that Your Word promises that You will never leave nor forsake those who love You.

THE GOD WHO HEARS

You, LORD, hear the desire of the afflicted; you encourage them, and you listen to their cry, defending the fatherless and the oppressed.
PSALM 10:17–18 NIV

Psalm 10 begins with the distressed cry of a man whose feelings tell him that his God has left him alone to deal with his troubles, who doesn't seem to even notice that he is in distress and suffering.

The rest of the Bible shows us that the psalmist's feelings of abandonment are just that—feelings, and nothing more. Scripture promises over and over that God is always with those who love Him, even when it doesn't *feel* like it.

But today's scripture passage takes these promises another wonderful step further. God not only promises to be with us forever and always; He promises to hear us when we call out to Him in our affliction, when we're hurting, when we need encouragement.

There's nothing this world or our spiritual enemies can throw at us that God doesn't understand—or that He isn't big enough or compassionate enough to handle...when we simply call out to Him.

. . . .

Lord God, strengthen and encourage me as I rest in the rock-solid truth that You hear me when I cry out to You. While You may not rescue me immediately when I call out, You will always deliver me in Your perfect way and perfect timing. Thank You!

YOUR SINS ARE FORGIVEN

"So I will prove to you that the Son of Man has the authority on earth to forgive sins." Then Jesus turned to the paralyzed man and said, "Stand up, pick up your mat, and go home!"
MATTHEW 9:6 NLT

Jesus shook up the spiritual sensibilities of some Jewish religious teachers when He said to a paralyzed man brought to Him for healing, "Be encouraged, my child! Your sins are forgiven" (Matthew 9:2 NLT). *That's blasphemy!* they thought. *Does He think He's God?*

Had Jesus not been who He truly was—the Son of God sent to earth to bring forgiveness of sins to humankind—these religious teachers would have been absolutely correct in labeling Him a blasphemer. But He was who He said He was, so He demonstrated His power and authority for all to see when He said to the paralyzed man, "Stand up, pick up your mat, and go home!"

As God in the flesh, Jesus had authority to do what God alone can do, namely forgive sin. So be encouraged! Your sins are forgiven!

. . . .

Lord Jesus, thank You that You still have the power and authority to forgive sin—my sin. I first came to You as a spiritual cripple, a man completely unable to so much as approach You. But because of Your great love for me, You reached down and healed me and forgave my sins. Your love is amazing!

REMAINING FAITHFUL

*Help, LORD, for no one is faithful anymore; those who are loyal have
vanished from the human race. Everyone lies to their neighbor;
they flatter with their lips but harbor deception in their hearts.*
PSALM 12:1–2 NIV

In a biblical scene depicting an utterly disheartened man hiding out
in a cave, the persecuted prophet Elijah lamented to his God, "I have
been very zealous for the LORD God Almighty. The Israelites have
rejected your covenant, torn down your altars, and put your prophets
to death with the sword. I am the only one left, and now they are
trying to kill me too" (1 Kings 19:14 NIV).

In today's scripture passage, David voices a very similar lament,
complaining that no one practices faithfulness or loyalty and that
everyone's mouths and hearts are filled with lies and deceit.

Perhaps you can identify with the words of Elijah and David.
Maybe you look around you and it seems as though you are alone in
loving the Lord and clinging to the truth of His Word. If so, don't be
discouraged. Instead, go to the Lord and ask Him for strength to cling
to Him and His Word—even when it seems like you're the only one.

*Lord God, I live in a world where it seems that there are very few
who value Your Word or desire to cling to speaking its truth. But I
know that You want to encourage me to be light in this dark world.*

GODLY SELF-AWARENESS

*Jacob prayed, "O God of my grandfather Abraham, and God of my father, Isaac—O L*ORD*, you told me, 'Return to your own land and to your relatives.' And you promised me, 'I will treat you kindly.' I am not worthy of all the unfailing love and faithfulness you have shown to me, your servant."*

GENESIS 32:9–10 NLT

The biblical patriarch Jacob was not a good man—at least early in his life. He wanted what he wanted, and he showed himself willing to lie, cheat, and deceive in order to get it. Yet God used this man in a profound way to accomplish His very important purposes.

At one point in his life, Jacob seemed to come to the realization that he wasn't worthy of the goodness God had extended him: "I am not worthy of all the unfailing love and faithfulness you have shown to me, your servant" (Genesis 32:10 NLT).

The truth of the matter is that none of us is worthy to receive anything good from the Lord. But God is gracious and loving, and He specializes in doing good for and through the unworthy.

Gracious Lord, I know that, like Your servant Jacob, I'm not worthy of the love, grace, and faithfulness You extend to me every day. Help me to always remember that anything good You've sent my way is only because of Your goodness and love.

WRESTLING WITH GOD

When the man saw that he could not overpower him, he touched the socket of Jacob's hip so that his hip was wrenched as he wrestled with the man. Then the man said, "Let me go, for it is daybreak." But Jacob replied, "I will not let you go unless you bless me."

GENESIS 32:25–26 NIV

Genesis 32 tells the story of Jacob's return to his home in Canaan—and of the strangest wrestling match ever. At one point one night, a mysterious man appears to Jacob and engages him in the match. Not long into the match, Jacob realizes that his "opponent" is no mere man but God Himself.

Jacob knew he was vastly overmatched, but he refuses to give up—even after God decides to dislocate Jacob's hip and demands that Jacob let go of Him. Though he was in what must have been searing pain, he wouldn't let go of God until he received a blessing.

God could have easily destroyed Jacob that night, but this encounter was part of His plan to bless Jacob by making him fully dependent on the Lord and not himself.

When you are contending with difficulties and trials, remember Jacob, who refused to stop clinging to his God, even though doing so meant serious pain and discomfort.

. . . .

Father in heaven, clinging to You isn't always easy. Yet I will refuse to let go of You, even when I'm tempted to do so.

WATCH YOUR WORDS!

LORD, who may dwell in your sacred tent? Who may live on your holy mountain? The one. . .whose tongue utters no slander, who does no wrong to a neighbor, and casts no slur on others.

PSALM 15:1–3 NIV

When most Christians think of the "big sins," their minds go to misdeeds such as murder, theft, adultery, and the like. But for many, the sin of gossip usually doesn't register as being all that serious. The Bible, however, says otherwise.

God takes the things we say to and about others very seriously. That's why the apostle James wrote, "Those who consider themselves religious and yet do not keep a tight rein on their tongues deceive themselves, and their religion is worthless" (James 1:26 NIV).

A man who controls his speech and who avoids gossip is a wise man indeed. He's a man who refuses to speak ill of others—even when what he might otherwise say is true.

Your words have tremendous power to help or to hurt others. So when you talk to or about someone, make sure you say only things that build up and hearten, not tear down or discourage.

. . . .

Father, thank You for providing guidelines and commands for living a life that pleases You. I will commit myself to making sure that I speak only words that encourage others and avoid critical speech, which only tears down what You are working to build up.

HE GIVES ALL GOOD THINGS

Keep me safe, O God, for I have come to you for
refuge. I said to the LORD, "You are my Master!
Every good thing I have comes from you."
PSALM 16:1–2 NLT

In his New Testament epistle, the apostle James says, "Every good and perfect gift is from above, coming down from the Father of the heavenly lights, who does not change like shifting shadows" (James 1:17 NIV).

Many centuries earlier, David began Psalm 16 with essentially the same message, proclaiming that he trusted the Lord his God and acknowledging that every good thing about him was the result of his relationship with God.

Like David, we can acknowledge that any good thing we have or can ever be is on account of the God who loves us and wants to do good things in us and make something good out of us. All we need to do is anchor our faith in Him and allow Him to mold us and make us what He wants us to be.

Lord God, thank You for giving me all good things.
Without You, I have no good thing. Without You,
I have nothing good to offer to anyone. You are
my everything, and I commit myself to coming to
You for protection, for direction, and for provision.

THE INTEGRITY OF JOSEPH

"With me in charge," [Joseph] told her, "my master does not concern himself with anything in the house; everything he owns he has entrusted to my care. No one is greater in this house than I am. My master has withheld nothing from me except you, because you are his wife. How then could I do such a wicked thing and sin against God?"

GENESIS 39:8–9 NIV

God calls each of His people to live lives of integrity and to be careful to make only choices worthy of a man who is part of His heavenly family. The patriarch Joseph understood the importance of making right choices, even when he might have gotten away with making a wrong one.

Joseph was a leading servant in the home of an important Egyptian man named Potiphar, whose wife tried desperately to seduce Joseph. Joseph resisted Mrs. Potiphar—and temptation—but he was still thrown in jail. But because Joseph acted with integrity, he remained on track to be used greatly in God's service and plans.

We should all be imitators of Joseph, always doing what is right in God's eyes simply because it is right.

Father in heaven, I want to follow the example of Your faithful servant Joseph, who was so committed to You and Your Word that he wouldn't even think of sinning against You—even though it cost him dearly.

GOD'S HEAVENLY FAMILY

But He answered and said to him who told Him, "Who is My
mother? And who are My brothers?" And He stretched out His
hand toward His disciples and said, "Behold, My mother and
My brothers! For whoever does the will of My Father who is
in heaven, the same is My brother and sister and mother."

MATTHEW 12:48–50 SKJV

In order to fulfill Old Testament prophecy, Jesus was born into a
Jewish family and was a descendant of King David. His mother was a
young virgin girl named Mary, and His earthly father was a carpenter
named Joseph. He also had earthly siblings.

The Bible shows that family is a big deal to God. Jesus no doubt
loved His mother and His earthly brothers and sisters. But one day as
Jesus was teaching, someone told Him that His mother and brothers
wanted to speak to Him. His response to that request is recorded in
the above scripture verses.

Yes, His earthly family was important to Jesus. But He made it
very clear that He had come to establish a heavenly family of people
who love, serve, and obey God.

Lord Jesus, I take great encouragement and joy in knowing
that I have, by faith, become part of Your eternal spiritual
family. You taught that this family consists of those who do
the will of their heavenly Father. Thank You for directing
me, guiding me, and enabling me to do His will.

CHOOSE HUMILITY

*You save the humble but bring low
those whose eyes are haughty.*

PSALM 18:27 NIV

What do you think is the worst sin a man can commit? Sexual immorality? Fits of anger? Greed? Drunkenness? All these sins—and many others—are serious affronts to a holy God. But they are, in the words of C. S. Lewis, "mere fleabites" when compared with the terrible, soul-destroying sin of pride.

It has been suggested that pride is at the heart of every sin a man commits. When you consider that pride can be defined as a heart attitude of independence from God, then you can see how the above definition rings true.

All humans grow up with a heart condition of pride. But there is hope. Jesus came to earth and died so that we could be freed from and forgiven for all our sins, including human pride. The Bible says, "God opposes the proud but shows favor to the humble" (James 4:6 NIV) and "Humble yourselves before the Lord, and he will lift you up" (James 4:10 NIV).

God loves humility and hates pride. So prayerfully and purposefully choose humility and the blessings God promises to the humble.

*Lord God, Your Word repeatedly teaches that You oppose
the proud and arrogant but extend grace and mercy to those
who humble themselves before You. Thank You for showing
me the blessings of choosing humility over pride.*

CONFIDENCE IN THE LORD

As for God, his way is perfect: The LORD's word is flawless;
he shields all who take refuge in him. For who is God
besides the LORD? And who is the Rock except our God?
PSALM 18:30–31 NIV

According to 2 Samuel 22:1, David—the future king of Israel—wrote Psalm 18 as a song of celebration after the Lord delivered him from the hands of all his enemies and from the hand of the murderous King Saul.

David knew the sole source of the strength he needed to defeat his enemies, and he set an example we should all follow when he took the time to write words of praise and gratitude to his God.

The Lord wants His people to take refuge in Him always, and especially during times of trouble or suffering. He wants to be our rock, the foundation of every part of our lives. He will never falter or fail us when we call out to Him for help—in our spiritual lives, in our emotional lives, or in our physical lives.

Take heart today, for you can always take confidence in the Lord.

* * *

Father in heaven, I take heart in knowing that You are perfect
in all Your ways, making You the perfect rock upon which
I can build my life. I choose to run to You for protection,
comfort, and direction. You alone are my God!

GOD'S GREATNESS ON DISPLAY

The heavens proclaim the glory of God. The skies display
his craftsmanship. Day after day they continue to
speak; night after night they make him known.
PSALM 19:1–2 NLT

In 1997–98, we earth dwellers were treated to a spectacular nighttime display in Comet Hale-Bopp, one of the brightest comets seen from earth for many decades. Hale-Bopp, also known as the Great Comet of 1997, was visible to the naked eye for a record eighteen months. What a sight it was!

Since about four thousand comets have been discovered in our solar system, it's not out of the question that David observed one of them and was in such awe that he was moved to write the words in the above scripture verses. What seems sure is that he looked skyward during a clear night in Israel and saw what we can see today: countless stars, planets, and other celestial bodies—all placed there by the Creator's hand.

Would you like to catch a glimpse of God's magnificence and glory? Just step outside. . .then look up.

Almighty Creator, sometimes all I have to do to appreciate
Your greatness is step outside, look up, and see the
magnificent beauty of the heavens You created. Thank You
for showing me Your greatness in what You've created.

GOD HEARS YOU

May the LORD hear you in the day of trouble.
May the name of the God of Jacob defend you.
May He send you help from the sanctuary
and strengthen you out of Zion.

PSALM 20:1–2 SKJV

Prayer is an essential, powerful part of our relationship with the Lord. Through prayer, we access God's immeasurable power and protection. Through prayer, we connect our hearts with the heart of our heavenly Father. Through prayer, we express our dependence on the Lord. And through prayers of faith, we make our requests known to God.

The Bible promises that "the prayer of a righteous person is powerful and effective" (James 5:16 NIV). So take time to connect with God in prayer every day. And don't pray just during times of difficulty. Pray also just to share with God in an intimate, loving way—just because.

Prayer—what a wonderful privilege it is for the man of God!

Lord Jesus, You promised that I would have troubles in this world, but Your Word also promises that God will hear my prayers and cries in those days when I am troubled and in need of comfort. Thank You for hearing me, encouraging me, and helping me when I call out to You.

A MATTER OF FOCUS

Joseph replied, "Don't be afraid of me. Am I God,
that I can punish you? You intended to harm me,
but God intended it all for good. He brought me to
this position so I could save the lives of many people.

GENESIS 50:19–20 NLT

How do you respond when you're faced with opposition or criticism because of your Christian faith? Or when you believe that you're treated unfairly...for no discernible reason? Joseph endured that kind of treatment—and worse—yet he kept his eyes on the Lord and on what He had planned for him.

If we're not careful, we can develop an attitude of "poor, pitiful me" when things aren't going our way. That happens when we focus on our circumstances and not on the amazing truth that "in all things God works for the good of those who love him, who have been called according to his purpose" (Romans 8:28 NIV).

Joseph could forgive his brothers for the wrong they had committed against him because he remained focused on the Lord and His plans and purposes. That makes him a great example to follow when we're facing tough times.

. . . .

Lord God, when I feel troubled or persecuted, encourage me and
strengthen me by reminding me that You really do use everything that
happens to me for my own good and for the good of Your kingdom.

EMPOWERING THE CALLED

*But Moses said to God, "Who am I that I should go to
Pharaoh and bring the Israelites out of Egypt?" And God
said, "I will be with you. And this will be the sign to you that
it is I who have sent you: When you have brought the people
out of Egypt, you will worship God on this mountain."*

Exodus 3:11–12 NIV

Moses had a heart for his Hebrew brothers and sisters languishing in
Egypt while he hid out in Midian. After all, he was forced to flee Egypt
after he killed an Egyptian slave master for abusing a Hebrew slave.

But when God spoke from a burning bush and commanded
Moses to return to Egypt and lead His people out of captivity, Moses
answered with a long list of excuses.

Moses' encounter with God at the burning bush teaches us an
important truth about how we should respond when God calls us to a
difficult—even humanly impossible—task, and it's this: It's not about
our human skills or abilities, or even about how we perceive ourselves.
Rather, it's about knowing that our God promises to be with us and
to give us everything we need to accomplish the task.

* * *

*Lord, strengthen me and encourage me every day to do all You call
me to do—especially when Your calling seems humanly impossible.
You are my God, so I know it's not about me but about whom I serve.*

A WILLING HEART

Then the LORD's anger burned against Moses and he said,
"What about your brother, Aaron the Levite? I know he can
speak well. He is already on his way to meet you, and he will be
glad to see you. You shall speak to him and put words in his mouth;
I will help both of you speak and will teach you what to do."
EXODUS 4:14–15 NIV

Moses had plenty of excuses when God spoke to him and assigned him the task of leading the Hebrews out of Egyptian captivity: "Who am I" (Exodus 3:11), "Who should I say sent me?" (3:13), "Suppose they will not believe me or listen to my voice" (4:1), and "I'm not an eloquent speaker" (4:10).

The Lord patiently answered each of Moses' objections, and one would think Moses felt assured that he could do the job. But the reluctant deliverer piqued the Lord's anger when he said, "Pardon your servant, Lord. Please send someone else" (Exodus 4:13 NIV).

When God gives us a special assignment, He won't become angry when we ask that He replace our doubts with His own special brand of assurance. But God asks that we always be willing, that we have a heart that always answers, "Here I am, send me!"

Lord God, You are most pleased with me when I hear You
when You speak and say yes to what You have for me.

YOUR GOOD SHEPHERD

The LORD is my shepherd; I have all that I need. . . . Even when I walk through the darkest valley, I will not be afraid, for you are close beside me. Your rod and your staff protect and comfort me.
PSALM 23:1, 4 NLT

David was not a perfect man, and he faltered many times in his walk with God. Yet his confidence was in the Lord, the one he recognized as his very own shepherd. A shepherd in biblical times was tasked with giving his flock protection and with moving the sheep from place to place so they could find adequate food and water.

As the sheep seemed to know they could trust their shepherd, David sensed in the deepest way that he could trust his God as his source of anything and everything he needed.

Centuries after David wrote Psalm 23, Jesus, God in the flesh, appeared on the scene, perfectly reflecting God's shepherd heart. "I am the good shepherd," He stated. "The good shepherd lays down his life for the sheep" (John 10:11 NIV).

Jesus is *your* Good Shepherd. He willingly laid down His life for you and continues leading, guiding, and protecting you all day, every day. He truly is everything you need.

. . . .

Lord Jesus, You are my Good Shepherd. You truly are all I need. You lead me and guide me through even the darkest, most difficult times in my life.

LISTEN TO HIM!

*But even as he spoke, a bright cloud overshadowed them,
and a voice from the cloud said, "This is my dearly loved Son,
who brings me great joy. Listen to him." The disciples
were terrified and fell face down on the ground.*

MATTHEW 17:5–6 NLT

In one of the most spectacular scenes in all the Bible, Jesus appeared to His three closest disciples—Peter, James, and John—in His true glory. This event, known as the Transfiguration, is traditionally believed to have taken place atop Mount Tabor in Galilee.

With the three disciples looking on, "his face shone like the sun, and his clothes became as white as the light" (Matthew 17:2 NIV). Just then, Moses and Elijah—the Old Testament's two greatest prophets—arrived on the scene. Then the voice of almighty God thundered from heaven, "This is my dearly loved Son, who brings me great joy. Listen to him."

Listen to Him. That was God's clear command to Peter, James, and John—and it's His command to us today. We are to keep listening for His voice, reading His words in the Bible—and then apply all He says to our lives here on earth.

*Lord Jesus, with Your three closest disciples watching and listening,
Your Father in heaven spoke His approval of You as His Son
and as the one we should always listen to. I choose to listen to
You daily and apply everything You have said to my life.*

TRUST IN GOD FROM THE HEART

*In you, LORD my God, I put my trust. I trust in you; do not
let me be put to shame, nor let my enemies triumph over
me. No one who hopes in you will ever be put to shame.*

PSALM 25:1–3 NIV

While it's not certain when David wrote Psalm 25, the biblical record makes it clear that he faced much trouble in his life—both before and after he took the throne as king of Israel. This psalm tells us that David had learned the importance of trusting God during difficult times. He knew that "no one who hopes in [the Lord] will ever be put to shame."

Even our most trustworthy friends can let us down, often through no fault of their own. People sometimes find themselves going through difficulties of their own and are therefore not in a place where we can fully trust them for help in times of trouble.

But it's not like that with our Father in heaven. He is in complete control of all things, and He can never be too troubled to come to our rescue. So put your complete trust in the Lord. He will never put you to shame.

* * *

*Lord God, I am heartened and strengthened to know
that when I choose to trust You, You will never let me down
or allow this world or my enemies to win out over me.
Thank You for being such a trustworthy heavenly Father.*

THE FAITH OF A CHILD

"Truly I tell you, unless you change and become like little children, you will never enter the kingdom of heaven. Therefore, whoever takes the lowly position of this child is the greatest in the kingdom of heaven. And whoever welcomes one such child in my name welcomes me."

MATTHEW 18:3–5 NIV

Those who have small children know better than anyone that they are, more than anything, pictures of complete dependency. Children have little to offer—other than love and outstretched hands ready to receive and open arms showing their need to be held and comforted.

When Jesus said, "Unless you change and become like little children, you will never enter the kingdom of heaven," He was letting His listeners know that they needed to be utterly dependent on God, in much the same way a child is dependent on its parents for all things. That, He said, was a requirement for entering God's eternal kingdom.

You can never earn God's favor based on your own merits or works. Rather, you receive all good things from God when you approach Him as a child approaches its parents.

Lord, I confess that I have nothing to offer You but a completely dependent heart. You desire that I humble myself like a child, extending nothing but empty hands longing to receive from You what I could never provide for myself. I trust You for everything I need to one day see Your eternal kingdom.

NO PEP TALK

*Don't be afraid! Stand your ground and witness how
the Eternal will rescue you today. . . . The Eternal will
fight on your behalf while you watch in silence.*
EXODUS 14:13–14 VOICE

God showed up every day in the Israelite camp. He was doing things that needed to survive in memories and shared around campfires. He was feeding and watering hundreds of thousands, but some thought giving up was a greater virtue. They'd been slaves after all. Maybe they felt that's all they were good for. But Moses declared that fear was off limits. He told the people to use their eyes to see what God would do, their minds to understand how He would rescue, and their mouths to close in honored silence in a view to a rescue.

Taking heart isn't a pep talk that you say to yourself hoping that someday you'll believe it. The idea of taking heart is a potent mixture of faith and hope that expands in the knowledge that God's got whatever you fear. It's more than self-encouraging, though many leave it there. You get to walk with God, knowing that He works on your behalf to bring good outcomes to bad circumstances. *Take heart.* Let it change the look on your face, the hesitancy in your step, and the downcast slope of your shoulders.

*Father, I want to stand tall, be brave and discover the
strength I need to do something more than make halfhearted
wishes. Help me stand, discover, and do—with You.*

SOMEONE WORTH KNOWING

*Jesus said, "Let the children come to me.
Don't stop them! For the Kingdom of Heaven
belongs to those who are like these children."*
MATTHEW 19:14 NLT

Imagine being a young boy excited about the possibility of seeing Jesus. You'd heard the stories, and it was easy to believe that Jesus was someone worth knowing. But when you got close enough to Him, to hear His voice, and touch His hand, the disciples scolded you, making you feel as if you'd done something wrong. In that moment, you felt the full weight of dejection. With hot tears threatening your eyes, you considered kicking rocks all the way home. But Jesus said something that made you believe that He actually cared about you. He didn't say the words to you, but to the men who scolded you. He wanted you to come close so you could hear Him. He wanted to see you.

This is a picture of the way every man should feel, knowing that Jesus wants you to come close, stay close, and learn from Him. You're not sent away. You aren't scolded for wanting to know more. He doesn't want anyone else stopping you from finding Him. This is the place where joy is discovered, curiosity is explored, and the gift of love is received.

*Lord, I don't have to hesitate for a moment when
I want to come to You. Guide my heart to the place
where You tell others, "Don't stop him!"*

THE HEART AND GOD'S PROMISES

God makes his people strong.
God gives his people peace.
PSALM 29:11 MSG

God hasn't broken a promise—*ever*. He says He'll give you strength—*He will*. He says He'll give you peace—*accept it*. The moment you believe Him is the moment you can take heart. This bold step realizes that God is absolutely dependable. It pulls the rug out from under every excuse you've ever had about waiting to follow, about stopping to consider and putting God off for now. You'll improve your level of courage when you get rid of the excuses for *failing to follow*.

Men are just as insecure as anyone, but it looks a little different in us. You might be more inclined to stuff emotions, hide personal struggle, and use anger instead of seeking answers to hard questions.

Taking heart means believing that God will deliver on His promises. It's a willingness to wait and the boldness to live life without second-guessing God. It recognizes struggles but also knows that there will be an end to the toil. It recognizes that worry has no place in the life of one who follows God. It remembers the promise maker is also the only perfect promise keeper.

- -

If my life is like a railway to You, God, then I have been off the rails far too often. Help me stay on track moving forward. Help me trust as You teach me to take heart.

SWALLOWING COURAGE

*All the people witnessed the thunder and lightning,
the sound of the trumpet, and the mountain surrounded by
smoke. When the people saw it they trembled and stood at a
distance. "You speak to us, and we will listen," they said to
Moses, "but don't let God speak to us, or we will die."*

EXODUS 20:18–19 HCSB

Taking heart isn't a one-and-done event. You can be strongly encouraged only to dance with discouragement once more. That happened to the Israelites. They'd seen God work and they experienced moments where they felt no fear because God was with them. In Exodus 20 they forgot what God could do and became *afraid* of Him. Afraid of God? The one who leads, guides, loves, and adopts? The one who shares, cares, prepares, and helps? That God?

The bold heart of the follower was replaced with something more timid and less courageous. God seemed too big, too mighty—and their own choices made it hard for them to believe that He would be patient with them.

Maybe you've felt that way. You love God and have chosen Him, and then suddenly you see your own imperfection and lose heart. The fear that you feel swallows your courage. The promises you've heard stand in stark contrast to the sin you know exists inside your own weak heart.

*You're strong, mighty, and perfect, Father. You're also loving,
kind, and compassionate. I never need to be afraid to come to You.*

WHAT'S THE BIG IDEA?

*Jesus stopped and called them. "What do you
want me to do for you?" he asked. "Lord,"
they answered, "we want our sight."*
MATTHEW 20:32–33 NIV

You have things you'd like to do and you might even give those plans a voice. You tell other people what you have in mind, but somewhere deep inside there's a voice you've heard before telling you it'll never happen. It says you're dreaming, you're not good enough, and it won't happen for someone like you. Taking heart sometimes means telling God about dreams you think are outlandish or too big to come true.

This is what Jesus asked a group of blind men to do. He didn't ask them to downplay their request. He wanted to hear their dream (however improbable). The men didn't hesitate—they wanted to see. Because of their belief, or because He was the Son of God, Jesus gave them the very thing they had been dreaming about. The men must have felt that He had given them a new life. *He had.*

You have a big idea, but it's nothing compared to God's big idea for you. Share your plan with Him and ask Him for help. God's answer might surprise you.

. . . .

*Lord, You want me to believe that big ideas come true.
It may be the thing I want or it could be the thing You
know I need. Help me believe in the big idea.*

OWNING COURAGE

*But I trusted in, relied on, and was confident
in You, O Lord; I said, You are my God.*
PSALM 31:14 AMPC

How many ways can you describe the term "take heart"? You'll find a year's worth of examples in this book. Here are a few descriptions to consider—possessing strength, holding hope, and owning courage.

Taking heart will always be more than acting brave for a moment. You can do that on your own when the need arises. No, taking heart sees that God alone gives real courage, hope, and strength. Taking heart proves you're not alone in this journey that can sometimes feel like a game of survival. Taking heart recognizes a companion that never leaves and never pretends He doesn't know you. Taking heart will change the elevation of your view.

David is credited as the writer of Psalm 31. He wrote the words at a time when he was fleeing King Saul. If David were to believe what he was told, the king was trying to kill him. But David trusted in the God who inspired him toward courage. David declared that his confidence came from God (not from David's personal storehouse of strength). This decision can be found in the many praise psalms you read in the Bible.

*God, I don't want to be convinced that You intentionally
wait for me to make a mess of things before You help me.
Sometimes I just need to be wise enough to ask You for help.*

REFUSING TO TAKE HEART

The chief priests and the Pharisees, the teachers and the elders,
knew that when Jesus told these stories He was speaking about
them. Not believing, they looked for a way to arrest Him—
a stealthy way, though. They were afraid to make too bold a move
against Him because all the people believed He was a prophet.

MATTHEW 21:45–46 VOICE

Matthew 21 is an exceptional example of what it looks like to refuse to take heart. The chief priests and Pharisees could have taken heart and learned from Jesus, but they chose hard-line unbelief. They could have been humble but chose to be proud. They could have asked questions but chose to accuse.

Defensive posturing will always make it difficult to take heart. When you make the choice to stand on a hill and defend personal opinion, you make it very difficult to be moved by God's truth. This isn't courage, and it sure isn't bravery. It bears the stench of decay and death. It's a wheezing and gasping for fresh air. It holds up the feeble sign "I know it all." And very few will believe it. You can make a better, bolder, clearer-thinking choice.

- -

When it comes to You, Father, I want to be all in. I want my
choices to be bold enough to look like choices You would make.
I want others to believe You, so let them see me believe You too.

A TIME TO TURN YOUR BACK

Finally, I confessed all my sins to you and stopped trying to hide my guilt. I said to myself, "I will confess my rebellion to the LORD." And you forgave me! All my guilt is gone.

PSALM 32:5 NLT

What do you believe are the benefits of confessing your sins to the Lord? You know that the Bible promises God's mercy and forgiveness when you confess your sins. But how can true confession help you?

You instinctively know that there is right and wrong and that someone greater than you decides what action fits in each category. It's easy to hide guilt and say that you get to decide what's right. It's easy to rebel while you shake a fist at heaven and shout, "You're not the boss of me!" But instead, turn your back on rebellion, and admit your guilt. This difficult-but-brave choice welcomes forgiveness and watches guilt walk away grumbling about its recent eviction.

The choice to hide doesn't change anything. The choice to rebel takes you further away from a good God. The choice to humbly tell God all about your poor choices is a perfect step in the the right direction.

So many choices and so many mistakes, Lord. It feels like I should give up and walk away. But You want everything to do with me. Help me be brave enough to accept Your forgiveness without running away.

THE GREAT KING'S RESIDENCE

"I'll move in and live with the Israelites. I'll be their God. They'll realize that I am their GOD who brought them out of the land of Egypt so that I could live with them. I am GOD, your God."

EXODUS 29:45–46 MSG

Before the Israelites could truly trust the Lord, He made Himself at home among the former slaves. They'd been ordered around and belittled, and then the Great King lived among them. Their past circumstances made it hard to believe a present reality. They had lived with dashed hopes and disappointed dreams for so long that it was difficult for them to believe that God really cared about them.

God provided food and they hoarded what He freely provided. It seemed they weren't convinced He would bring the food trucks of heaven back daily—but He kept providing. He tried breaking their habit of viewing everything from the lens of slavery. It remained an ever-present stumbling block.

Your mom or dad once made promises that you chose to believe or disbelieve. Maybe they proved trustworthy and you found it easy to trust them. Maybe not. But God has never been untrustworthy. He always keeps His promises, and that's why it just makes good sense to trust Him.

. . . .

Every man has been in bondage at least once in life, God. Give me a willingness to believe enough so I can believe more. To trust enough to see You move. To have faith enough to witness You—moving mountains.

LIFE ASSURANCE

We wait for Yahweh; He is our help and shield. For our hearts rejoice in Him because we trust in His holy name.

PSALM 33:20–21 HCSB

The more you know about God, the more you can feel encouraged. The more you feel encouraged, the more you'll trust Him. The more you trust Him, the more impressive your story becomes. And it is that story that can encourage others to follow your example.

There's a sigh of relief waiting for those willing to get to know God. He cares deeply for you, and His rescue plan waits for you to notice, recognize your need, and then accept His offer. Not everyone will. Not everyone has.

You can discover the motivation you need to move in God's direction. That happens when you recognize Him for who He is and then agree to make your life an example of a man who follows God. This isn't a supplemental life assurance policy. It's not a "just in case" way of thinking. It is the only way to discover freedom from a broken past and the freedom to follow a better plan.

Be patient. Help is on the way. Protection is yours. Rejoice and trust in God. Take heart. That's an impressive list of takeaways from Psalm 33.

* * *

There's nothing about You that I should be suspicious of, Father. Help me trust You enough that I'll see following You as my only option.

PEOPLE DON'T ALWAYS KNOW BEST

*The LORD replied, "My Presence will
go with you, and I will give you rest."*
EXODUS 33:14 NIV

It had been a tense day for the people of Israel. They had witnessed God's miracles before leaving Egypt. They had witnessed His presence as they made their way through the wilderness. They had even witnessed their leader, Moses, walk up the side of a mountain to meet with God. Then? They suffered spiritual amnesia.

While Moses was away, the people made the wrong assumptions of a forgetful mind. Since Moses was with God and they suffered a memory lapse, they gathered all the gold they could find and then asked Moses' brother, Aaron, to make a god from rings, earrings, and other jewelry.

The people were not secure or encouraged in their relationship with God. They felt abandoned. They decided any god would do, even when it was a non-god. When confronted, Aaron made excuses—so did the people. God was not amused—neither was Moses.

God gave Moses reason to take heart. Read this encouragement again, "My Presence will go with you, and I will give you rest." God didn't say He would gather all His gifts and go home. He didn't suggest that He would abandon Moses. God would keep Moses company. He promised better days to come. You have the same promise. *Be encouraged.*

. . . .

*I don't want to forget that You are with me always, Lord.
Give me the reminders I need because I will forget.*

SOON

Watch therefore [give strict attention and be cautious and active], for you know neither the day nor the hour when the Son of Man will come.
MATTHEW 25:13 AMPC

You can find encouragement in the Lord anytime you need to. When you're feeling overwhelmed, disheartened, or disturbed, you'll always find relief in remembering the goodness of God.

When you feel alone or abandoned, when you lose heart or question your future in the Lord, He wants you to understand that you have believed a lie. There will come a day when He returns. Knowing the exact time when He'll return is less important than knowing and believing that He *will* return.

This is just one example of a way that you can hold tight to the supernatural courage that keeps you anchored in this moment and then gives you hope for every moment between now and the promised return of God's Son.

Watch, pay attention, use caution, and be active in preparing for the day simply called "soon." God wants you to be ready. That means keeping your hold on things here very lightly. This isn't your forever home. Taking heart for a coming reunion with God will always be a most excellent decision.

....

*I believe Jesus came. I believe He died for my sin, God.
I believe there's life after life and a place for me—
with You. Encourage me to keep following until then.*

VACATE PAIN

Reassure my soul and say, "I will deliver you."
PSALM 35:3 VOICE

Sometimes the Bible gives you a front-row seat to the prayer life of others. What was on their heart? How did they approach God? Were their prayers honest or filled with words that just sounded like prayer? You'll find prayers throughout the Bible, but the book of Psalms contains more prayers than other books of the Bible.

The best prayers are ones where the individual praying comes to the place where they take heart. It's a turning point that takes them from the dark place that led them to prayer to a glimpse of God's goodness that then leads them to a place of worship.

Prayer can be your best reminder to take encouragement in the Lord. Psalm 35 is a deeply honest prayer from David, and apart from the angst, you discover that the one praying wanted a reassured soul. That reassurance would need to come from God. The reassurance would need to be that he would not be left to face his struggle alone.

You see, in order to take heart you will need to vacate a part of your heart that was crushed, bruised, and burdened. It's a great reason to tell past hurt to move on.

. . . .

Be my deliverer, Father. Take me from the pain I have suffered. Give me peace, hope, and help. I want to remember that You are always worthy of my trust.

THE HESITANCY

[David said to God,] I will give you full credit
when everyone gathers for worship; when the people
turn out in force I will say my Hallelujahs.
PSALM 35:18 MSG

Was David refusing God's gift? *Maybe.* Is he a bad example? *Not necessarily.* He trusted God but didn't trust humans so much. Critics were everywhere. Enemies were plentiful. He needed relief, and the king struggled with discouragement.

It might sound like the king was bargaining with God. Was he setting conditions for his faith? "When everyone gathers. . .when the people turn out in force." Those were the two elements the king needed in order to give God credit and lead a hallelujah cheer.

David wasn't much different than most of us. He believed, but there was more to learn. There were others like him in the Bible, and their responses are summarized by the simple phrase uttered by a father who believed in Jesus but found circumstances impossible: "I believe. Help me with my doubts!" (Mark 9:24 MSG).

There's something freeing knowing you aren't the only person who's ever doubted. Trust is important to every relationship, but it's not easily given. On this Valentine's Day and on your journey toward Easter, remember you're asked to love God and then take heart by trusting Him more each day.

. . . .

It's easy to be weary, Lord. It's harder to take heart. But that's
what You want me to do. Would You help me do that?

MOSES DID

Moses did everything just as the
LORD had commanded him.

EXODUS 40:16 HCSB

Taking heart is all about belief, isn't it? After all, you don't join a cause you don't believe in. You don't follow someone if you don't trust what they say. You don't tell other people about ideas you don't accept as truth. You won't obey things you believe are wrong.

Moses had seen plenty of examples of God's faithfulness. There were the accounts of how God protected him from a death sentence as a baby, of Him speaking from a burning bush, and of the miracles He performed to set His people free from slavery. Moses had a long history of observing God's faithfulness.

When the Lord gave him instructions on how to assemble the tabernacle, Moses didn't have to ask for God's résumé and there was no need for references. God's job was taken and it was secure. Moses needed to follow God—and he did.

Each day of your journey with God should make you more and more willing to take heart. Obedience becomes second nature, and trust is an easy gift. What if you had the same kind of legacy as Moses? Fill in your name and read the following sentence personally.

_____ did everything just as the Lord commanded.

Obeying You means believing You, God. I believe
You're worth following, have answers to my
questions, and are completely trustworthy.

WEAK FLESH

[Jesus said,] "Watch and pray so that you will not fall into temptation. The spirit is willing, but the flesh is weak."
MATTHEW 26:41 NIV

Nine disciples weren't invited. Jesus asked only three to follow Him and pray that night. Peter, James, and John likely believed they were up to the challenge. They were invited to a private retreat with the Son of God. They would not be denied the stories of being with Him. This was big, important, and a mission they enthusiastically embraced.

They thought they were ready for the challenge, but their best intentions failed. They probably started with prayer, but sleep sent them a more urgent invitation and they accepted.

You might have wanted to follow God closely but somehow get sidetracked too. It may not be sleep while praying (although it's common), but maybe a quick redirect to Pornography Place, Seductress Street, or Gossip Cul-de-sac.

It's disheartening to begin strong only to discover far too quickly how weak you really are. It can even make you wonder if following is really worth it. Yet if you spend time evaluating what you know to be true, you might recognize that life isn't better without Jesus. Walking away sends you back to a place of defeat.

So keep following. It's worth it!

. . . .

My flesh is weak, Father. You give a man like me Your strength. Thank You for picking me up when I fall.

A PRESENCE PRECIOUS

How precious is Your steadfast love, O God!
The children of men take refuge and put their
trust under the shadow of Your wings.
PSALM 36:7 AMPC

Praise is released from the lips of those God has heartened and encouraged. They're in the best position to recognize miracles. Why? They have chosen an investment strategy that pays dividends.

Resist a surface relationship with God. It doesn't please Him. It never helps you.

You might have wondered if God can be trusted, if His love is forever, and if His refuge has room for you. But when you choose a deeper relationship with Him, you have access to the right answers. You can enjoy the tangible benefits of God's care for you. You can share what you're learning with people who need to take heart and have no idea how to do it, if they can, or why it's important.

When you encounter people unsure about whether they can or should follow God, just know they may be wrestling with these same issues. They may be under the impression that God is unapproachable.

Psalm 36 gives you the hope that there is rest, peace, and love in the presence of God. He wants to be known—by you.

I want to view You as amazing, Lord. Not just in this moment, but in every moment of every day. Give me the peace that's more complete than I could imagine and a hope that knows one day I will meet You face-to-face.

CIRCUMSTANCES UNCONTROLLED

[The chief priests, scribes, and elders mocked Jesus, saying]:
He saved others, but He can't save Himself. If He's really
the King of Israel, then let Him climb down from the cross—
then we'll believe Him. He claimed communion with God—
well, let God save Him, if He's God's beloved Son.

MATTHEW 27:41–43 VOICE

Peer pressure can take your faith and ask you to toss it in the dustbin of failed ideas. You could hear a comment like "You don't really believe that stuff about Jesus, do you?" That question makes it seem like the only answer is to deny that Jesus means *anything* to you.

This happened on a hill near Jerusalem when Jesus hung dying on a cross. The religious leaders were doing their best to impact the faith of Jesus' followers: "He saved others, but He can't save Himself." They even did the first-century version of the triple dog dare by mocking Jesus and telling Him to get down from the cross on His own—*if He could.*

That wasn't God's plan. If Jesus was to be the sacrifice for all sin, then He would need to die. You can take heart in believing in an outcome more impressive than the tragedy, in trusting an outcome to God during circumstances you can't control.

I don't want to give up or give in when others mock You,
God. Strengthen me and embolden me to stand for You.

PSALM 37 INSTRUCTIONS

Be still in the presence of the LORD, and wait patiently
for him to act. Don't worry about evil people who
prosper or fret about their wicked schemes.
PSALM 37:7 NLT

The message from Psalm 37 is impressive—and a good one for a Christian man to follow. Start with being still. Move on to waiting patiently. Add the command to refuse to worry about or concern yourself with sinners who make evil plans. *See? Good instructions.*

But this passage continues with further directives. "Stop being angry! Turn from your rage!" (v. 8 NLT). "It is better to be godly and have little than to be evil and rich" (v. 16 NLT). "The LORD directs the steps of the godly" (v. 23 NLT). "The godly always give . . .and their children are a blessing" (v. 26 NLT).

You're asked to behave differently once you know, serve, and follow God. If you take these instructions to heart, your present life will look very different from the old life God helped you to leave behind. Today and every day, it's good to remember that God can help you every day to make the good choices Psalm 37—and the rest of the Bible—encourages you to make every day.

Father, keep me from those things that sidetrack me.
Thank You for making big changes in me and
helping me to make good choices.

AN INVITATION OVERLOOKED

The angel spoke to the women: "There is nothing to fear here. I know you're looking for Jesus, the One they nailed to the cross. He is not here. He was raised, just as he said. Come and look at the place where he was placed."

MATTHEW 28:5–6 MSG

God very often extends invitations to receive encouragement. But it's possible for you to miss the invitation—or maybe you just refuse to receive it. Sometimes you're confused enough that you don't understand the value of what's being offered.

A group of women arrived at Jesus' now-empty tomb and received an unbelievable invitation to receive encouragement. They were disheartened because they were certain Jesus was dead. They were dismayed because they wanted to honor Him but He wasn't there. They were confused because meeting an angel wasn't something that happened every day. Circumstances caused them to delay their hope acceptance speech. They failed to recognize encouragement.

Were they even listening when the angel told them, "Jesus is not here. He was raised. Take a look for yourself"?

Think about what distracts you from accepting the encouragement God has waiting for you. When you identify the distractions, then you can do something about them. You don't have to let them stick around or keep you from the great things God has for you.

I don't want to be confused, Lord. I don't want to be distracted, dismayed, or disheartened. Help me recognize that You want to encourage me.

THE STRUGGLE ADMISSION

*LORD, do not abandon me; my God, do not be far
from me. Hurry to help me, Lord, my Savior.*
PSALM 38:21–22 HCSB

When you read Psalm 38, you might be left to wonder how it could possibly help its readers to take heart. How can anyone be encouraged when some of the points of David's prayer included punishment (v. 1), sickness (v. 3), and sin (v. 4)? It was an admission of a messy life, and there's little feeling that David was experiencing much in the way of encouragement. On the contrary, it feels like an appointment with depression with a long recovery ahead.

But tucked away at the tail end of the chapter is something incredibly important: a request for God's companionship. David didn't want to be abandoned, and he was bold enough to ask for help. He may not have been heartened by verse 22, but he stated something profound. The king of Israel told God that he *wanted* God to encourage him.

You can't wish away life circumstances. You may not feel better just because you *want* to feel better. You can admit to God that you're struggling and then confess that you want to be heartened. That means having the courage to trust in Him to be your source of encouragement.

*It can seem like taking heart means that I
never struggle, God. But I do. I need to trust You.
Give me the strength to ask for Your presence.*

EMBARRASSED BY FAILINGS

Look away from me so I might have a chance to recover my joy and smile again before I lay this life down and am no more.
PSALM 39:13 VOICE

King David may have been nostalgic or near the end of his life, but Psalm 39 shows a desperate king who recognized his personal guilt. He had broken the laws of the God who was the only example of perfection. If God was light, then David was darkness. If God was hope, then David was depression. If God was love, then David was loathing.

The king of Israel was nothing that God was, yet the Lord referred to him as someone who could reflect His heart (see 1 Samuel 13:14). God's example was so perfectly wonderful that it made the king remember who he was without God—and he was not the shining example God wanted him to be. Verse 13 suggests that the king was embarrassed by his failings. He needed the chance to recover and wanted a fully restored friendship with God.

It's good to know that God shows up in unlikely places in scripture to prove that the struggle you feel is just as real as it was to men of God whose stories you read in the Bible. Therein lies hope.

Father, sometimes it's a struggle to take heart. May my moments of struggle keep leading me back to You. Do something with my mess. Give me the courage to be encouraged.

HE BELIEVED

*A leper came to [Jesus], begging Him on his knees and saying
to Him, If You are willing, You are able to make me clean.*

MARK 1:40 AMPC

The first chapter of Mark contains the words of a man whose simple faith heartened him enough to seek out a miracle healing. He essentially told Jesus that he knew He could heal and that the healing would happen if He was only willing. The man with a skin condition called leprosy didn't say whether he'd heard about the good things that Jesus had done for others. He didn't suggest that Jesus might not want to heal a guy like him. He just dropped to his knees, was not above begging, and *believed*.

This man recognized that healing was possible and that Jesus was the healer. He expressed trust in Him. He believed in an outcome that, for most, seemed impossible. Do you believe that God loves to see this kind of faith?

It's easy to stare at the ground, use your shoe to move some dirt around, and, instead of asking God for help, feel embarrassed as you turn and walk back to your pain—and away from His help.

Every day you get to make that choice. You can be embarrassed or believing. You can be timid or bold. You can stay broken or discover healing.

*Help me make a bolder choice, Lord.
If You're willing, You can help me.*

BEYOND THE MESS

Me? I'm a mess. I'm nothing and have nothing:
make something of me. You can do it; you've got
what it takes—but God, don't put it off.
PSALM 40:17 MSG

When you make the choice to believe God, you might find yourself in some very open conversations with Him. You define who you are and then define who you think He is. You compare and contrast. Make sure you have a clear understanding, knowing that you aren't asking as an equal to God. You are asking because you're certain that you literally can't do what you're asking Him to do. If you're a mess—tell Him. If you have sinned—confess to Him that you were wrong. If you've walked away—declare your return.

And if you feel needy, you should remember that you are. That's why you're praying. That's why you're asking God for help. That's why you abandon your own best effort. God's plans for you aren't the result of your own work but His.

God is making you into His masterpiece (see Ephesians 2:10), but that only happens when you come to the end of your efforts, hand Him the paintbrushes, and let Him take over as the master artist. Masterpiece status happens because of what God does. *Always.* One hundred percent of the time.

My time with You is always well spent, God.
Teach me to bring my mess to You. Give me the
assurance I need to be certain You're the one changing me.

MORE THAN FEEL-GOOD WORDS

Then Jesus said, "Whoever has ears to hear, let them hear."
MARK 4:9 NIV

Paying attention to Jesus is a great way to be encouraged and strengthened in your faith. Jesus wanted life change for those who met Him, and listening allowed them to gain enough information to avoid discouragement and embrace something better. And it was more than just listening, wasn't it? The phrase used at the beginning of this reading was "paying attention," meaning truly connecting what God says in His Word with what you understand in your mind. The words you read in the Bible are just feel-good quotes when they don't connect from your lips to your heart.

Take God's words. *They are yours without cost.* Do something with them. *They have the power to make you new.* Connect them to your actions. *They can teach you how to represent God in everything you do.*

If you have ears, then listen. If you have eyes, read and understand. If you have a heart, let what you hear and see impact what you believe. When this trifecta of engagement occurs, you will find yourself taking heart.

. . . .

Father, there are things I can do to receive courage and strength. I want to do them and not neglect them. I want to use them to find the encouragement I need to keep my feet walking in Your steps.

IN THE MAJORITY

By this I know that You delight in me:
my enemy does not shout in triumph over me.

PSALM 41:11 HCSB

It's easy to lose heart when you feel like you're being bullied. You flop inside like those tall inflatable tube men you see waving their arms outside car dealerships. There isn't much holding you up, and whatever help you find in personal effort can leave you more quickly than it arrived.

Psalm 41 shows that David was in this kind of place. He was angry over the success of those who had bullied him. He recognized that what was going on wasn't fair. Revenge would have been David's preference, but he also knew that no one had the ability to triumph over him without God's permission.

So the king was all in, committed, and encouraged to trust—completely, persistently, and with ongoing determination. David knew that God was with him and that with God he was in the majority. Any minority opinion didn't matter in view of eternity. It was simply a short-lived season of trouble dismissed by God's helping hand.

There's a lesson here for you. There's hope in this instruction. There's joy in holding on.

* * *

There's just one You, Lord. You know more, do more, and teach more than I ever will. Help me learn what You teach, watch what You do, and understand more about You and Your ways.

A JESUS ENCOUNTER

One of the rulers of the synagogue came up, Jairus by name;
and seeing Him, he prostrated himself at His feet and begged
Him earnestly, saying, My little daughter is at the point of death.
Come and lay Your hands on her, so that she may be healed and live.

MARK 5:22–23 AMPC

Jairus wasn't supposed to express anything close to faith when he encountered Jesus. If he followed the example of fellow synagogue leaders, he should have treated Jesus with disdain. However, Jairus was in a place of desperation. His daughter was dying and he had nowhere left to turn. It was either Jesus, who had already healed many, or the death of someone he loved very deeply.

Jairus chose what appeared foolish to his peers but what was in reality the only sensible choice. He took heart in what others had rejected. He humbled himself, he begged, and he believed that Jesus, and only Jesus, could do something for him. That may sound redundant, but it holds a key to understanding the reason *you* can take heart. God (Jesus) can do what you can't. When you recognize that He cares about you and wants the best for you, then coming to Him for help is no longer a matter of desperation.

Let me care more about You and what You can do, God,
and less about the opinions of those who won't ask You for help.

REJECTING CHAOS

It was Your strength—Your right hand, Your arm, and the light of Your presence that gave them success, for You loved them.
PSALM 44:3 VOICE

Psalm 44 was written by the sons of Korah. They were closely related to Moses and were singers. They were responsible for around 10 percent of the psalms. Their words in this psalm were reminders that no matter what difficulty they faced, if they would simply remember the goodness and love of God, they could trade in uncertainty for encouragement. The internal sea of fear would recede, anxiety would release its grip, and peace could make the heart God's home.

When your inner turmoil over your difficulties is not tempered this way, you will find yourself walking on edge or in a state of internal chaos and out-of-control external impulses. It will leave you in a weakened state.

Most scholars believe there were at least three brothers who were involved in writing the psalms attributed to the sons of Korah. It seems possible that as they wrote together, they remembered together and were encouraged together. You might find that taking the time to share your struggles with like-minded Christians can help you recover your spiritual senses when circumstances threaten to take you where you don't want to go.

Father, I don't want to be out of control, but I can't always control myself or my actions. When I'm tempted to join Team Chaos, help me remember You.

THE SENSIBLE AND HELPFUL CHOICE

Rise up! Help us! Ransom us because of your unfailing love.
PSALM 44:26 NLT

You just read one more bit of wisdom from the sons of Korah on this extra day of the year. These men were inviting God to join them in their struggle. They weren't asking Him to just give them strength in the struggle (although it is wise to ask for that). No, these men were asking God to show up with might, power, and glory. They needed Him to step in and take charge of something they knew they could not handle on their own.

These men were giving God permission to take their mess and redeem their shortcomings. They needed to learn more from God, but they first needed to be rescued. They needed to follow God, but they first needed to find a place of refuge. They were in deep trouble and needed to remember who made the rescue plan possible.

You face the same real and present battle every day. You might be quicker to ask for help or you might wait until it seems too late. Of course, those are choices you can make, but only one is truly helpful.

Thank You, Lord, for giving me an extra day this year. Help me use it to place my chaos under Your control. Give me the peace that comes with knowing that You are in control of everything.

REST IS RESTORATION

*"This is to be a lasting ordinance for the generations
to come, wherever you live. It is a day of sabbath
rest for you, and you must deny yourselves."*
LEVITICUS 23:31–32 NIV

When you finish a project, you step back and admire a job well done. But you also know that you're shifting roles from creator to manager—now you have to take care of the work you've done. That's the idea behind the Sabbath—not stepping away from working as much as stepping into a new role.

God made humans to be stewards of His creation. By ordaining a day of rest from the week's labors, He wasn't telling us to check out but to enjoy Him. Rest isn't relaxation in this sense but recommitment to knowing God. A sabbath is meant to help us manage our trust, to set aside daily labors and believe that God will hold things together.

It's not a legalistic warning to avoid anything that might be construed as work. Resting in God—acknowledging His good care and provision—is part of how He restores us to His original plans in the garden. God wants fellowship with you, and the Sabbath is part of how He meant for that to happen.

. . . .

*Lord God, thank You for all the ways You take care of me
each day. You are worth the effort it takes to set aside time
to enjoy You and remember who You are and all You've done.*

EXPECT THE UNEXPECTED

When they saw Him walking on the sea, they thought it was a ghost and cried out; for they all saw Him and were terrified. Immediately He spoke with them and said, "Have courage! It is I. Don't be afraid."

MARK 6:49–50 HCSB

We're so used to the idea of Jesus walking on the waves that it's easy to miss the context. We need to put ourselves in His disciples' sandals to get at the deeper reality in play here. When was the last time you were on a boat in a storm and saw someone walking toward you on the water? You wouldn't be saying, "Oh, finally—here's Frank!" You'd be freaking out.

But if the disciples were alarmed because they thought they saw a ghost, it went up a level when they saw it was Jesus. After this, there was no denying that He was not just a miracle worker but God Himself.

To follow Jesus means expecting the unexpected. He is always going to be who He is and act according to His character and nature, but the way He does things is seldom what we expect. Our comfort level with Jesus often hinges on our willingness to be in awe of Him, to trust His ways are better and higher than ours.

Jesus, I want to always be blown away by who You are and what You've done, are doing, and will do.

YOUR OWN PERSONAL SAVIOR

*"I'll set up my residence in your neighborhood; I won't avoid
or shun you; I'll stroll through your streets. I'll be your God;
you'll be my people. I am GOD, your personal God."*
LEVITICUS 26:11–12 MSG

Christians are still subject to seeing the physical world through sin-stained glasses. Jesus will fix us eventually, but till then, we can't afford to act as if we're above falling to temptation. In the context of Leviticus 26, we can't take God's blessings for granted.

The law was a conditional covenant, so God's blessings were contingent on His people obeying His commands. In Christ, God's grace overrides our inability to do so consistently—but we can't ever forget His grace. God wants relationship with us so much that He died for it—just so someday, He could walk through our neighborhoods and we would all be glad to see each other.

We show God our love for Him by obeying His commands. Jesus didn't get rid of the law; He fulfilled it. He made it possible for His Spirit to live in us, guiding us into His truth and leading us to live lives of love and grace. No matter how often we go off track, we can get back on and into that life-giving relationship with Jesus.

. . . .

*God, thank You for wanting a real, meaningful
relationship with me. Help me love You more than
anything else so I can love others the way You do.*

LET GOD BE GOD

Let be and be still, and know (recognize and
understand) that I am God. I will be exalted
among the nations! I will be exalted in the earth!
PSALM 46:10 AMPC

Psalm 46 reminds God's people that He is still in control, still in charge of the outcome—of *all* outcomes. That includes natural disasters—the changing earth, shaking mountains, and roaring waters—and international conflict—raging nations and tottering kingdoms.

God wants to remind us that His plans include a future free of strife—God at the center of our lives, in His holy city, a place flowing with peaceful waters and praise to our King.

And yet, the famous verse "Be still and know that I am God" doesn't just mean quietly hoping that God will do something. In Hebrew, *be still* also means "let go" and "stop." It implies surrender. Everyone will at one point surrender to God, but only some do so willingly. God will *still* His enemies' futile struggle against Him, but He will strengthen and give hope to His people when we let Him be who He is and do what He does. We know He is God when we stop resisting the pull of the urgent and trust Him to ride out the craziness with us. In the end, He wins. . .and so will we.

Almighty God, sovereign and unshockable, I put my life
and the madness of the world in Your hands today.

PRAISE HIM LIKE YOU KNOW HIM

*God is the King of all the earth; sing praises in
a skillful psalm and with understanding.*
PSALM 47:7 AMPC

Like Psalm 46, Psalm 47 keeps the theme of God's sovereign power but shifts our response from trust to praise. In ancient times, a song was most often a story. The psalms often set God's exploits to music—how He famously delivered His people from slavery and protected them from the most fearsome army in the known world.

The reason is simple: We need reminders. We need to tell ourselves early and often that God is God, all-powerful and all-knowing. His character is evident in His deeds too, and in His great mercy and kindness, along with His holiness and majesty.

Greatness inspires us. Whether it's an excellent performance or a fruitful project, we want to witness meaningful things done well. That's God's stock-in-trade, so the things that make us stand and shout in joy and approval should point us to Him. Even better, we know Him—the great Creator, Physician, Engineer, and Artist—so we should let Him know we know.

God's greatness demands our proper response: "Applause, everyone. Bravo, bravissimo! Shout God-songs at the top of your lungs! GOD Most High is stunning, astride land and ocean. . . . Sing your best songs to God" (Psalm 47:1–2, 7 MSG).

*God Most High, I celebrate You—Your majesty and power, Your
gracious sacrificial love, Your ultimate victory. No one is like You.*

WORTH THE STRUGGLE

*"Everyone will be salted with fire. Salt is good, but if
it loses its saltiness, how can you make it salty again?
Have salt among yourselves, and be at peace with each other."*

MARK 9:49–50 NIV

Jesus brought serious challenge in Mark 9, starting with the hard aspects of His mission: His rejection and suffering, the lack of belief limiting His work, and how the greatest among them must be the servant of all. He addressed our tendency to overcomplicate faith by eliminating the childlike wonder at its core, and the divisiveness that results even among believers because of a desire for superiority.

Even when we believe that God is God and Jesus is His Son and our Savior, we still battle our sinful tendencies. Fortunately, by God's grace, there's a bigger picture—one where we overcome our old selves, learn to love serving others, and confidently express God's great truth with equally great love.

All these challenges are what Jesus called salt, a refining fire that burns away everything that doesn't ultimately matter and brings peace, both within us and with others. If we resist the struggle that comes with following Him, we lose our saltiness—our connection to His mission. It's hard, but it's worth the effort.

*Lord Jesus, I receive both Your challenge and Your support.
Bring Your salt into my life, preserving Your truth in me and
enabling me to walk in peace and grace with You and others.*

TOUCHING THE SORE SPOT

*Jesus looked at him and loved him. "One thing you lack," he said.
"Go, sell everything you have and give to the poor, and you will
have treasure in heaven. Then come, follow me." At this the man's
face fell. He went away sad, because he had great wealth.*

MARK 10:21–22 NIV

For all the young man's good behavior, Jesus knew the one thing he
kept closer to his heart than God. We all have one thing that threatens
God's place on our heart's throne.

Jesus made it personal with the young man, but with love. That's
His way. He came to save all of us; but by His Spirit, He continues that
saving work on an individual basis. Jesus knows what makes us tick
and what's keeping us from knowing God and truly putting Him first.

Respecting God is not enough. He wants all of us, so as gently
as Jesus could while keeping the hard truth front and center, He
revealed the man's sore spot. How the Lord's heart must have fallen
as the man walked away. When Jesus touches that one thing in your
life, whatever it is, fight that urge to resist. What He has for you is
harder but far better than anything the world can offer.

*Jesus, if there is anything in my heart keeping me
from truly putting You first, show it to me so
I can confess it and trust You with all I am.*

CALLED OUT AND UP

Jesus stopped and said, Call him. And they called the blind man, telling him, Take courage! Get up! He is calling you.
MARK 10:49 AMPC

Jesus has the power to heal all types of blindness—the physical but also the mental, emotional, and spiritual. In fact, the latter types of healings are ultimately the most impressive. Whether we regain physical sight or not, we can always use correction and healing in our minds and hearts.

That's why there's a difference between calling someone out and calling him up. Calling a guy out means you're busting him on some fault or misdeed (often so you can feel superior), but calling him up means you're also offering suggestions for improvement and support along the way, because you want what's best for him. We need both redirection and help, but we also need to be willing to receive it when it's offered.

Jesus exemplified such a leader, one who both tells us when we're off target and helps us hit the mark, one worth following. We all have our blind spots, and none of us likes to have them revealed. But with God, we can always trust that He does so for our highest good.

Merciful God, You see the areas I don't, the ones that keep me from knowing You and loving others more completely. When You reveal my blind spots, give me the courage to deal with them.

FAITH IN GOD ALONE

If you don't doubt, but trust that what you say will take place, then it will happen. . . . Whatever you pray for or ask from God, believe that you'll receive it and you will.

MARK 11:23–24 VOICE

Jesus' point is that God can do mountain-sized works in our lives— problems we thought we'd never overcome or relationships we feared would never heal. We can pray mountain-sized prayers or miniscule ones—no detail escapes God's notice. Even a little bit of faith on our part sets Him in motion, so it makes no sense to doubt Him.

Doubt comes when we approach God without humility, seeking our agenda instead of His will. Doubt hardens our hearts when we fail to recall God's promises or refuse to confess any sins that might be blocking the path between us.

Once our hearts are in order, we can pray with trust that, from there, God will sort out what He can do. And while He can do anything in keeping with His character and nature, He is also aware of every person at every point along history's time line—past, present, and future—and He will do what pleases Him and brings Him glory. And few things bring God greater glory than loving you well.

Father in heaven, almighty God, You can do anything, including helping me with the tough situation I'm in now. Get my heart right with You so I can rejoice in Your will.

GRATITUDE CAN BE A SACRIFICE

"Make thankfulness your sacrifice to God, and keep the vows you made to the Most High. Then call on me when you are in trouble, and I will rescue you, and you will give me glory."

PSALM 50:14–15 NLT

Most God-fearing people will admit that, at some point, God has disappointed them. An important prayer went unanswered—or came back with an answer we didn't like. Without His power and perspective, thankfulness is hard. But such moments are testing grounds for our faith. For some, God's *wait* or *no* is the final straw. That's a transactional approach to relationship—giving to get—which makes gratitude impossible.

However, God makes it clear that our gratitude is the response He wants—especially when it isn't easy to be thankful. God owns the cattle on a thousand hills, but our thanks is a meaningful sacrifice that honors Him.

Even when we don't understand or like God's response, will we still trust Him? For those who do, it's a growth moment, an acknowledgment of God's thoughts and ways being higher than ours and an acceptance that He is still good and still doing good. We are then able to thank Him with full hearts, even in our momentary disappointment.

. . . .

Lord God, even when I don't get all that You're doing, I still trust You. I still believe that You are good and You are doing good. Thank You for taking care of me.

MINDFUL GIVING

*Jesus called his disciples to him and said, "I tell you the truth,
this poor widow has given more than all the others who are
making contributions. For they gave a tiny part of their surplus,
but she, poor as she is, has given everything she had to live on."*
MARK 12:43–44 NLT

The story of the widow's mite is more than a commendation of good intentions or a model for how we should give. The facts are there: What the widow gave hurt her more than the offerings of the rich helped them. But is Jesus commending her or warning us?

Context helps. Jesus had spent some time lambasting the corrupt religious leaders, who loved the spotlight and long prayers but leveraged the last few coins from widows to buy their fancy robes and maintain the temple complex. He saw the widow as a poor woman left with nothing, someone the leaders should have been caring for, not bleeding dry. Jesus was criticizing the system—greed supplants generosity.

That's why the Bible makes giving a heart issue. When we are grateful for who God is and all He has done, we give gladly to support His work. We want in on the life-changing things He is doing—including standing up to repression and grift.

*Lord, check my heart to make sure I am giving
to causes that promote and support what
matters most to You—people, not profits.*

TRUTH FROM THE INSIDE OUT

You long to enthrone truth throughout my being;
in unseen places deep within me, You show me wisdom.
PSALM 51:6 VOICE

The key to David's psalm of repentance is that he acknowledges that no one is more offended by his sin than God. Others were certainly affected; that's always the case. But as David noted in Psalm 51:4 (VOICE), "It was against You, only You, that I sinned, for I have done what You say is wrong."

Forgiveness is hard because it puts the power to make things right in the hands of the offended party. Asking for it means accepting the consequences of the wrong we've done. To extend forgiveness is to take the offense on our own shoulders—something we have to do for our own sake so we don't become bitter from hanging on to the wrong done to us.

The good news is that God has gone to extensive lengths to make things right between us and Him. When He sits as King of our hearts and His truth is saturated throughout our being, we know that His grace is greater than any sin. We can confess with confidence that He will forgive us, and we can take the consequences in stride.

Merciful Lord, I confess my sins to You. Forgive me.
Work out Your truth in my heart in a deep and true
way that changes me to be more like Jesus.

A BORN-AGAIN HEART

Create in me a clean heart, O God, and renew a right,
persevering, and steadfast spirit within me.
PSALM 51:10 AMPC

More than asking for forgiveness for his sin with Bathsheba and Uriah, David longed for God to take away sinful desires altogether. He knew that was the only way he wouldn't hurt and offend God with his selfish, shortsighted behavior again. David was anticipating the Messiah, the one who would make such an incredible dream a reality.

Ezekiel 36:26 (NIV) revealed this was God's desire too, as He promised His people, "I will give you a new heart and put a new spirit in you; I will remove from you your heart of stone and give you a heart of flesh." It was a double prophecy: first, of the Messiah coming to make it possible for us to be born anew; and, ultimately, of the eternal age in which we will not have to fight our sinful natures to do what's right.

David also understood that the Holy Spirit was crucial to such a revitalization of our spirits, begging God not to take His Spirit from him. As believers, we have the Holy Spirit dwelling in us, our constant companion, helper, and guide into God's truth. He prompts us to confess our sins and assures us of God's forgiveness.

God, keep building the heart of Christ in me—to love You
first and best and to love others the way You love me.

COURAGE OVER COWARDICE

"Only do not rebel against the LORD. And do not be afraid of the people of the land, because we will devour them. Their protection is gone, but the LORD is with us. Do not be afraid of them."

NUMBERS 14:9 NIV

Twelve scouts returned from the Promised Land having seen the same things. But ten of them freaked out, causing panic throughout Israel's camp. Caleb and Joshua insisted that these hurdles were not enough to keep them from conquering the land. Everyone else thought they were dangerous nuts who might lead them into disaster—and if God hadn't been involved, they might have had a point. But God *was* involved, and the situation was clearly a test of faith.

The difference was in how each side viewed God. The majority saw giants and towering walls and said, "No way! God led us out here to die." Caleb and Joshua said, "But the Lord is with us." The majority said, "Stone these two before they get us all killed," but in the end, only Caleb and Joshua, who begged the people not to rebel against God, entered the Promised Land. Everyone else died in the wilderness.

What a difference it makes to live like God is who He says He is.

. . . .

Lord, You are the difference maker, the one who helps me overcome my doubts and fears so I can stand for You and Your truth when it counts most.

WATCH AND PRAY

*"Watch and pray, lest you enter into temptation.
The spirit truly is willing but the body is weak."*

MARK 14:38 SKJV

Jesus knew what was coming: betrayal, denial, torture, and an excruciating death. But even in His darkest hour, when His friends fell asleep on Him, when soldiers and criminals mocked Him, He chose forgiveness and compassion.

In Gethsemane, Jesus felt the weight of what He was about to do—absorb all the hell every person who has ever lived deserves—and had He only been a man, it would have crushed Him. Instead, as the God-Man, He chose the Father's will—to be separated momentarily from the Trinity for the first time ever so that we would not have to be separated from God eternally.

Because of His choice, we have a hope and strength that the world can't give or take away. We suffer in this life, but because of Jesus' suffering and resurrection, we know that God does great things through the worst circumstances. We're not hoping He might work all things together for good; we know it. Jesus chose to take on the cross; all that's left is for us to choose Him. When our flesh doubts and struggles with sin, let His Spirit in us respond with faith.

*Jesus, You gave up everything to give me everything.
I can only respond by giving You all that I am.
By Your Spirit, keep me from giving in to sin.*

FOR GOD'S SAKE

God, for your sake, help me! Use your influence to clear me.
Listen, God—I'm desperate. Don't be too busy to hear me.
PSALM 54:1–2 MSG

The Bible's histories never say if David got sick of being hunted by Saul—but David said so in the psalms he wrote about those hard days. He poured out his heart to God, leaving no stone unturned, no emotion unexplored or hidden from the Lord. The results are raw and real, the kinds of prayers many Christians think are NSFC (not safe for church).

David wasn't just complaining for complaint's sake—he was crying out for God to deliver him for the sake of God's good name. That's why the pattern of the psalms always includes a return to worship. David let God know that he was struggling and scared and angry, but then he recalled God's character and history as the helper and ally of the faithful, as the just one who never abandons those who are faithful to Him.

God knows the struggle you're in, but it can feel like He has withdrawn His presence and strength. In those times, pray with honesty and expectation. No enemy, whether external or deep in your heart, can keep Him from you.

Almighty God, faithful Father, You are my help. You saved me from hell, and You will be with me as I face the trials of this world. Glorify Your name by coming to help me again.

BALM FOR THE DEEPEST WOUNDS

Cast your troubles upon the Eternal; His care is unceasing!
He will not allow His righteous to be shaken.

PSALM 55:22 VOICE

Few wounds cut more deeply than a friend's betrayal. Psalm 55 addresses such a betrayal—a friend become foe, smooth words masking surprising hatred, a stunning turn that cut David to the quick. And so, he turned to God.

The psalms remind us that God cares about every detail of our lives, that He is worthy of our praise in all the ups and downs. If you haven't yet suffered a blow that you think you might never get up from, you will. This world is hard and cruel, but with God, there is always hope—even if you would rather die than take another breath.

Never forget that Jesus understands everything you go through. He knows sorrow and loss, emotional and physical agony, and the deepest betrayals and rejection. Because He overcame them, you will too. Life will shake you, but He won't let you be knocked off your post at His side. If all you can do is rasp out a single-word prayer—*help* or *please* or *Father*—He hears and He is there. You're going to be okay.

* *

Father, the pain from old wounds feels like it might
kill me. Heal me, please, and let me know You're
still there and that You're not going to ditch me.

ALWAYS IN HIS HANDS

*Tell the Israelites to bring you a red heifer without spot,
in which is no blemish, upon which a yoke has never
come. And. . .Eleazar the priest. . .shall bring her outside
the camp, and she shall be slaughtered before him.*

NUMBERS 19:2–3 AMPC

What's the deal with the red cow? An unblemished heifer that never saw rider or yoke, its sacrifice performed outside the camp of Israel, its blood sprinkled toward the altar, its ashes used to purify anyone who'd been in contact with the dead—strange, but it all points to the sacrificial, healing death of Christ.

The crazier the world gets—the more divisive and godless and violent—the easier it is for people, even Christians, to say, "Where is God?" The red cow reminds us: *everywhere.* When we return to God's Word and look for His fingerprints on history, our confidence in His sovereignty is renewed. If it's not all okay yet, it's because He isn't finished yet. History is indeed *His story,* and the Bible shows us the remarkable tapestry He has been weaving since before He invented time—and it all centers on the Messiah, Jesus Christ.

Since God can handle all those details, He can tend to every detail of your life too. It's all in His hands.

. . . .

*Lord God, no detail goes unnoticed by You. Thank You
for sending Jesus to save us, for everything You have
ever done to reveal the good news to the world.*

BACK IN BLACK

You've kept track of my every toss and turn through
the sleepless nights, each tear entered in your ledger,
each ache written in your book. . . . Fearless now,
I trust in God; what can mere mortals do to me?

PSALM 56:8, 11 MSG

It's comforting to know God keeps a record of all your sorrows and sufferings. As an adopted son through Christ, your overall account has gone from red to black. You are no longer in debt to God for your sin but blessed, as Ephesians 1:3 (NLT) says, "with every spiritual blessing in the heavenly realms."

Because the Holy Spirit is working in you to bear spiritual fruit—all the good things listed in Galatians 5:22–23—you can walk with confidence that your hardship is repurposed toward God's good will. No tears are wasted, no heartache ends in hopelessness. Nothing anyone can do to or say about you will change God's mind about you, and that liberates you from basing your worth on accomplishments or others' opinions.

Your Father has written your name in the most important ledger of all, the Book of Life. Your eternity is secure, and so is your present. He tracks every loss, assuring you that, when you trust Him with your suffering, you will come out vindicated and victorious.

Faithful God, thank You for taking such good care of
me, especially when I'm down. I give all my grief to
You. Do Your work and will in my heart and life.

CAN'T CURSE THE BLESSED

Balak said to Balaam, "What have you done to me? I brought you
to curse my enemies, but you have done nothing but bless them!"
He answered, "Must I not speak what the LORD puts in my mouth?"
NUMBERS 23:11–12 NIV

Balaam was a hired prophet, engaged by Balak to curse Israel and drive them from his territory. Balaam took the gig but soon found himself in a pickle: He could only say what God told him to say. Three times he attempted to curse Israel; three times God compelled him to speak blessing over them instead.

When even a mercenary, whose livelihood is based on getting the job done and getting paid, can't go against God's blessing, it's safe to say God's people are secure. Safe in Christ, we're protected not from every hardship but from the ultimate adversity of separation from our Maker. He is with us and watching over us, and He will see us through anything or anyone that comes against us.

Furthermore, there's a reminder for us about speaking God's truth. Our culture demands compliance with its views, but we can't water down God's Word. Love without truth isn't love, and vice versa. When you're loyal to God, He's got your back.

Lord God, Your truth and love are shaping me into the image
of Jesus. Give me courage to share Your good news and not
to back down from speaking Your truth with Your heart.

CHANNEL THE ANGER

The godly will rejoice when they see injustice avenged.
. . . Then at last everyone will say, "There truly
is a reward for those who live for God."
PSALM 58:10–11 NLT

Most Christians have an anger problem: the lie that a good Christian doesn't get mad. To be sure, anger is a double-edged blade. Too often we stuff our frustrations down until we hulk out and damage relationships and trust. But Ephesians 4:26 (SKJV) gives us the appropriate reaction: "Be angry and do not sin." That's the blade's other edge: an honest but productive response.

Psalm 58 is an imprecatory psalm—David raging against his enemies and the world's injustice. It's raw, even violent stuff. God can handle our anger, even though He isn't obliged to do what we ask if it doesn't align with His will. But He knows about anger. Psalm 7:11 says God is angry with the wicked every day. But the cross shows us what He did with His anger at our sin—taking our just punishment on Himself so we could avoid the brunt of His righteous wrath.

We know things aren't the way they're supposed to be. The Bible calls us to channel our anger into setting things right, aligning with God's desire for reconciliation and justice.

. . . .

Father, help me as a new creation in Christ to channel my
frustrations into words and works that acknowledge
the problem but also honor You and Your desire for
repentance, redemption, and restoration.

HUMBLE DEVOTION

*[Simeon] was a just and pious man, anticipating
the liberation of Israel from her troubles. He was
a man in touch with the Holy Spirit.*

LUKE 2:25 VOICE

There was nothing fancy or flashy about Simeon and Anna. They weren't out in front of the people as leaders, and yet God saw them. That they are remembered eternally in God's Word tells us how much God values those who serve Him because of who He is and not for the praise of men.

These two quiet servants loved God with all their hearts, trusting Him through thick and thin, regardless of practicality or popularity. It's easy for us to feel guilty reading about such people because our desire to be recognized for our service gets in the way. But any guilt should prompt us to seek God for who He is and not what He can do for us.

Jesus said in Matthew 6 that our private devotion to God will be rewarded. Anchored in Him privately, we can serve Him publicly without wanting the spotlight. The accounts of Simeon and Anna remind us that He sees our quiet service to Him, our heartfelt worship, and He will reward us in His way and His timing just for faithfully waiting on Him.

* * *

*God, You alone are worthy of all my praise and devotion.
Cleanse me of any desire for the spotlight and fill
me with a passion to know You better.*

TAKE A BREATH

*I will watch for You, for You keep me strong. God, You are
my security! My God is one step ahead of me with His mercy;
He will show me the victory I desire over my enemies.*

<small>PSALM 59:9–10 VOICE</small>

Psalm 59 has a violent edge, as David calls for God to show no mercy
to those who attack the innocent and slander God's name. But then,
David pulls back into a more patient posture, awaiting God's ultimate
vindication and triumph.

That shift is essential for Christians facing a world increasingly
hostile to the gospel. When we see good being called evil and evil
being called good, often our initial thought is to lash out and blast
such foolish people with Bible verses or social media vitriol. But as
James 1:20 reminds us, our anger doesn't produce God's righteousness.

Remember: God sees all of it. His patient heart is to see as many
as possible come to repentance in Christ. Until Christ returns and
reigns with righteous justice on earth, He may well rescue us from
persecution and increasing godlessness—but our call in Christ is to
love God first and best and then love others the way He loves us. That
requires His patience and acting on His kingdom-increasing objectives.

*Lord, Your timing is perfect and Your justice is certain.
Help me to focus on the mission You've given me
and to trust You with the outcomes.*

LIVING THE GOOD NEWS

"Prepare the way for the Lord, make straight paths for him. . . . The crooked roads shall become straight, the rough ways smooth. And all people will see God's salvation."

LUKE 3:4–6 NIV

In Luke 3:8 (NIV), John the Baptist said, "Produce fruit in keeping with repentance." Turning from sin and toward God must have such an impact on our hearts that it leads to life change. We act differently than we used to, and Jesus is the difference.

We love His words more—enough to obey them when it's not easy. We love family, friends, and coworkers better—we relentlessly seek what's best for them. We even begin to do the same for strangers and enemies, treating them fairly, giving them the benefit of the doubt, trusting God to sort out the outcomes when we obey His call to love like He does.

Like John, we do it all for one whose sandals we're not worthy to untie—one who saw our sinful state and said, "I'm going to fix that." John's fiery words and deeds stemmed from his passion for his Messiah. He correctly saw the gospel for what it is—good news that God is making all things new, and He starts with us.

. . . .

Jesus, You are worth whatever it costs me to follow You. Restore my sense of wonder and awe at the gospel. Let it refresh my heart to serve You and love others like You do.

BREAD WITH AN EDGE

Jesus answered [the devil], saying, "It is written, 'Man shall not live by bread alone, but by every word of God.'"

LUKE 4:4 SKJV

To be human is to be tempted. That's a big takeaway from Jesus' spiritual battle with Satan in the desert. Jesus was showing His foe that He was fully human, as well as fully God. He was tempted just like we are, and because He overcame it, we know we can too.

God's Word is our chief weapon against the enemy of our souls. In the wilderness, Jesus parried Satan's temptations with scripture. He could've said, "I'm God, so shut up and leave Me alone." Satan would've had to obey Him. But Jesus, as always, had us in mind, even during this terrible forty-day period.

Jesus called Himself the Bread of Life, meaning He alone can satisfy our deepest needs. To benefit from His provision, though, we need to know His words, which cut like a sword. That's what He gave us in the wilderness: bread with an edge. When we obey His commands, we sharpen the edge of His blade. When His words live in us, they cut through enemy attacks and seemingly unbreakable bonds to our old ways.

. . . .

Jesus, when I rely on what You have said and done, I can stand against anyone who attacks me, starting with the devil. I submit to You. Let Your Word work in me for Your glory.

YOUR IMPENETRABLE FORTRESS

You are the One I will call when pushed to the edge, when my heart is faint. Shoulder me to the rock above me. For You are my protection, an impenetrable fortress from my enemies.
PSALM 61:2–3 VOICE

Behind all physical conflict is a spiritual enemy, God's former worship leader turned traitor, Satan. From Eden to the cross, the devil tried to thwart God's plan to rescue humankind from sin. When he failed there, he shifted his formidable resources to the destruction of Jesus' church.

When you became a Christian, you joined the body that is Satan's primary target. He loves nothing better than to see you weakened, doubtful, and neutralized in the mission Jesus gave you—namely to live out His values and share His good news with all who will hear it.

All everyday problems carry a spiritual undercurrent because of who you are in Christ. Troubles at home and work, division in the church, conflict with the culture—all of it is the world, your own flesh, and the devil trying to push you over the edge.

Satan loves a quitter. On your own, you're no match for him. But when you seek the shelter of God—provided through His Word, your prayers, and His people—the adversary is no match for you. Lean hard into God in troubled times. He won't let you down.

. . . .

*God, You are my strength and refuge.
In troubled times, I turn to You first and foremost.*

ROOM FOR ALL

Jesus answered them, "It is not the healthy who need a doctor, but the sick. I have not come to call the righteous, but sinners to repentance."

LUKE 5:31–32 NIV

Politics is one of the most divisive issues in the church today. But the body of Christ must not limit itself to one side of the political tracks. Jesus exists for the benefit of the entire world. No man-made system can fully encompass the scope of the gospel, and Jesus would likely have praise and critiques for all parties involved.

People of strong faith on either side of the aisle are doing their best to follow Jesus. Consider the group that Jesus Himself first chose to represent Him to the world. Fishermen come to mind first, humble, hardworking souls who set aside their livelihood to follow Jesus. But Jesus also picked a Jewish tax collector (a collaborator with Rome) and a Zealot (a committed idealist who sought to bring down Rome). He selected two who would throw Him under the bus, only one of whom would repent. Jesus countered social norms by counting women among the people He discipled.

Diversity is a crucial part of being the body of Christ. Surrender your political opinions to the Lordship and leadership of Jesus. That's where you'll find true peace and freedom.

. . . .

Jesus, forgive me for putting any man-made ways and ideas above You and Your ways. Open my heart to looking for the possibilities You see in people.

WHAT SUITS THE SABBATH?

Jesus addressed them, "Let me ask you something:
What kind of action suits the Sabbath best? Doing good
or doing evil? Helping people or leaving them helpless?"
LUKE 6:9 MSG

One of the most significant ways Jesus tweaked religious expectations was how He handled the Sabbath. God instituted a day of rest right after He finished His creation, but throughout Israel's history, they had ignored it, trusting in themselves rather than their God, until God enforced a seventy-year Sabbath by sending them into exile in Babylon. By Jesus' day, the Sabbath had become a legalistic blockade, with strict punishments rigorously enforced over the detailed and bizarre interpretations of what constituted work.

The religious leaders repeatedly tried to catch Jesus breaking one of their arcane Sabbath rules—and He obliged them, picking grain from a field one time and healing a crippled man's hand on another. His defense? "The Son of Man is Lord of the Sabbath" (Luke 6:5 NIV).

Where Jesus is Lord, there is freedom from doing things the way they've always been done just because that's how they've always been done. Trusting the Lord by taking a day to honor and celebrate Him is good, but what better way to do both than obey His command to love others well, to help where we can in Jesus' name?

Lord God, You deserve honor and obedience
every day, but You desire sacrifices of praise
and love more than rigid adherence to tradition.

THAT'S A TOUGH ONE

*"Love your enemies, do good to them. . . . Then your
reward will be great, and you will be children of the Most
High, because he is kind to the ungrateful and wicked."*

LUKE 6:35 NIV

Love your enemies. Is this the hardest thing Jesus told us to do?
Maybe. But this command distinguishes Christianity from all other
religions. No other god or religious leader ever took on the reality of
what it means to save sinful people by being "kind to the ungrateful
and wicked." And make no mistake—that's us. We all fall short of
God's standard, but even when we were His enemies, He sent His
Son to die for us.

We may have people who don't like us, who attack us on social
media, and our temptation is to respond in kind. But like Jesus, we
only have one enemy, who hates us as deeply as God loves us. With
Jesus at our side, we can stand against the devil.

The reward? A life without regrets, full of purpose, fueled by
being forgiven and forgiving others. In other words, we become like
Jesus Himself. But to do so, we need to walk His path of suffering,
and that means loving the way He loves and loving who He loves.
That's all of us too.

. . . .

*Lord Jesus, You love the unlovable, including me.
Guide me by Your Spirit to love like You do.
It's the only hope for improving the world.*

SKIP THE SELF-PRESERVATION

*"Don't pick on people, jump on their failures, criticize their
faults—unless, of course, you want the same treatment.
. . . Be easy on people; you'll find life a lot easier."*
LUKE 6:37 MSG

It's human nature to judge others. Fear drives this instinct to protect
ourselves. We tell ourselves that others will always choose what's
best for them over what's best for us, so we must do the same. But
that only works if God isn't in the picture. If we believe we are left
to our own devices, that God is too busy or disinterested to get involved, then self-preservation makes sense.

But the Bible tells us that God cares deeply about us. He is Lord
of all, but He also gets down in the weeds of life with us. The least
self-preservational act in history was Jesus becoming human—God
saying, "Though I need nothing, I love you enough to die for you."
Because He cares, He wants us to care too.

When we resist judging others, we are recalling our debt to the
one who alone can judge righteously but instead chose to save us. We're
trusting He will continue to preserve us and shape us into people who
live in the rhythms of grace and seek what's best for others.

*God, Your grace fuels me to love like You do. I trust
that You will preserve and protect me, so I can
focus on living out Your kingdom values.*

YOUR FAITHFUL GOD

Know that Yahweh your God is God, the faithful God who
keeps His gracious covenant loyalty for a thousand generations
with those who love Him and keep His commands.

DEUTERONOMY 7:9 HCSB

Under the new covenant of grace, we are not bound to obey the law of Moses to have God's blessings. But the principles of the law are eternal, because God is. He doesn't change, so why would His Word? So, because of grace, we obey His commands, particularly as summed up by Jesus: to love God with all you are and to love others as He does.

Because Jesus fulfilled the law, we can look at God's commands to Israel and find His heart in them. We see that He is holy, but that His holiness compels Him to take care of those who love Him—to the extent of building a bridge over the chasm of sin that separates us from Him.

Our part is to offer God the only offering He truly wants in response to His great sacrifice: our thoughts, dreams, deeds, and desires. His loyalty to us is unquestionable, and when we respond in kind, His faithfulness will shape us into the best versions of ourselves—someone only He can see right now, but someone worth the effort and the wait.

. . . .

Great is Your faithfulness, God Almighty. You remain
the same, now and forever, and You deserve all of
me. Here I am, Lord. Shape me as You will.

WHEN YOU'RE CHASTENED

"You shall also consider in your heart that as a man chastens his son, so the LORD your God chastens you."
DEUTERONOMY 8:5 SKJV

After forty years in the wilderness, the Israelites were ready to enter Canaan, which God had promised to Abraham's descendants. The book of Deuteronomy contains Moses' final instructions before the people crossed the Jordan River to possess the land.

With his decades of God-ordained leadership, Moses had credibility. His listeners were a younger generation of Israelites—the children and grandchildren of those who'd escaped slavery in Egypt. Because the older Israelites had complained and rebelled, God decreed that only two of that entire generation—the faithful spies Caleb and Joshua—would live to enter Canaan.

Not even Moses would step foot in the land. He'd been banished for dishonoring God in an angry outburst as the people whined about water. But in his own disappointment, Moses saw God's chastening as good, and he encouraged the people to welcome discipline as a father's loving guidance.

Even the best human father will fail at his job. But God, in His complete knowledge and selfless love, chastens His children for their perfect benefit—now and forever. When you're going through hard times, ask God what He's trying to teach you. Consider in your heart that He's being a very good Father.

Lord, I don't always enjoy chastening, but I know I need it. Guide me in Your perfect ways.

GOD CHOSE YOU

Blessed is the man whom You choose and cause to approach You, that he may dwell in Your courts. We shall be satisfied with the goodness of Your house, even of Your holy temple.

PSALM 65:4 SKJV

Many people struggle with the idea of God choosing His own, yet the idea appears throughout scripture. Certainly God chose David, the author of today's scripture, for relationship and blessing in a very powerful way.

The Bible also teaches human responsibility for sin. It goes to our very conception (Psalm 51:5), affects everyone (Romans 3:23), and puts us all under a sentence of death (Romans 6:23). Apart from God's intervention, we are doomed.

Exactly how and why some people are saved is known only to God—and His grasp of such mysteries is a huge distinguishing factor between Him and us. If we could understand everything about God, He wouldn't be God. . .we would. Clearly, that's not the case.

So, trusting as Abraham did that "the Judge of all the earth" will do right (Genesis 18:25 SKJV), let's be grateful that God looked with kindness on each of us who follow Jesus. We as Christians enjoy God's greatest mercies—which we should be eager to pass along to others.

Heavenly Father, thank You for choosing me and causing me to approach You. May I always appreciate Your gift of salvation. Please empower me to share this good news with others.

YOU ARE JESUS' LITTLE BROTHER

He replied, "My mother and brothers are those
who hear God's word and put it into practice."

LUKE 8:21 NIV

What a few guys enjoy in life—a fantastic older brother—every Christian man has in Jesus. Even if you were an only child, or you just had sisters, or your brothers were younger, or your older brother wasn't that great, Jesus is everything you could hope for: Kind. Helpful. Protective. Wise. Generous. Loving. The list goes on and on.

And those benefits are available to any man who simply obeys Jesus. In today's scripture, Jesus' biological family sought Him while He traveled around teaching. We all know Jesus' mother was Mary; perhaps His brothers are less familiar: James, Joseph, Judas, and Simon (Matthew 13:55). Jesus also had sisters, though they are unnamed in scripture (Mark 6:3).

While He undoubtedly loved His flesh-and-blood family, Jesus was most concerned with His *spiritual* siblings, those who would accept His teaching and receive His gift of salvation. For some time, "even his own brothers did not believe in him" (John 7:5 NIV).

Happily, at least some of Jesus' brothers ultimately believed. And we who have made the same commitment can count on Him to be the big brother who excels all others—the one who is truly perfect.

So when trouble comes calling, just say, "Buzz off! I'm Jesus' little brother!"

Lord Jesus, thank You for making me Your
little brother. Keep me always by Your side.

GOD IS STILL IN CONTROL

Say to God, "How awesome are your deeds!
Your enemies cringe before your mighty power."
PSALM 66:3 NLT

Today's scripture must be read in ultimate terms. Not all God's enemies are currently cringing before Him...in fact, they're more like the angry nations of Psalm 2, with rulers who "plot together against the LORD and against his anointed one. 'Let us break their chains,' they cry, 'and free ourselves from slavery to God'" (vv. 2–3 NLT).

But a day is coming when those who oppose God and trouble His children will regret their folly. "The one who rules in heaven laughs. The Lord scoffs at them. Then in anger he rebukes them, terrifying them with his fierce fury" (Psalm 2:4–5 NLT). They'll cringe while the rest of us celebrate.

"Everything on earth will worship you; they will sing your praises, shouting your name in glorious songs" (Psalm 66:4 NLT). Note the future tense of those verbs—we are not at present in this stage of history. But Jesus said He's "coming soon" (Revelation 3:11; 22:7, 12, 20), and the world's current trajectory seems to indicate His return is closer than ever. All the sin and sadness, fear and frustration of this world will be wiped away. God will make everything right in His good time.

Until then, keep your chin up. God is still in control.

Lord, how awesome are Your deeds! Remind me
today of Your greatness and goodness.

TRUSTWORTHY PREDICTIONS

The LORD your God will raise up for you a prophet like me from
among you, from your fellow Israelites. You must listen to him.

DEUTERONOMY 18:15 NIV

How often predictions are proven wrong. Economists prophesy growth, but output falls. Sportswriters back a team for the championship, but it finishes down the standings. The forecasters miss today's actual weather by a country mile.

Isn't it great to serve a God who truly knows the future?

Really, it's only future to us. As the timeless Creator of time, God is above and beyond all physical restraints. He sees the entire picture at once, so He can bat a thousand on His predictions—like the one He shared through Moses in today's scripture.

As Moses readied the Israelites to enter Canaan, he said God would one day provide another prophet like himself. God then elaborated, saying, "I will put my words in his mouth. He will tell them everything I command him. I myself will call to account anyone who does not listen to my words that the prophet speaks in my name" (Deuteronomy 18:18–19 NIV).

Who is this? Clearly Jesus, as the early Christian leaders Peter and Stephen confirmed (Acts 3, 7).

God makes His plans, then makes His plans known, then makes His plans come to pass. With that kind of God, we have no reason for fear.

. . . .

Lord, I praise You for Your power and knowledge.
Give me the confidence to believe everything You say.

PSALMIST'S PRAYER GUIDE

Come and listen, all you who fear God, and I will tell you
what he did for me. For I cried out to him for help, praising
him as I spoke. If I had not confessed the sin in my heart,
the Lord would not have listened. But God did listen!
He paid attention to my prayer. Praise God, who did not
ignore my prayer or withdraw his unfailing love from me.
PSALM 66:16–20 NLT

These verses describe "3 C's" of effective prayer: first, the confidence we have in God; second, the conditions we must meet; and third, the conclusion we'll enjoy.

Through the first fifteen verses of Psalm 66, the writer praises God for His awesome glory and might. This is a God who could lead His people out of slavery in Egypt on a dry path through the Red Sea (v. 6), a God who brought them "through fire and flood" into "a place of great abundance" (v. 12 NLT).

With confidence in God's power and goodness, the psalmist ensured his right standing. By meeting the condition of prayer—confession of sin—he knew God would listen.

The beautiful conclusion? "God did listen! He paid attention to my prayer." And God never removed His unfailing love.

Thousands of years have passed since this psalm was written. But God has not changed. He still welcomes the confident, clean-hearted prayers of His people.

Lord God, You are great and powerful!
Please hear my honest, humble pleas.

SAY WHAT?

Peter had no idea what he was saying.
LUKE 9:33 VOICE

Since the apostle Peter once fished for a living, Roman Catholics identify him as the patron saint of fishermen and net makers. Because Jesus said He would give the keys of the kingdom to Peter (Matthew 16:19), he's also the patron saint of locksmiths. Even cobblers claim Peter, perhaps because he was the guy who walked on water with the Lord.

What if the rest of us make Peter the patron saint of our own dumb reactions?

If you've ever said something you regretted, spoke out irritably, or fibbed in a moment of fear, Peter's your guy. He definitely earned his reputation for speaking first and thinking later. If you've ever done that, you're in good company.

But we don't want to stop there. Just knowing that others have failed doesn't make *us* any better. It's important to remember that Jesus always stuck by Peter—even after Peter tried to protect himself by insisting he didn't even know His Lord.

After the resurrection, Jesus found Peter and restored their relationship (John 21:13–22). The Lord led His impetuous apostle into three affirmations of love, one for each earlier denial. And Peter, the guy who sometimes "had no idea what he was saying," began speaking words that led countless people to faith in Jesus.

If we let Him, Jesus will gladly do a similar work in our lives.

Lord, please control my tongue, using it for Your honor and glory.

NEVER GO BACK

*"No one who puts a hand to the plow and looks back
is fit for service in the kingdom of God."*
LUKE 9:62 NIV

In the classic 1944 sci-fi story "Desertion," Clifford Simak envisioned attempts to mine Jupiter despite its ammonia rain, slashing wind, and immense atmospheric pressure. Since the giant planet was deadly to humans, workers were biologically converted into native "Lopers"—but the first five test subjects left their protective dome never to return. Project manager Kent Fowler feared a glitch in the conversion process.

Miss Stanley, the grim converter operator, disagreed. She accused Fowler of selfishly wasting lives and was incredulous when he requested two additional conversions—one being his loyal old dog, Towser. Fowler then explained that *he* would accompany Towser.

As a Loper, Fowler was surprised to find the atmosphere pleasant. The winds seemed mild, the air fresh, the crashing waterfalls musical. And he was enjoying deep telepathic conversations with Towser! They soon agreed to pursue a bigger, better, more beautiful life in the wild, abandoning their previous home. "They would turn me back into a dog," Towser said. "And me back into a man," Fowler replied.

"Desertion" dismisses God's image in humanity. But Christian readers may sense a parallel to God's own conversion process—of making lesser (sinful) beings into something far better (sanctified followers of Jesus).

Once you've been converted, never go back.

*Lord, I thank You for the bigger, better, more
beautiful life You offer. Keep me on track!*

BUMPER CROP

*"The harvest is plentiful, but the workers are few.
Ask the Lord of the harvest, therefore, to send
out workers into his harvest field."*

LUKE 10:2 NIV

Jesus said these words to seventy-two disciples He'd commissioned to teach and heal. Separate from the Twelve, this group went out in pairs to places Jesus Himself would soon visit.

Luke 10:2 is often used to stir Christians to greater concern for the lost. That's appropriate, since all of us could probably do more to share the gospel.

Maybe this topic creates stress or guilt in our hearts. If so, reread the first four words of the verse: *The harvest is plentiful.* Though Jesus' disciples would encounter apathy and opposition, they would also find people who welcomed their message. Many people were ready to hear the good news. That's true in our day too.

We can't let this dark world depress or irritate us and keep us from reflecting Jesus' light to our unsaved family, friends, and neighbors. Jesus hasn't yet returned because God "is patient with you, not wanting anyone to perish, but everyone to come to repentance" (2 Peter 3:9 NIV). As we see from the parable of the vineyard workers (Matthew 20:1–16) and the account of a thief crucified beside Jesus (Luke 23:39–43), God will save people at literally the final hour.

Let's pray for workers in God's harvest. . .and be sure we're part of the answer.

Jesus, use me to draw many to Yourself.

TEAM LIFT

May the Lord be praised! Day after day He bears our burdens.
PSALM 68:19 HCSB

Heavy boxes at the home improvement store often sport a black-and-yellow TEAM LIFT label. For the safety of what's inside—the box and your body—you'll want to enlist another person's help in moving it.

When it comes to our heavy spiritual burdens, the Lord is always ready to help. Sometimes He bears them all, as today's scripture indicates. A New Testament counterpart is 1 Peter 5:7 (HCSB): "Casting all your care on Him, because He cares about you."

But often the Lord wants us to carry the weight *with* Him. In the words of Jesus, "My yoke is easy and My burden is light" (Matthew 11:30 HCSB). He does the heavy lifting, like a father who asks his toddler to "help" move something. Dad could handle it himself, but he wants his little one to learn to work and stick with a job. That's why God calls us to persevere in hardships—whether in marriage or family or job or church or any of a thousand other challenging situations. We'll discover His own strength, which is always available if we get overwhelmed.

When we "team lift" with the Lord, we'll never hurt ourselves or fail to accomplish the goal. Those are great reasons to praise Him.

. . . .

*Lord, I thank You for helping me carry life's heavy
burdens. May I do my part, knowing that You
always have the whole weight in hand.*

OUR OBLIGATION

"The LORD our God has secrets known to no one. We are
not accountable for them, but we and our children are
accountable forever for all that he has revealed to us,
so that we may obey all the terms of these instructions."

DEUTERONOMY 29:29 NLT

The invasion of Canaan was to begin shortly. God's people, the Israelites, would soon enter the land God had promised to their forefathers. As the forty-year leadership of Moses wound to a close, the people gathered to hear the great prophet's final instructions. This is Deuteronomy in a nutshell.

With a name meaning "second law," Deuteronomy contains many reminders of the rules God laid down in Exodus and Leviticus. The repetition was purposeful and needful, since the Israelites who originally heard the law were dead. They'd been punished for their rebellion, leaving Canaan to a new generation.

Moses wanted these younger Israelites to understand their obligation to God—they were accountable for knowing and obeying whatever He had revealed to them. So are we.

Many aspects of our infinite God are beyond us—infinitely so. But we need not worry over those things. God's reasoning, timetable, and methods are often "secrets known to no one." His utter supremacy, His way of salvation, and His moral rules are clearly revealed in scripture, so we must live accordingly.

Our God is sometimes mysterious. Our obligation to Him is not.

Lord, thank You for Your clear expectations.
Give me the courage to walk in them.

ANYONE CAN BE BLESSED

Jesus: No, how blessed are those who hear God's voice and make God's message their way of life.
LUKE 11:28 VOICE

Money, it is said, makes the world go 'round. But a good argument can also be made for connections.

Successful people make sure their relatives are well provided for. Kings hand down the throne to their own offspring. Business leaders make sure their families have jobs (or simply cash). Influential people engineer opportunities for their spouses, siblings, and kids. If you're "in," life is good.

It's nice to know that Jesus takes an entirely different approach.

One time when He was teaching, a woman in the crowd interrupted Jesus by shouting, "How blessed is Your mother's womb for bearing You! How blessed are her breasts for nursing You!" (Luke 11:27–28 VOICE).

What the woman said was true. Mary herself, after learning she would give birth to the Messiah, praised God by saying, "Now and forever, I will be considered blessed by all generations" (Luke 1:48 VOICE).

But Jesus' response to that enthusiastic follower—the words of today's scripture—broadened the opportunity for blessing. You don't have to be Jesus' flesh-and-blood kin to enjoy God's favor. Just listen for His voice and apply His Word to your life. No special connections are needed. *Anyone* can be blessed.

Lord Jesus, it's so nice to know that You welcome everyone. I don't have to be "anyone special" to be blessed. I just need to follow You.

WHEN YOU'RE WAY DOWN

"It is mine to avenge; I will repay. In due time their foot will slip; their day of disaster is near and their doom rushes upon them."
DEUTERONOMY 32:35 NIV

The most famous sermon not preached by Jesus is probably Jonathan Edwards' "Sinners in the Hands of an Angry God." Delivered at Enfield, Connecticut, in July 1741, an instigator of America's first "great awakening," it centered on today's scripture.

Deuteronomy 32 is a song of Moses, sung as Israel prepared to enter the Promised Land. The lyrics hammered God's people for their unfaithfulness, for making Him "jealous with their foreign gods" (Deuteronomy 32:16 NIV). Moses' song quoted the Lord saying, "I will heap calamities on them and spend my arrows against them" (v. 23 NIV).

But partway through, around verse 35, the warnings shift to Israel's enemies. No matter how angry God was at His own people, He loved them. He would defend them against other nations that corrupted and harassed them. God will avenge His people "when he sees their strength is gone" (Deuteronomy 32:36 NIV).

In good times, the Israelites forgot God. Often, we do too. So God sends difficulties to get His people's attention. Sometimes, we're knocked so far down we can't imagine getting back up. But that's when God in His mercy steps in again, offering yet another chance to return to His love.

Are you way down? That's exactly where God works.

Father, please lift me up, close to Your heart.

FEEL LIKE A NUMBER?

"Are not five sparrows sold for two pennies? Yet not
one of them is forgotten by God. Indeed, the very
hairs of your head are all numbered. Don't be afraid;
you are worth more than many sparrows."

LUKE 12:6–7 NIV

In the late 1970s, rocker Bob Seger's "Feel Like a Number" lamented the depersonalization of human beings. "I got the idea for the song after watching a show about computer banks and how many names were in them," he said. "It's about identity and trying to survive."

And that was years before the internet, before your every web search was tracked by a multidigit IP address, every purchase identified by your fifteen-or sixteen-digit credit card number. We simply can't avoid being a number.

Unless. . .we're part of God's family through faith in Jesus Christ. Sure, God is numbering our hairs—a relatively easy job with many of us. But the awesome Creator who "brings out the starry host one by one and calls forth each of them by name" (Isaiah 40:26 NIV) also knows exactly who His children are. Jesus, having described Himself as the good shepherd, said He "calls his own sheep by name" (John 10:3 NIV). And someday, He'll even give each of us a new name, "known only to the one who receives it" (Revelation 2:17 NIV).

You're not just a number. You're a completely known, much-loved son of God.

Lord, thank You for paying such deep, personal attention to me.

THE 12:33 PLAN

*You can have a different kind of savings plan: one that
never depreciates, one that never defaults, one that can't be
plundered by crooks or destroyed by natural calamities.*
LUKE 12:33 VOICE

An estimated 32 percent of Americans have 401(k) plans. Likely
100 percent of them get heartburn when the stock market tumbles.

Jesus offers a far better investment option: the 12:33 Plan. Want
eternal gains and no chance of loss? Study the prospectus in this
passage of Luke.

The Lord was warning His disciples against worry. There's no
need to stress over food and clothing, since the Father generously
cares for birds and flowers—and people are of much greater value. In
fact, God will gladly share His entire kingdom with us (Luke 12:32).

That's the return. The investment is found early in Luke 12:33
(VOICE): "You can sell your possessions and give generously to the
poor." Cheerful giving, not frenzied accumulating, should characterize
our lives. This kind of investment, Jesus promised, never goes bust,
never drops in value, never disappears due to theft, fire, or flood. It's
stored up in heaven (v. 34), where God makes sure it's safe. And, soon
enough, you'll be safe there with Him.

Jesus' final word: "Since you don't need to worry—about security
and safety, about food and clothing—then pursue God's kingdom
first and foremost, and these other things will come to you as well"
(Luke 12:31 VOICE).

Lord, please manage everything—it all came from You anyway.

GOD HELPS THOSE WHO
HELP THEMSELVES

*When Joshua was near the town of Jericho, he looked up and
saw a man standing in front of him with sword in hand.
Joshua went up to him and demanded, "Are you friend or foe?"*

JOSHUA 5:13 NLT

You won't find the title of today's reading in scripture. But the famed
Bible commentator Matthew Henry (1662–1714) applied the aphorism
to Israel's leader Joshua.

Just ahead of Israel's conquest of Jericho, Joshua saw an unknown
man holding a sword and immediately challenged him: "Are you
friend or foe?"

The man's response was "neither." He was no enemy, but he was
also much more than a friend. "I am the commander of the LORD's
army," he told Joshua (Joshua 5:14 NLT), who immediately fell to the
ground in reverence. "Joshua was in his post as a general," Matthew
Henry observed, "when God came and made himself known as
Generalissimo." Joshua quickly requested orders, and the Lord shared
plans for defeating Jericho, the first obstacle in the Promised Land.

God is always near, always ready to help us do any job He
commands us to do. But *we* have to take the first step. Even the faith
and courage for that first step come from God, so when His Spirit
prompts you, obey. You'll have all of God's army in support.

*Lord of heaven's armies, what would You have me do?
Give me Your direction, courage, and power.*

ARE YOU POOR AND NEEDY? GOOD!

But as for me, I am poor and needy; come quickly to me,
O God. You are my help and my deliverer; LORD, do not delay.

PSALM 70:5 NIV

Question: Why did the Israelites wander so long in the wilderness? Answer: Because Moses refused to stop and ask for directions.

The older you are, the better you'll understand the joke—GPS and mapping technology have made asking for directions a thing of the past. But whatever our age, many of us guys still hate to admit weakness of any kind.

Humility, however, is essential for our Christian growth and happiness. In fact, we'll never even be saved unless we come to God "like little children" (Matthew 18:3 NIV). Since pride is the root from which all other sin grows, God despises it. Isaiah prophesied of a time when "the arrogance of man will be brought low and human pride humbled; the LORD alone will be exalted in that day" (Isaiah 2:17 NIV).

Though King David's pride occasionally got him into trouble— consider his sin with Bathsheba and the foolish census that brought a plague on Israel (2 Samuel 11, 24)—he always returned to God in humble dependence. Today's scripture is an example of the attitude we should consciously develop in our own lives. Let's pray, like David did,

"But as for me, I am poor and needy; come quickly
to me, O God. You are my help and my deliverer;
LORD, do not delay" (Psalm 70:5 NIV).

THE OTHER SIDE OF WARNING

"Unless you repent, you too will all perish."
LUKE 13:3 NIV

Many prefer the "gracious" Jesus of the New Testament to the "harsh" God of the Old Testament. They argue that God is angry and vindictive; Jesus is all love and acceptance.

There are sound theological reasons (such as the doctrine of the Trinity) to dismiss that argument. But even a quick skim of scripture reveals many examples of God's patience and tenderness "before Christ," as well as Jesus' own tough approach to sin and holiness. Today's scripture, repeated verbatim in Luke 13:5, is an instance of the latter.

When informed of the Roman governor Pilate's violence against certain Galileans, Jesus didn't criticize the perpetrator or sympathize with the victims. Instead, He told the crowd around Him, "Do you think that these Galileans were worse sinners than all the other Galileans because they suffered this way?" (Luke 13:2 NIV).

Then Jesus mentioned another news headline: "Those eighteen who died when the tower in Siloam fell on them—do you think they were more guilty than all the others living in Jerusalem?" (Luke 13:4 NIV). To both questions He said, "I tell you, no! But unless you repent, you too will all perish" (v. 5 NIV).

Jesus was harsh when warning about sin. But He was actually being gracious, helping us to meet God on His own terms. . .which is the only way we can.

Holy God, loving Lord, help me honor
Your perfection by my humble submission.

AN OPENING FOR YOU

"People will come from east and west and north and south, and will take their places at the feast in the kingdom of God."
LUKE 13:29 NIV

Chances are the vast majority of guys reading this devotional are Gentiles. Out of around eight billion people on earth, only some fifteen million are Jewish.

Jesus Himself first brought the good news of salvation to the Jews—and then to the Gentiles—so we Gentiles thank God for including us in His family—not through any physical descent but simply by faith in Christ.

Jesus Himself described the opening the Gentiles would enjoy. In Luke 13, the Lord is asked, "Are only a few people going to be saved?" (v. 23 NIV). He responds by noting that many in Israel would assume, mistakenly, that their physical proximity and interactions with Him would guarantee their salvation (vv. 26–27). In contrast, faithful Jews of Old Testament times *would* enjoy eternity with God (v. 28), as would both Jews and Gentiles—people from "east and west and north and south" (v. 29)—who made "every effort to enter through the narrow door" (v. 24).

An opening is available to you. Have you made every effort to go through it?

. . . .

Lord Jesus, I thank You for making salvation available to everyone. Please confirm my place in Your kingdom, and draw many others—Jew and Gentile alike—to Yourself.

LIFE IS HARD. . .

Though you have made me see troubles, many and bitter, you will restore my life again; from the depths of the earth you will again bring me up.

PSALM 71:20 NIV

Some people see "life is hard. . ." and finish with "then you die." Christians should read "life is hard. . ." and conclude, "but God is good."

Troubles are inevitable and, as the psalmist notes, "many and bitter." We slog through the "depths of the earth" due to Adam and Eve's original sin as well as our own personal rebellion. Happily, the story doesn't end there.

If we truly follow Jesus, God will restore our lives. There's a good chance He'll bring us up from the difficulties we face in this world. But if not, there's a 100 percent chance He'll make everything right in heaven.

Let's be realistic about the world we live in. It's broken by sin and filled with troubled people, and that affects even those of us who love and follow God. But He's well aware of our trials (see the story of Job) and is working out every detail for our good (see the story of Joseph and Romans 8:28). Here's how Jesus summarized the situation: "In this world you will have trouble. But take heart! I have overcome the world" (John 16:33 NIV).

Lord God, this life is hard. . .but You are good. Please keep my focus on You and what You're accomplishing amid the trials.

NO EXCUSES!

He told him: "A man was giving a large banquet and invited many. At the time of the banquet, he sent his slave to tell those who were invited, 'Come, because everything is now ready.' But without exception they all began to make excuses."
LUKE 14:16–18 HCSB

Though generations of American children have been told they could grow up to be president, that's really not true. Through the United States' first 246 years, only 46 men have held the office. . .and the current national population is around 330 million.

Really, there are many things a guy just can't do. No matter how hard you flap your arms, you'll never fly like a bird. Try as you might, you can't lift a railway locomotive with your bare hands. There's no shame in saying, "I can't," and no need to make excuses.

But the things we can and should do can and should be done—without excuse. That's especially true in the spiritual realm, where God calls us to salvation, sanctification, and service. Today's scripture describes the Jewish leaders of Jesus' day who all offered "reasons" to avoid the Lord's invitation to follow Him in faith. Let's avoid their mistake and cheerfully do as Jesus says. When He commands, He also empowers. Our excuses only hinder His blessing.

Lord God, please break my tendency to make excuses.
Help me to do what You say, right away.

PRAY FOR YOUR LEADERS

Give your love of justice to the king, O God,
and righteousness to the king's son.
PSALM 72:1 NLT

Psalm 72 contains the God-inspired words of a God-ordained king for his God-beloved son and successor. David, the second and greatest king of Israel, God's chosen people, wanted his son Solomon to lead the nation in peace, prosperity, and justice. If you know much of Israel's history, you'll recall that Solomon—whom God called Jedidiah, or "beloved of the LORD" (2 Samuel 12:25 NLT)—started well but ultimately faltered.

Still, David's prayer was a good one, the kind of prayer we should offer for our leaders today. Of course, many things have changed since Solomon's time. But the apostle Paul taught all Christians to pray "for kings and all who are in authority" (1 Timothy 2:2 NLT). What better request could there be than to ask God to give our leaders a love of justice and righteousness?

Benjamin Franklin's adage "Nothing is certain except death and taxes" might be amended with "and selfish, corrupt politicians." But shouldn't that truth spur us on to even greater prayer? Never forget that "the king's heart is like a stream of water directed by the LORD; he guides it wherever he pleases" (Proverbs 21:1 NLT).

King Jesus, I look forward to the day that You rule the world
in perfect righteousness. Until that time, please restrain the
evil impulses of our leaders and guide them in wisdom.

CONFLICT AMONG BROTHERS

"The Mighty One, God, the LORD!
He knows! And let Israel know!"

JOSHUA 22:22 NIV

Though scripture calls Christians to live in peace, we don't always live up to God's standard. Saved by His grace, we're still fallen men in a broken world—often succumbing to the temptation to speak carelessly, judge unfairly, even consciously pursue advantage over others. When this happens, the ancient Israelites provide an example for moving forward in brotherhood.

After helping their countrymen fight for the Promised Land, the tribes of Reuben and Gad, plus half the tribe of Manasseh, returned to Gilead, a region east of Canaan. They had specially requested this excellent pastureland.

Moses had sharply questioned their original request. Now, under Joshua, the two and a half tribes again raised eyebrows by building a replica of the Lord's altar near the Jordan River. They were accused of turning from God through divisive worship.

The accused quickly called on God as their witness, then humbly explained that the altar was just a reminder to their descendants to worship at the one true altar with the whole Israelite community. Happily, the other tribes accepted the rationale in the spirit it was offered. A crisis was averted and fellowship restored.

As we face conflict, may we also look quickly to God, answer gently (Proverbs 15:1), and pursue restoration. The Lord will guide us into the brotherhood He desires.

Father, temper my pride so I can live in peace with my brothers.

GOD KNOWS HEARTS

*But He said to them, You are the ones who declare yourselves
just and upright before men, but God knows your hearts.
For what is exalted and highly thought of among men is
detestable and abhorrent (an abomination) in the sight of God.*

LUKE 16:15 AMPC

The idea that "God knows hearts" can be either frightening or comforting. You choose.

If, like the Pharisees of Jesus' day, you think your relationship with God is all about power, prestige, and putting others down, be afraid. Be very afraid. That is not at all what faith in Christ means or leads to.

But if you take Jesus' teaching seriously—if you honestly and humbly seek His strength to live up to His principles, however imperfectly—you can take heart in the knowledge that God recognizes and rewards such pursuits. You'll be part of the crowd the apostle Paul described to Timothy: "Shun youthful lusts and flee from them, and aim at and pursue righteousness (all that is virtuous and good, right living, conformity to the will of God in thought, word, and deed); [and aim at and pursue] faith, love, [and] peace (harmony and concord with others) in fellowship with all [Christians], who call upon the Lord out of a pure heart" (2 Timothy 2:22 AMPC).

God already knows your heart. What would you like Him to find there?

*Heavenly Father, I want a pure heart, one that
consistently pursues Jesus and pleases You.*

ULTIMATE JUSTICE

*When you arise, O Lord, you will laugh at their silly
ideas as a person laughs at dreams in the morning.*
PSALM 73:20 NLT

"Cheaters never win." Yeah, right.

These days, playing by the rules seems like a quaint, old-fashioned notion. Watch the news—or observe neighbors and coworkers—and you may conclude that living honorably just holds you back.

But that's nothing new. The author of Psalm 73 grappled with the same frustration centuries before Jesus' birth. "I envied the proud when I saw them prosper despite their wickedness," the psalmist complained. "They seem to live such painless lives; their bodies are so healthy and strong. They don't have troubles like other people; they're not plagued with problems like everyone else. They wear pride like a jeweled necklace and clothe themselves with cruelty" (vv. 3–6 NLT).

Of course, that's not the whole story. The psalm writer had an epiphany in the temple when he realized the destiny of the proud oppressors (v. 17). Though they could hurt their fellow man seemingly with impunity, they would not escape God's justice (v. 19). In fact, the Lord would chuckle at their ridiculous bluster, turned so quickly into terror.

As Christians, we are called to love and pray for our enemies, not gloat over their demise. But those who steadfastly refuse God's mercy will face justice. We can be sure that God will make proper retribution and vindicate His own.

Lord, help me to trust in Your perfect justice.

WHY WE MUST FIGHT

These are the nations that GOD left there, using them to test the Israelites who had no experience in the Canaanite wars. He did it to train the descendants of Israel, the ones who had no battle experience, in the art of war.

JUDGES 3:1–2 MSG

Good parents sometimes let their kids struggle—even fail—as an important lesson. God treats His own children similarly.

Though we'll never perfectly understand God, we occasionally get a biblical explanation of His ways. In Judges, we read that He used enemy nations to train His people in "the art of war." Previous Israelites had fought battles, but the present generation was untested. They would need toughening to become the enduring nation God intended them to be. Sadly, the Israelites often failed the test, choosing to imitate, rather than dominate, the wicked cultures around them.

Similar challenges and opportunities face us. For His own reasons, God doesn't take us to heaven as soon as we're saved. He leaves us in a battle zone, where we'll need to learn the art of war if we're to survive. We may not understand His purpose—and even wish it were different—but God calls us to fight the evil attitudes and philosophies of the world around us.

There's no guarantee that we'll prevail on this battlefield. But our obedient efforts will certainly be rewarded.

Lord, You call me to battle. Equip me with courage and cunning to fight with honor.

LIFE NOT MAKING SENSE?

"Will not God bring about justice for his chosen ones, who cry out to him day and night? Will he keep putting them off? I tell you, he will see that they get justice, and quickly. However, when the Son of Man comes, will he find faith on the earth?"

LUKE 18:7–8 NIV

Whether it's another mass shooting or simply our personal budget, much of life doesn't add up. We want things to make sense, but many circumstances resist our best efforts at understanding: the illness or death of loved ones, our own emotional and relational challenges, the incomprehensible behaviors of individuals and nations.

That's why we need faith.

Jesus spoke a parable to show His disciples "that they should always pray and not give up" (Luke 18:1 NIV). He described a downtrodden widow who continually pled with a judge for justice. Though the judge "neither feared God nor cared what people thought" (v. 2 NIV), he ultimately ruled for her just to make her go away. God the Father, who is nothing like that judge, will certainly care for His own, as today's scripture indicates.

God allows trouble and confusion in our lives to build our faith—if things always made sense to us, why would we pursue Him? The key is simply to trust His wisdom and timing. Keep the faith. . .it's what pleases God (Hebrews 11:6).

Lord, help me to trust You in every situation. I want to keep the faith!

POSSIBLE WITH GOD

"What is impossible with men is possible with God."
LUKE 18:27 HCSB

Got any impossible situations in your life? Any depressing circumstances for which there is no human hope? At one time or another, we'll all answer yes to such questions.

We who follow Jesus, however, always have hope. The baffling, bewildering, befuddling barriers to our own desires are totally within God's power. "What is impossible with men," to reiterate Jesus' teaching, "is possible with God."

Creating an entire universe from nothing was no problem to Him. Overseeing trillions of living things doesn't tax Him in the least. The Lord can certainly handle our impossible situations.

But read Jesus' words one more time. Notice that what is "impossible with men" is not "*guaranteed*" with God". . .it's simply "possible." For His own wise reasons, the Lord sometimes says no to us, or perhaps "wait." Whatever His response to the impossible situations that try our souls, we know well that God knows best.

In context, today's scripture discusses the salvation of hard-to-reach people. If that's your impossible situation, keep the faith. If it's a health or financial or relational issue, keep praying and obeying. God may ultimately give you what you want, or He may redirect your hopes in a better direction. Whatever the case, never doubt that all things are possible with God.

Lord, I know You can do all things. Please give me what I long for—or change those longings to align with Your will.

DAY IS COMING

The day is Yours; the night also is Yours.
You have prepared the light and the sun.
PSALM 74:16 SKJV

Most of us, at some point in childhood, are afraid of the dark. Part of "growing up" is shedding that particular fear.

But even men can dread the nighttime—not for presumed monsters under the bed but for the frightening things that inhabit our own minds. Minus the distractions of the day's activity, we might worry over career and finances, our marriage or kids, the state of the world, or any of a million other topics that disrupt sleep. What's a guy to do?

Psalm 74 offers both sympathy and hope. Clearly referencing the Babylonian destruction of Jerusalem, the psalm writer spends the first eleven verses bemoaning God's anger and seeming rejection of His people. Bad people were oppressing God's people, and the Lord was allowing it to happen.

But then the psalm writer changed his mindset entirely. "God is my King of old, working salvation in the midst of the earth," he wrote (v. 12 SKJV). The Lord possessed enough power to divide seas, dry up rivers, and break open fountains, all to help His people. There would be times of darkness, as today's scripture indicates. . .but God is always preparing light and sun to follow.

Every night gives way to day. This is God's plan, in both the natural and spiritual realm.

Father, allay my fears and remind me that Your day is coming.

WHEN GOD GETS WEARY

*But the Israelites said, "We have sinned. Deal with us as You see fit;
only deliver us today!" So they got rid of the foreign gods among them
and worshiped the LORD, and He became weary of Israel's misery.*
JUDGES 10:15–16 HCSB

Creating and maintaining the universe is no challenge to our infinite,
almighty God. A familiar passage from Isaiah emphasizes the Lord's
strength and stamina: "Do you not know? Have you not heard? Yahweh
is the everlasting God, the Creator of the whole earth. He never grows
faint or weary" (Isaiah 40:28 HCSB).

So why does the book of Judges say God *can* be wearied?

Reread today's scripture and watch carefully for what wearies the
Lord: it's the misery of His people. In the time of the judges, that
misery was self-inflicted, due entirely to Israel's idolatry and rebellion.
But as soon as the people admitted their guilt and changed their ways,
God admitted His pain and changed His people's fortunes.

If you are in Christ, God the Father loves you with an everlasting
love (Jeremiah 31:3). Even when you sin, He longs for you to return
to His side. And as soon as you make the first move, He rushes to
welcome you back. God is never weary to forgive and restore.

*Heavenly Father, it's amazing to realize that my misery wearies
You. May I always avoid sin so that neither of us needs to suffer.*

FROM THE HAND OF GOD

*No one from the east or the west or from the
desert can exalt themselves. It is God who judges:
He brings one down, he exalts another.*

PSALM 75:6–7 NIV

We men tend to like recognition. If we've accomplished something of note, we want others to notice it and call us out by name. And if we're successful in our jobs, we feel that we deserve a promotion.

Today's scripture verses, however, tell us that God is the one who exalts. The psalmist Asaph was teaching the proud (and reminding the humble) that their success and exaltation come from the Lord, not as a result of their own ambition and initiative.

If you are successful, even by human standards, it's a good idea to avoid boasting but instead humbly thank God for what you've been able to accomplish. That is part of what the apostle James was getting at when he wrote, "Every good and perfect gift is from above, coming down from the Father of the heavenly lights, who does not change like shifting shadows" (James 1:17 NIV).

God isn't against success or accomplishment. But always remember that whatever good things you enjoy in this life are from His generous hand.

. . . .

*Father in heaven, You are in control of all things, including my
life circumstances and any success I enjoy. I humbly submit
myself to You so that You may do with me as You will.*

JUDGMENT ON WICKEDNESS

But as for me, I will always proclaim what God has done; I will sing praises to the God of Jacob. For God says, "I will break the strength of the wicked, but I will increase the power of the godly."

Psalm 75:9–10 NLT

Asaph, the writer of Psalm 75, recognized that the world around him was filled with defiant, wicked men whose hearts and minds were set on all sorts of wrongdoing.

If Asaph had lived today, he would certainly have made the same observations. But, unlike so many who feel discouraged at what they see going on around them, Asaph confidently proclaimed, "I will always proclaim what God has done; I will sing praises to the God of Jacob."

Asaph's confidence was based in his realization that God was aware of the state of the world, and of humanity, and that He would one day judge all evil and lift up the godly.

Today's scripture verses give you hope. It won't be like this forever. One day, the Lord will break the power and strength of the wicked and lift up the righteous—those who believe in and follow Jesus.

. . . .

Father in heaven, sometimes I find myself feeling a deep sense of sadness and discouragement at all the sin, injustice, and violence going on in the world today. But I am heartened when I read Your promises to one day righteously judge the world, defeat evil, and set all things right.

GIVING ALL FOR JESUS

While Jesus was in the Temple, he watched the rich people dropping their gifts in the collection box. Then a poor widow came by and dropped in two small coins. "I tell you the truth," Jesus said, "this poor widow has given more than all the rest of them. For they have given a tiny part of their surplus, but she, poor as she is, has given everything she has."

LUKE 21:1–4 NLT

Jesus directed His followers' attention to a poor widow who had dropped her last two coins into the temple collection box—and contrasted her sacrifice with those who gave only their surplus. "This poor widow has given more than all the rest of them," He said.

Jesus commended this impoverished widow for giving everything she had. Hers was a huge financial sacrifice (it was everything she had), but there's a principle here beyond the giving of money—as important as that is. God wants us to dedicate everything we have—our money, our time, our mental energy...*everything*—to glorify Him and to bring others into His eternal kingdom.

Father in heaven, even when I don't have much to give,
You still see my sacrifices to You. May I always be faithful to give
You all I have, even when what I have to give seems relatively
small and insignificant. May I always find encouragement in
knowing that You always see when I give of what little I have.

YOUR SALVATION IS NEAR

*"Everyone will see the Son of Man coming on a cloud with
power and great glory. So when all these things begin to
happen, stand and look up, for your salvation is near!"*
LUKE 21:27–28 NLT

In Luke 21:5–24, Jesus talks to His followers about events that would take place prior to His second coming. Then, He makes the blessed promises found in today's scripture verses.

Jesus is coming back. It has been two thousand years since He made that promise, and we're still waiting. But Jesus' promise to return is as sure and as dependable as it was when He first made it.

We don't know when the things Jesus predicted, including His return, will come to pass. They could begin to happen in another century, or they could begin to happen tomorrow. In the meantime, we are to be watchful, hopeful. . .and ready.

Jesus died, but He was raised from the dead. He ascended back to heaven, but He's coming back! We who follow Him can take heart in the wonderful truth that the day He returns will be our first day of eternity in God's heavenly kingdom.

*Jesus, I take great encouragement in Your promise that
You will return one day and finally and eternally redeem
me and others who faithfully follow You in this life here on
earth. May I always be ready for Your return, knowing that
it could happen at any time. What a day that will be!*

TRUE GREATNESS

Jesus told them, "In this world the kings and great men lord it over their people, yet they are called 'friends of the people.' But among you it will be different. Those who are the greatest among you should take the lowest rank, and the leader should be like a servant. Who is more important, the one who sits at the table or the one who serves? The one who sits at the table, of course. But not here! For I am among you as one who serves."

Luke 22:25–27 nlt

The word *servant* isn't held in as high of regard as it should be these days. When many people hear that word, they think of someone who is of lower rank, someone who is tasked with the most menial and humbling responsibilities.

Jesus, however, has a much different take on what it really means to be a servant. He told His followers that the one who wants to be greatest should humbly serve. In the words of the apostle Paul, "serve one another humbly in love" (Galatians 5:13 niv).

While Jesus was on earth, He set the perfect example of a servant. Now, we should take His example to heart and take on the role of a humble, loving servant.

. . . .

Lord Jesus, You set the perfect example of taking the role of a lowly servant. May I always purpose to follow Your example and make myself a servant above all things.

HIS WILL BE DONE

"Father, if you are willing, take this cup from me; yet not my will, but yours be done." An angel from heaven appeared to him and strengthened him. And being in anguish, he prayed more earnestly, and his sweat was like drops of blood falling to the ground.

LUKE 22:42–44 NIV

As Jesus prayed in the garden of Gethsemane, He was in a sort of anguish we have no way to comprehend. He knew the pain and suffering He would endure in the coming hours, and His human side wondered if there was another way to rescue humankind from the consequences of sin. But Jesus was submitted to His Father's will and plan.

"Not my will, but yours be done." This was the perfect prayer for a perfect Savior who was fully committed to obeying His heavenly Father in every way, even when that obedience came at the cost of horrific suffering.

Jesus gave Himself up to die a horrible, ugly, humiliating death on a Roman cross because it was the Father's will for Him to do so—and because He loved us so deeply. And He also set a perfect example of obedience to God's will.

Lord Jesus, You set an amazing example of submission to God the Father when You prayed this anguished prayer: "Not my will, but yours be done." Help me to follow Your example of love, obedience, and submission, especially when my heart and soul are hurting.

WORDS OF BLESSING

*Just then Boaz arrived from Bethlehem and
greeted the harvesters, "The LORD be with you!"
"The LORD bless you!" they answered.*
RUTH 2:4 NIV

The Bible has much to say about the power of words spoken. Our words have the power to tear others down—or to build them up and bless them.

Consider Boaz, a wealthy, powerful man who lived in Bethlehem and who plays a key part in the biblical story of Ruth. When Boaz makes his first appearance in the story, his words make quite the impression on the reader. "The LORD be with you!" he greeted his field hands, who answered with a hearty "The LORD bless you!"

Boaz's words to his workers give the impression that he loved the Lord and that he cared about the men who worked for him, and they also show us that positive words spoken can help a man to have a great influence for the Lord.

Just look at how Boaz's workers responded to his greeting!

Do you want to bless, build up, and encourage others? Do you want to give yourself an "in" so you can introduce someone to Jesus? Start by going out of your way to speak words of blessing, especially to those who desperately need to hear them.

*Father, I want to be like Boaz and always make a great impression—
for You. May my words and actions always encourage and bless
everyone You bring into my life—even for a fleeting moment.*

WITH JESUS IN PARADISE

And he said to Jesus, "Lord, remember me when You come into Your kingdom." And Jesus said to him, "Truly I say to you, today you shall be with Me in paradise."

LUKE 23:42–43 SKJV

Two dying criminals hung from wooden crosses, one on either side of Jesus. They had both joined in the hateful mocks and jeers of the crowd gathered to witness Jesus' crucifixion. Until. . .

We don't know what these two malefactors had done to earn their terrible fate that day. But the Bible tells us that one of these recognized two things: that he deserved the punishment he was suffering that day *and* that he was in the presence of his only hope for something better on the other side of the grave. "Lord, remember me when You come into Your kingdom," he begged. Then came Jesus' response: "Today you shall be with Me in paradise."

Consider the word Jesus used for His eternal kingdom that day: *paradise*. Then think about this: if Jesus, the Son of God, who was there when God created the entire universe, called that place paradise, then the place that is now the eternal home to the penitent criminal must be far greater, far more beautiful, than anything we can dare imagine.

And that same place will be your eternal home too!

Jesus, thank You for reserving for me a place with You in paradise.

RECEIVING UNDERSTANDING

But they were terrified and frightened and supposed that
they had seen a spirit. And He said to them, "Why are you
troubled? And why do thoughts arise in your hearts?"

LUKE 24:37–38 SKJV

On more than one occasion, Jesus told His disciples that He would suffer and die at the hands of the Jewish and Roman authorities but also that God would raise Him from the dead—all according to Old Testament prophecy.

After all Jesus had said to the Eleven, you might think that they waited expectantly to see their risen Lord's appearance. Somehow, though, the truths Jesus shared hadn't sunk in. When the resurrected Jesus appeared to them, their response was one of fear, not joy.

Jesus knew what the disciples needed, so He supernaturally "opened their minds so they could understand the Scriptures" (Luke 24:45 NIV).

All men of God need the same thing the disciples needed: understanding of the scriptures. The good news is that God has promised understanding of spiritual things through the Holy Spirit to those who ask for it. So as you open your Bible today, and every day, ask God to open your mind and give you the understanding you need.

. . . .

Lord God, I want to know You and Your written Word better
each day. As I read and study the scriptures, open my mind
to its truths and how I should apply them to my own life.

SEEK GOD FIRST

*When the soldiers returned to camp, the elders of Israel asked,
"Why did the LORD bring defeat on us today before the Philistines?
Let us bring the ark of the LORD's covenant from Shiloh, so that
he may go with us and save us from the hand of our enemies."*

1 SAMUEL 4:3 NIV

After losing a battle (and about four thousand soldiers) to the rival
Philistines, the leaders of Israel were in a state of shock and wondered
why God had brought defeat on their army. Why hadn't He brought
them success on the battlefield like He had so many times? But while
they asked a valid question, they failed to stop and ask God why they
had been defeated and what they needed to do next. They neglected
to issue a call for repentance so that God would show them favor.

Instead of doing any of those things, the leaders hatched a plan
to carry the ark of the covenant into a second battle, presuming that
its power would carry them to victory. The plan failed. Miserably.

We Christian men should be careful not to make the same mistake
Israel's leadership made in 1 Samuel 3. That means seeking the Lord
first for what we should do when we're faced with trials and difficulties.

*Loving heavenly Father, when things aren't going well for
me, when life seems like a constant struggle, remind me
to turn to You first for answers and for direction.*

JESUS THE LAMB OF GOD

*The next day John saw Jesus coming toward him and said,
"Look, the Lamb of God, who takes away the sin of the
world! This is the one I meant when I said, 'A man who comes
after me has surpassed me because he was before me.'"*

JOHN 1:29–30 NIV

In modern times, religious animal sacrifice seems cruel, even backward.
But in Old Testament times, God required the sacrifice of valuable
animals to atone for people's sins. God's requirement that the sacrifice be a perfect (and therefore most valuable) specimen remindedz
the people of two things: God wanted and deserved the very best *and*
sin always came with great cost.

When John the Baptist saw Jesus approaching him, he made a
first-time public declaration of Jesus' true identity, calling Him "the
Lamb of God, who takes away the sin of the world!"

John understood that God had sent Jesus to earth to be the perfect
sacrifice for our sin.

Jesus lived a perfectly sinless life here on earth (see Hebrews
4:15). But He would die a horrible, violent death so that we could be
forgiven and then live forever with Him in heaven.

So take heart in knowing who Jesus really is—and thank Him
every day. . .for what He alone could do for you.

*Dear Jesus, thank You for being the perfect, sinless Lamb
of God. Thank You for giving Your life for me.*

THE COMPARISON TRAP

But the people refused to listen to Samuel's warning. "Even so, we still want a king," they said. "We want to be like the nations around us. Our king will judge us and lead us into battle."

1 Samuel 8:19–20 nlt

A human king wasn't God's very best for the nation of Israel. He wanted to be the people's King. But even though the leaders of Israel had the very best King in the Lord, they wanted a human king, and He said to the prophet Samuel, "Listen to all that the people are saying to you; it is not you they have rejected, but they have rejected me as their king. As they have done from the day I brought them up out of Egypt until this day, forsaking me and serving other gods, so they are doing to you" (1 Samuel 8:7–8 niv).

Samuel relayed God's words to Israel's leaders; they refused to listen, instead telling him, "Even so, we still want a king. We want to be like the nations around us."

Like Israel, we too can fall into the trap of desiring things those around us have—things God has said He doesn't want us to have. When we do that, we find ourselves missing out on the satisfaction we are to find in God alone.

Loving Father, may I seek satisfaction and fulfillment in You alone. Protect me from falling into the trap of comparing myself with others.

NO CONDEMNATION

"For God did not send his Son into the world to condemn the world, but to save the world through him. Whoever believes in him is not condemned, but whoever does not believe stands condemned already because they have not believed in the name of God's one and only Son."

JOHN 3:17–18 NIV

It's probably safe to say that every Christian man has had those moments of self-condemnation, moments when he feels convinced that God still holds his sins against him and is ready to "drop the hammer" and consign him to an eternity in hell.

If only the one who is in Christ but condemns himself would read and believe what the Bible says about God's love and how He poured out that love on humanity by sending His Son to die for our sins, then that self-condemnation would fly away. The apostle Paul put it perfectly when he wrote, "Therefore, there is now no condemnation for those who are in Christ Jesus" (Romans 8:1 NIV).

You may find yourself suffering under sometimes intense self-condemnation. But it doesn't have to be that way. When you feel afraid or unsure about your eternal destination, open your Bible and read what it says about you and where you are headed.

When you do that, rejoicing will replace your fear.

Loving heavenly Father, thank You for the blessed assurance that since I belong to You, I never need to fear condemnation or eternal punishment for my past sins.

FAITHFUL INTERCESSION

"As for me, far be it from me that I should sin against the LORD by failing to pray for you. And I will teach you the way that is good and right."

1 SAMUEL 12:23 NIV

Samuel had reluctantly anointed Saul as king of Israel, marking a huge transition for the nation of Israel. As he ceded the nation's leadership to Saul, he addressed the people, challenging them to serve God under their new king. As he ended his speech, he declared that he would continue to pray for the nation and its people, for to do otherwise would be a sin against God.

Samuel understood something that the man of God needs to grasp today, namely that the very best thing we can do for people is to pray for them. Samuel didn't agree with Israel's choice to have a king to rule over them, but he knew that God wasn't going to abandon His people. He knew that the best way to promote God's work in the people's hearts was to pray for them.

Several Bible passages encourage—or command—God's people to pray for others, a type of prayer called intercession. If God has moved your heart toward prayer for someone, take heart in knowing that He will hear your faithful, persistent prayers.

* *

Father in heaven, You desire that all men of God pray for others. May I always be faithful to that calling.

DOING YOUR PART

"You know the saying, 'One plants and another harvests.' And it's true. I sent you to harvest where you didn't plant; others had already done the work, and now you will get to gather the harvest."

JOHN 4:37–38 NLT

As a born-again believer, you should have a heart for winning souls for Jesus. The Bible teaches that you can do that by loving, serving, and speaking the message of salvation through faith in Jesus Christ.

But what if you've done all those things but haven't seen any results? What if you haven't seen anything in the way of a "harvest"? Well, don't be discouraged.

When you take the time to tell someone about Jesus, don't believe that you've failed just because you don't see an immediate conversion. Instead, take heart. . .and continue to faithfully and consistently speak the truth of salvation through Jesus Christ—and don't forget to pray, because you can't know for sure what God is doing in the heart of a man who doesn't yet know Jesus.

Lord Jesus, I want to bring people to You. Please give me the opportunities to speak Your name and message to those who need to hear it. Remind me, as You did Your followers, that it's not my job to convert anyone. My responsibility is simply to love others and tell them about You, even though I may not see the end results of doing so.

OBEDIENCE BEFORE SACRIFICE

But Samuel replied: "Does the LORD delight in burnt offerings and sacrifices as much as in obeying the LORD? To obey is better than sacrifice, and to heed is better than the fat of rams."

1 SAMUEL 15:22 NIV

Saul's reign as king of Israel was a disaster, not because he wasn't a strong, talented, gifted, appealing leader (he was all those things) but because he lacked a heart of true, unreserved obedience to the Lord.

Today's scripture verse is part of the prophet Samuel's rebuke of the king for his disobedience. God had commanded Saul to destroy the Amalekites, but he spared their king and captured their best livestock, which he claimed would be used for sacrifices to God. But Samuel saw through Saul's excuses, and so did God. Saul had focused on outward acts of worship and not on obedience.

We Christian men today do well to avoid the kind of mistake Saul made. While outward signs of devotion to God—such as attending church, singing worship songs, or giving financially—can be good things, they cannot be substitutes for a life of true obedience.

. . . .

Lord God, may I never try to substitute outward signs of faith to take the place of true and complete obedience. Create in me a pure heart that seeks to serve You and obey You completely.

UNDESERVED FORGIVENESS

*Help us, O God of our salvation! Help us for the glory of your
name. Save us and forgive our sins for the honor of your name.*

PSALM 79:9 NLT

The Bible's message of salvation begins with the terrible truth that
each and every one of us is a sinner in need of forgiveness. The apostle
Paul put it this way: "All have sinned and fall short of the glory of
God" (Romans 3:23 NIV). Furthermore, the Bible teaches that no one
deserves God's forgiveness and that we are all deserving of eternal
condemnation.

Now for the good news.

God has freely and generously offered sinners forgiveness and
mercy, not because we deserve it but because He is a loving, merciful
God who forgives "for the honor of [His] name."

We have nothing to offer God except our extended empty hands,
but because of His love and mercy, we can confidently ask Him to
forgive our sins, knowing that He is "faithful and just and will forgive
us our sins and purify us from all unrighteousness" (1 John 1:9 NIV).

Are you in need of God's forgiveness today? If so, take heart, for
God not only can forgive you—He *wants* to.

*Lord God, I know I don't deserve Your forgiveness or
mercy. But You extend forgiveness to me simply because
it's in Your amazingly loving and merciful nature to do so.
Thank You for loving and forgiving a sinner like me.*

OUR SOURCE OF LIFE

*"The Father has life in himself, and he has
granted that same life-giving power to his Son."*
JOHN 5:26 NLT

As the eternal God and the Creator of all living things, the Lord
our God is the source of all life—both physical and spiritual. And in
today's verse, Jesus stated that God the Father had granted the Son
the power and authority to give eternal life to anyone who comes to
Him in faith.

Think about the amazing miracle of receiving new life in Christ.
At one time, you were in a hopeless, helpless state of spiritual death.
Sin had separated you from God, and there was nothing you could
do about it. But God's only Son came to earth, where He died and
was raised from the dead so that you could be made alive in Him.

The apostle John gave us reason to take heart when he wrote,
"Whoever has the Son has life; whoever does not have the Son of
God does not have life" (1 John 5:12 NIV). Do you have Jesus? Then
you have life—abundant life here on earth and eternal life with Him
in heaven.

*Lord Jesus, today and every day, I want to thank You and praise Your
name with everything I have for giving me life. I was once spiritually
dead, but You made me alive. Thank You for Your amazing love.*

FAITH TESTING

*[Jesus] said to Philip, "Where shall we buy bread for
these people to eat?" He asked this only to test him,
for he already had in mind what he was going to do.*
JOHN 6:5–6 NIV

Jesus was about to perform one of His greatest miracles—the feeding
of five thousand hungry people, the only one of His miracles recorded
in all four Gospels. John's account of this miracle includes a lesson in
faith for the disciple Philip.

Jesus knew what He was going to do and how He was going to
do it, but first He asked Philip how they could possibly buy enough
food to feed such a large crowd. Philip couldn't answer Jesus' question
directly but instead pointed out the problem: "It would take more
than half a year's wages to buy enough bread for each one to have a
bite!" (John 6:7 NIV).

Philip's problem was that he was focused on the material resources
they needed to solve the problem when he should have been focusing
on the solution standing right in front of him. He failed the test, but
he learned a valuable lesson about faith.

When God asks you to do something that is beyond your means,
do you focus on the problems the task presents, or do you focus on
the one who provides everything you need?

*Jesus, whenever You give me a tough assignment,
help me to focus on You and Your provision.*

JESUS' EARTHLY MISSION

*"For I have come down from heaven not to do my
will but to do the will of him who sent me."*

John 6:38 niv

Jesus' three-year earthly ministry was coming to an end. In everything He said and everything He had done, down to the last detail, He had set the perfect example of complete submission and obedience to the will of His Father in heaven. In doing that, He made Himself the perfect servant, the perfect sacrifice for the sins of all men.

At the moment of truth, as His human side longed for a way to avoid the horrible suffering He knew was ahead, Jesus showed His commitment to the Father's will when He prayed from His heart, "Not my will, but yours be done" (Luke 22:42 niv).

The apostle Paul wrote of Jesus' life—and death—here on earth: "He made himself nothing by taking the very nature of a servant, being made in human likeness. And being found in appearance as a man, he humbled himself by becoming obedient to death—even death on a cross!" (Philippians 2:7–8 niv). When Jesus prayed His prayer of complete submission to His Father's will, He set the perfect example of obedience—and He also showed us what He was willing to suffer on our behalf.

. . . .

*Lord Jesus, thank You for being so committed to Your
heavenly Father's will by dying in my place so that I
could have an eternal home in heaven with You.*

THE BREAD OF LIFE

"I tell you the truth, anyone who believes has eternal life. Yes, I am the bread of life! Your ancestors ate manna in the wilderness, but they all died. Anyone who eats the bread from heaven, however, will never die."

JOHN 6:47–50 NLT

Just as each of us needs literal food to sustain us physically, we need Jesus to sustain us spiritually and give us eternal life. Jesus came to earth to minister to spiritually hungry and thirsty people, and in the above verse, He identified Himself as "the bread of life," meaning that He alone would be the spiritual nourishment each man so desperately needs.

Speaking to a big crowd gathered on the shores of the Sea of Galilee, Jesus once spoke this promise: "Blessed are those who hunger and thirst for righteousness, for they will be filled" (Matthew 5:6 NIV). He would be the one to meet that hunger.

The people who heard Jesus' words in today's scripture passage knew that God had provided their ancestors manna (bread) to keep them from starving. Every one of those people eventually died, but Jesus said that those who partook of Him, the bread of life, would live forever.

Jesus is your bread of life. What can you do to share that bread with others?

....

Dear Jesus, only You can satisfy a man's spiritual hunger. May I always live in that truth and also have the courage to speak it to others.

TRUST HIS TEACHING

*Jesus answered, "My teaching is not my own. It comes
from the one who sent me. Anyone who chooses to do
the will of God will find out whether my teaching
comes from God or whether I speak on my own."*

JOHN 7:16–17 NIV

For the three years of Jesus' earthly ministry, He spent His time ministering to the sick, the crippled, the hungry, and those weighed down by sin. But He also comforted and challenged those He encountered with some amazing, life-changing teaching.

Today, even those who embrace the "secular" Jesus acknowledge that He was a historically great teacher who offered great wisdom concerning how people should treat and relate to others. Jesus was indeed a great teacher, but He was so much more than that. He was the very Son of God, and His ability to speak life-changing words into the lives of His followers proved it.

In the above scripture passage, Jesus stated that all of His teaching—every word of it—was straight from the mouth and heart of the God who had sent Him to earth in the first place—not as a result of His own learning or credentials.

You can trust Jesus' wisdom and teaching because of where it comes from.

*Father in heaven, I thank You for giving Jesus the words to say as He
imparted teaching and wisdom to those who would listen to Him.
With Your help I will apply everything He said to my own life.*

SENT BY GOD

While Jesus was teaching in the Temple, he called out, "Yes, you know me, and you know where I come from. But I'm not here on my own. The one who sent me is true, and you don't know him. But I know him because I come from him, and he sent me to you."

JOHN 7:28–29 NLT

Jesus boldly and confidently made claims that set Him apart from other men, namely that God the Father had sent Him from heaven, where He had enjoyed a very special bond with both the Father and the Holy Spirit. Later, the apostle John summarized God's purpose for sending Jesus to earth: "He sent his one and only Son into the world that we might live through him" (1 John 4:9 NIV).

Jesus, the Son of God who came to earth to die and then rise again, is the one and only mediator between a holy, loving God and sinful humanity—and the ultimate expression of God's love.

You can take heart in the wonderful truth that Jesus wasn't just a good man who delivered amazing moral teaching. He was God's only Son, sent by the Father so that He could give you a forever home in His heavenly kingdom.

Loving heavenly Father, thank You for sending Your only begotten Son so that I can have close, intimate fellowship with You—and so that I can have my sins forgiven and then spend eternity in Your eternal kingdom.

THE LIGHT OF THE WORLD

Jesus spoke to the people once more and said, "I am the light of the world. If you follow me, you won't have to walk in darkness, because you will have the light that leads to life."

JOHN 8:12 NLT

In today's scripture verse, Jesus identified Himself as "the light of the world," meaning that He came into the world to be the one true source of spiritual light.

Since sin entered into the world through Adam and Eve's disobedience, our world has been shrouded in terrible spiritual death, darkness, and sin. Men are without hope of getting right with God— no hope except for Jesus!

Jesus wanted His listeners to understand that they didn't have to live lives of hopelessness, darkness, and slavery to sin. Instead, if they would simply believe in and follow Him, He would give them the transforming, restoring "light that leads to life."

Decades after Jesus had returned to heaven, the apostle John wrote, "If we are living in the light, as God is in the light, then we have fellowship with each other, and the blood of Jesus, his Son, cleanses us from all sin" (1 John 1:7 NLT).

Jesus has promised to give you light, a light you have the privilege of sharing with the world around you.

Thank You, Jesus, that I can walk in Your light every minute of every day. Help me, through Your Holy Spirit, to shine that light into the world around me.

FOR GOD'S GLORY

"Neither this man nor his parents sinned,"
said Jesus, "but this happened so that the
works of God might be displayed in him."
JOHN 9:3 NIV

One day, Jesus and His disciples encountered a man who had been born blind. Immediately, His followers jumped to a conclusion: "Rabbi, who sinned, this man or his parents, that he was born blind?" (John 9:2 NIV).

Jesus, knowing that the Twelve were wrong in their assumption, corrected their thinking, telling them that the man's blindness wasn't the result of any individual's sin but happened "so that the works of God might be displayed in him."

It's sometimes easy to look at our own problems as results of our own wrongdoing, as God's punishment for our sin. But Jesus' words in today's scripture verse suggest that our difficulties can actually allow God to bring glory to Himself.

The apostle Paul wrote: "And we know that in all things God works for the good of those who love him, who have been called according to his purpose" (Romans 8:28 NIV). That means all things, including our own suffering and hardships.

So when you find yourself in a tough spot in life, ask God to use that situation to bring Himself glory.

. . . .

Lord Jesus, help me to see my own hardships and
suffering as opportunities to glorify You and point
others to You as I endure those difficulties.

REVIVE US!

*Restore us again, God our Savior, and put away your
displeasure toward us. Will you be angry with us forever?
Will you prolong your anger through all generations? Will you
not revive us again, that your people may rejoice in you?*

PSALM 85:4–6 NIV

In the 1730s and 1740s in Colonial America, an event called the First
Great Awakening swept through the colonies. This revival resulted in a
surge in devotion to the Christian faith among church-going believers,
including an intense awareness of personal guilt over sin as well as
a deeper commitment to the message of salvation through Christ.
The Awakening made the faith more personal to the average person.

Today's scripture verses are part of a prayer asking God to bring
spiritual revival to the people of Israel. It acknowledges that God was
not pleased with the spiritual condition of the Hebrew nation, and it
also recognizes that God Himself is the source of revival and shows
us that we can and should pray for spiritual awakening.

Do you feel a need for personal revival? Do you recognize the
need for revival in your church or in our nation. Then talk to God and
ask Him to send revival. That's a request He will honor.

*Lord God, please keep me sensitive to Your Spirit's prompting
and direction so that I can know when I need revival. When
I need revival, remind me that You love me and want me to
enjoy a strong and growing relationship with You.*

A RICH AND SATISFYING LIFE

*"The thief's purpose is to steal and kill and destroy.
My purpose is to give them a rich and satisfying life."*
JOHN 10:10 NLT

When Jesus talked about the "rich and satisfying life," He was referring to those many things He promises to do within us, starting with the wonderful gift of salvation. That's a life of blessings beyond measure, a life of joy and peace and fulfillment.

The devil—the one Jesus called "the thief"—wants to rob even those who follow Christ of the rich and satisfying life. But we don't have to let him succeed. We can choose to receive every good thing Jesus has for us.

Our part in receiving that rich and satisfying life is to follow Jesus' command: "Remain in me, as I also remain in you. No branch can bear fruit by itself; it must remain in the vine. Neither can you bear fruit unless you remain in me" (John 15:4 NIV).

Remain in me. That means refusing to allow yourself to be distracted—by the pleasures of this world or by your own problems—and following hard after Jesus. That's the way to enjoy that rich and abundant life.

. . . .

*Jesus, I confess that my life in You doesn't always feel rich and
satisfying. I know that the devil wants me to feel defeated—
or at least discouraged. But I want the rich and satisfying
life You promised. Help me to focus on You alone.*

A VOLUNTARY SACRIFICE

*"The reason my Father loves me is that I lay down my life—
only to take it up again. No one takes it from me, but I lay it down
of my own accord. I have authority to lay it down and authority
to take it up again. This command I received from my Father."*

JOHN 10:17–18 NIV

We can imagine that the devil believed he had achieved an
overwhelming victory when Jesus died at the hands of the Jewish
and Roman authorities who condemned Him, sentenced Him, and
executed Him on a wooden cross.

Yet Jesus' death was anything but a defeat. In the above scripture
passage, Jesus plainly stated that no one—not even the most powerful
worldly entities of the time—had any authority over Him. He
would die willingly, and His willingness to die on a cross and then
be raised from the dead would clearly demonstrate His own power
and authority.

At the time, many—including Jesus' own followers—saw His
death as defeat for Him. But it was instead the victory He had come
to declare over Satan and his works of evil.

. . . .

*Lord Jesus, You died at the hands of both the Jews and the Gentiles,
but You died willingly—for me. Your death and resurrection would
give me and others victory over sin and death and would secure an
eternity in heaven with You. Thank You for what You did for me.*

WHOLE-HEARTED DEPENDENCE

Teach me your ways, O Lord, that I may live according to your truth! Grant me purity of heart, so that I may honor you.
PSALM 86:11 NLT

David wanted to honor God by living according to His truth, but being a humble man who knew his own limitations, he knew he needed to fully depend on Him to do that. In the above verse, David entreats the Lord, asking Him for teaching and for a pure heart.

David understood that God loved him and wanted to help him live a life and speak words that honored Him. In making the requests in Psalm 86:11, David showed himself to be a man Jesus would call "poor in spirit" (Matthew 5:3)—in other words, a man who knew how much he needed God, a man who needed to approach a holy but loving God as a beggar with empty hands outstretched in hopes of receiving from Him.

God desires that you honor Him in all your words and all your deeds. But He never intended for you to go it alone. On the contrary, He wants you to fully depend on Him for teaching, wisdom, and purity of heart so that you can live according to His truth.

Lord, I want to honor You every day and in every way. Please teach me Your ways and purify my heart that I may do just that. I praise Your name and thank You for hearing my prayers.

DO YOU BELIEVE THIS?

Jesus said to her, "I am the resurrection and the life. The one who believes in me will live, even though they die; and whoever lives by believing in me will never die. Do you believe this?"

JOHN 11:25–26 NIV

Jesus' close friend Lazarus had died, and when He arrived in Lazarus' hometown of Bethany, He spoke the most beautiful—and meaningful—words of condolence ever spoken. Lazarus' sister Martha ran to meet Jesus as He entered Bethany. Martha believed that her brother would one day be raised from the dead, but Jesus was about to show her that He had power over death.

With nothing but the command "Lazarus, come forth!" Jesus brought Lazarus from a darkened tomb into the daylight. Jesus, the man who had just called Himself "the resurrection and the life," proved that death was no obstacle for Him.

Jesus is our one and only source of resurrection and eternal life. Without Him, we have neither, but with Him we will one day be raised from the dead and will have everlasting life.

Do you believe this? If so, take heart! Because Jesus has defeated death, you will see God's eternal kingdom.

Lord Jesus, You truly are my source of everlasting life. I know that I will die one day. But I know without a doubt that at the moment I draw my last breath I'll be with You in heaven.

WHEN LIFE IS AT ITS WORST

O LORD, God of my salvation, I cry out to you by day.
I come to you at night. Now hear my prayer; listen to my cry.
PSALM 88:1–2 NLT

There's not a lot in Psalm 88 that will lift you up when life has you down, when you're struggling to feel a sense of hope, when it *feels* like God has forgotten you—or worse yet, has turned against you.

In this dark psalm, the writer declares...

..."I am overwhelmed with troubles" (v. 3 NIV).

..."I am set apart with the dead, like the slain who lie in the grave, whom you remember no more" (v. 5 NIV).

..."Your wrath has swept over me; your terrors have destroyed me" (v. 16 NIV).

But there is a glimmer of hope, and it's found at the beginning of the psalm. The psalmist addresses the Lord as "God of my salvation" and declares that he will continue to "cry out to you" day and night and entreats Him to "hear my prayer; listen to my cry."

Whatever difficulties we face, we can turn to the Lord, knowing that He is the God of our salvation and our source of comfort and encouragement.

God of my salvation, use my life's difficulties to remind me to turn to You first in all situations. Thank You for Your unfailing love.

REVELATION—NOT REVENGE

Someone told David that his wise counselor Ahithophel was conspiring with Absalom. So David prayed. David: O Eternal One, I ask that you turn Ahithophel's counsel into foolishness.

2 SAMUEL 15:31 VOICE

David often wanted God to bring justice to someone who stood in the way of his plans. Second Samuel 15 seems tempered by bad life circumstances. David had an adviser that turned his back on him and was giving counsel to the adversary. There had been a time when David would have asked for justice, but this passage includes a prayer asking that his adversary would see Ahithophel's advice as foolishness. David knew his adviser was wise and that his wisdom would help his enemy. But David didn't ask for something horrible to happen to his former adviser; he just didn't want to see the enemy benefit from good advice.

It's wise to pray that God would allow the truth to be known when you know someone is telling lies. It's kind to pray that a person you count as an adversary would have a change of heart. It's loving to pray for those who hurt you. When anger isn't your motivation for prayer, it will be much easier to discover encouragement from a God who loves you more than anyone else could ever hate you.

Thank You, Lord, for giving me the choice to love. Love is a commandment that helps me take this journey more seriously.

THE CLARITY LIGHT

"I have come as a light to shine in this dark world, so that all who put their trust in me will no longer remain in the dark."
JOHN 12:46 NLT

You have a choice to make, and it isn't a difficult one. Yet many will hesitate and push the decision to a future date or simply reject the idea altogether. What is the choice? *Trusting God.* The positive result of this trust? *Clarity.* To make the other choice would be like trying to read in a dark room. There's a light switch, but when you refuse to use it, you can't see to read—and because you can't read, you cannot learn.

Turning on the light helps you to see spiritually. That's *clarity,* which makes the things you have previously misunderstood understandable. It allows you a glimpse into God's plan and purpose for your life. It suggests wisdom is yours if you use the light to learn truth.

Some people get so used to living in this world's darkness that they can never understand anything but heading toward a future filled with nothing but futility. But the light Jesus gives helps you see where you're going, move beyond where you've been, and discover that there's hope in this very moment.

I don't want to live in darkness, God. Help me seek the light of Your Son and see a future that's good. This is the clarity of Your kindness.

BE VOCAL

Who is like you, LORD God Almighty? You, LORD, are mighty, and your faithfulness surrounds you.
PSALM 89:8 NIV

What would it be like to be so convinced that God is everything you can never be that your mouth refuses silence on the issue? Well, one thing is certain: your conversations would have a purpose—even in the awkward moments between what you're saying and how others respond.

When you follow God with all your heart, it no longer matters what anyone else thinks. You are not in a popularity contest, and you are not responsible for making others believe the good news you know to be true. Yes, God can use your words, but you need to say them first.

Psalm 89 describes a God clothed in might and faithfulness. The psalm is written by someone equally impressed with God (the writer of this psalm is a wise man named Ethan).

Even when people don't want to understand, you can (and should) speak. If they reject God, it's not because they never had a chance to accept Him. There's only one whose approval you should seek, and He wants you to tell others about Him. Be strong. Be courageous. Be vocal.

. . . .

It's easy to keep quiet, Father. Let me learn something from Ethan and be so impressed with You that others will hear about You from me.

LOVE'S BACKSTORY

[Jesus said,] "If you love me, show it by doing what I've told you. I will talk to the Father, and he'll provide you another Friend so that you will always have someone with you. This Friend is the Spirit of Truth."

JOHN 14:15–17 MSG

If John 14 were a cup, it would be overflowing with examples of how the disciples were encouraged to take heart. Let's settle in on verse 15. The backstory came in John 3, where we read that God loved everyone (no one left out). Between chapters 3 and 14 Jesus had taught His followers many things. That would mean that those followers should have understood *cause and effect* a little better than they seemed to.

How about a refresher on what Jesus said. If you want to show that you love Jesus, then pay attention to what He said you should do. And then? *Do that.* Obedience will be hard, so a Helper will take up residence in your life. He will be a friend. He will teach truth.

This is an impressive list of reasons to take heart. You're not asked to fake it until you make it, try hard and then try harder, or even believe something else that seems easier. Trust. Obey. Take heart.

. . . .

Let me work with You, Lord, not against You.
Don't let me try to be perfect on my own. Help me
take heart because I always have Your help.

THE CANDIDATE

*For the waves of death engulfed me; the torrents of
destruction terrified me. The ropes of Sheol entangled me;
the snares of death confronted me. I called to the LORD
in my distress; I called to my God. From His temple He
heard my voice, and my cry for help reached His ears.*

2 SAMUEL 22:5–7 HCSB

If you identify with the words of 2 Samuel 22, then you're a good candidate to know more about receiving encouragement from the Lord. David felt that death and destruction had followed him and he was left with distress. In this place, David spoke God's name—and God listened.

You have been—or will be—in that place. Pressure mounts as circumstances rip you from your comfort zone. If you're a car, you've wrecked. If you're a house, an earthquake struck. If you're a road, a river eroded your course. This isn't the makings of a feel-good movie, and it won't be remembered as the subject from the good ole days. Like David, you need to take heart. You can only do that when you take the God who gave you a heart. Call His name believing He exists and that He has the power to help when you're left feeling like death and destruction are the best you can hope for.

*Lord God, I need to be reminded that life here can
never be perfect. Help me call whenever trouble comes.
May Yours be the first name I say and the one I trust most.*

THE KNOWING

I assure you, most solemnly I tell you, that you shall
weep and grieve, but the world will rejoice. You will
be sorrowful, but your sorrow will be turned into joy.
JOHN 16:20 AMPC

John 16:20 says that you will suffer sadness, but it also says that the world will rejoice. What? Is this verse really saying that people will make fun of you? *Yes.* The things that cause you sorrow may convince people to kick you while you're down. This too is common, isn't it?

How is it possible to come back from universal ridicule? You can take heart in knowing something that those who make fun of you overlook. God is good, loves you, and what He thinks is all that should matter to you.

People might respond to your pain with what they don't know. They will make assumptions and draw conclusions that are far from accurate. When they toss their ridicule like a vial of acid, it may leave you wondering why. On the other hand, God knows you and deals with you with compassion, mercy, and grace. The sorrow you suffer at the hands of others can turn to joy when you determine that God's thoughts about you count more. *They always have.*

. . . .

Heavenly Father, what others think of me can be faulty or downright
wrong, but You know and love me perfectly. Give me the wisdom
to know the difference and then discover encouragement.

GOD'S TRUTH

O Lord, where is the unfailing love You showed in times past?
And where is the proof of Your faithfulness to David?
PSALM 89:49 VOICE

Let's check back in with Ethan the psalmist today. His bad day continues. If you take what you think is true about Christianity, then Ethan's words don't seem to match that truth. But his words are in the Bible, the inspired Word of God.

If you believe that Christians never struggle, then you will be challenged by reality. If you think you will never experience loneliness, then you might be challenged again today. Ethan wrote honestly about not feeling God's love and not seeing His faithfulness. Was Ethan right? *No.* Was he being honest? *Yes.* But his feelings didn't match God's truth. You can take heart based on these truths. God doesn't leave or abandon His people—*truth.* God has always been faithful—*truth.* God's love never ends—*truth.*

God's truth will never fail you, but your feelings might. The truth is God's job, but feelings show you how human you actually are. Truth creates sound decision-making. Feelings do not. When your feelings are confused, take heart in God's truth.

. . . .

I need to remember that Your truth can be trusted, Lord,
even when it doesn't feel like it. Give me that kind of trust even
when what I experience makes it feel as if I've been abandoned.

FINAL INSTRUCTIONS

*[David told his son Solomon,] "I am about to go the way
of all the earth," he said. "So be strong, act like a man, and
observe what the LORD your God requires: Walk in obedience
to him, and keep his decrees and commands, his laws and
regulations, as written in the Law of Moses. Do this so that
you may prosper in all you do and wherever you go."*

1 KINGS 2:2–3 NIV

David was impressive (yet not perfect) in his role as king of Israel.
His legacy was rich with trust in his God. Psalm 90 is an excursion
to the end of his life. In this passage, he gave a gift—a blessing of
sorts—to the son who would be the new king. Solomon had heard
many words from his father about God's faithfulness. David's parting
advice was as strong as just about anything young Solomon had ever
heard from his dad. There was a list of things like adopting the legacy
of obedience and following God. In his own way David was reminding
Solomon that following God faithfully would allow him to prosper
in the way God defines prosperity. This advice from an ancient king
as one of his final instructions is for you too.

*Lord God, when my life is nearing an end, may I have the wisdom
to tell those I love to follow You. May my encouragement cause
them to take heart and learn from You as they walk with You.*

EMBRACING ADVENTURE

*One of the Chief Priest's servants. . .said,
"Didn't I see you in the garden with him?"
Again, Peter denied it. Just then a rooster crowed.*
JOHN 18:26–27 MSG

Peter was so close to the adventure of a lifetime. Jesus had been arrested and Peter followed Him. Was the disciple going to attempt a rescue? That could have been his plan, but instead Peter hung out in a crowd listening for what may be happening to Jesus but doing everything he could to be invisible. One person noticed him and asked if he was with Jesus. Peter said no. Then, a second person asked the same question and was met with a not-so-silent eruption of denial. Then a third time is recorded in John 18:26–27. Peter wasn't the rescuer he imagined he would be. He adopted the role of a coward who was given three opportunities to stand with Jesus but couldn't bring himself to do so. Jesus had assured him that would happen.

Peter would still have the adventure of a lifetime, but he couldn't be the hero he imagined himself to be. He would need to be the servant Jesus knew he could be. In the proper role, Peter could be useful. Peter could embrace adventure. These are things you can do.

*I don't need to chase my own adventure to find Yours,
Father. Help me take heart when my plans fail. It just
means I need to keep looking for Your plan.*

THE DAILY STRUGGLE

*He Himself will deliver you from the hunter's net, from the
destructive plague. He will cover you with His feathers; you
will take refuge under His wings. His faithfulness will be a
protective shield. You will not fear the terror of the night.*

PSALM 91:3–5 HCSB

The psalms are a collection of real life, real struggle, and real praise.
David wrote more of the psalms than anyone, but many believe that
Psalm 91, though it isn't attributed to anyone specific, was penned
by Moses.

Moses spent decades in the wilderness on his own and decades
more with the Hebrew people, who never seemed to be satisfied.
He was the deliverer of Israel, but even he needed a deliverer from a
laundry list of personal struggles. He had to contend with the people
he led, the people in the lands they passed through, and the poor
decisions of both.

If Moses hadn't been strengthened and encouraged every day of
this journey, it would have been easy for him to give up.

Despair might be a choice you've considered, but the same faithful
God of Moses rescues from destruction, offers rescue, demonstrates
faithfulness, and deals with the terror you experience. So, is it time
for life redirection?

. . . .

*Lord, I want to learn to trust You more every day. Encourage me when
I'm down and let my life praise You in more than just good times.*

AN IMPORTANT ELEMENT

But by the cross of Jesus stood His mother, His mother's sister,
Mary the [wife] of Clopas, and Mary Magdalene.
JOHN 19:25 AMPC

Taking heart should be contagious. When you see someone with a belief in God's goodness that changes everything about them, it's inspirational. It can position you to make the same choice. Friends can be an important part of personal encouragement.

Three women stood in view of a cross made of crude timbers. Jesus—who taught in the synagogue, performed miracle after miracle, and gave wisdom a new face—was dying. His hands fastened to splintered wood, His feet similarly held in place, and His body struggled to bear His own weight so He could catch a breath. They listened in as He forgave; they heard the ridicule of the criminals also dying on that hill. These women watched Jesus bow His head as His human life ended.

They would need each other in those moments and in the days that followed. Most of the disciples, overcome with grief and disappointment, stayed away. But these women were strengthened by the presence of other believers and in knowing that Jesus truly meant something more than what they had witnessed on that hill.

The friends you keep can be crucial in helping you take heart when some say doing so is a choice that doesn't make sense.

Send me good friends, God. I need to remember they can
help me take heart or encourage something less honorable.

VACATING JUNK ROOMS

[Solomon] prayed, "O Lord, God of Israel, there is no God like you in all of heaven above or on the earth below. You keep your covenant and show unfailing love to all who walk before you in wholehearted devotion."

1 Kings 8:23 NLT

If you really want to amp up your own personal encouragement, then it may be time to use your mind to remember. Solomon was the wisest human king this world ever knew. God helped him, and this king accepted God's help. Solomon took materials assembled by his father, David, and had a temple made to honor God. In his prayer, Solomon made sure he spent time remembering. The glory days the king remembered were not about the things he excelled at but the good things God had done, the good God He is, and the many reasons to worship the God who rescues.

When you focus on God, the cobwebs of concern get brushed away, the soot of selfishness is removed, and the pot of pride is no longer left to simmer. You can take heart as you remember those times when God's encouragements populated the places in your life that before had been storing junk.

Father, I'm not always aware that I stand in the way of Your encouragement. I can think I know so much that You aren't my first call but a useful resource for on-call services. I need to remember—You are more.

A GARDEN ENCOUNTER

[Jesus said,] Mary, you cannot hold Me. I must rise above this world to be with My Father, who is also your Father; My God, who is also your God. Go tell this to all My brothers.

JOHN 20:17 VOICE

Two days ago, you read that Mary Magdalene was on a hill looking on as Jesus died. She was encouraged by having two friends with her. Two agonizing nights passed. On the third day, Mary went to Jesus' tomb, but when she arrived, she experienced confusion.

She was told by angels that Jesus was no longer there; she made an assumption without asking questions. She thought someone had taken Jesus' body. This was a cruel act, and if it were true, it simply amplified her grief.

Mary met a man she thought was a groundskeeper and begged him to tell her where Jesus had been taken. Mary was losing heart. But the man standing before her was Jesus.

Everything Mary had assumed was impossible was proven possible, and her heart was filled to overflowing with joy and encouragement. Jesus told her to take her full heart and "go tell this to all My brothers."

Don't keep silent about what you know. Let God speak good news through your voice, in the words you write, and in the things you do. Taking heart means never keeping God and His goodness to yourself.

. . . .

I don't want to keep good news hidden, Lord.
When You encourage me, help me encourage others.

LIVE WITH THE LONG VIEW

Your throne was established long ago;
you are from all eternity.

PSALM 93:2 NIV

Today is Flag Day in America, a day when we remember the adoption of the American flag of the United States. Yes, there is a feeling of pride associated with the commemoration, but it also gives Americans a day to think about our beginnings as a nation. There were people who believed enough in the idea of freedom that the flag was adopted less than a year after the founding of America.

Psalm 93 invites you to a different commemoration. Every day is a reason to remember the King of kings. He has always existed, and His kingdom was established, in part, to benefit mankind. Live with the long view of a coming kingdom, even though it can't be seen with physical eyes or recognized by the average man.

Take heart, knowing that there's a kingdom where God rules and is making things ready for His people to live there with Him. He has given us His instructions for life—the Bible—to help prepare you to one day take up eternal residence there. Accept the courage to believe, the boldness to act, and strength that comes with an active and vibrant faith.

. . . .

Lord God, I want to commemorate Your goodness today. Remembering Your gifts helps me make that choice. Thank You for Your kingdom and for the home You're preparing for me to enjoy forever.

NO CHAINS

The king's answer was harsh and rude. He spurned the counsel of the elders and went with the advice of the younger set, "If you think life under my father was hard, you haven't seen the half of it. My father thrashed you with whips; I'll beat you bloody with chains!"

1 KINGS 12:13–14 MSG

Wisdom isn't hereditary. You only need to read 1 Kings 12 to find evidence. Solomon was the wisest king ever. His son Rehoboam? Not so much. This new, young king wanted to leave his own legacy. When the people asked if he could make things a little easier in his reign, the new king promised he would think it over. Rehoboam then got advice from men who worked with his father and then from people closer to his age. The two bits of advice were very different. The older men thought he should make things easier, but the younger people thought it was time to get tough with people they viewed as slackers.

What you read in 1 Kings 12:12–13 is how the new king responded. The people lost heart. When Rehoboam's rule is remembered, it is rarely for anything good.

You have lost heart and taken heart at various times in your life. The bad actions of people can cause the first, but God always inspires the second.

Father in heaven, Your love defines You and also encourages me. Help me remember Your burdens are light and You always step in to help.

CERTAINTY

As [the disciples] strained to see [Jesus] rising into heaven,
two white-robed men suddenly stood among them. "Men of
Galilee," they said, "why are you standing here staring into
heaven? Jesus has been taken from you into heaven, but someday
he will return from heaven in the same way you saw him go!"

ACTS 1:10–11 NLT

You need signposts to direct you and encourage you when you're uncertain. Jesus told His disciples that He would rise from the dead. They were uncertain because that wasn't typical. Mary Magdalene thought the body of Jesus was stolen. Jesus talked to her that morning, but she didn't recognize Him at first because it couldn't be possible—she had seen Him die. The disciples watched Jesus ascend to heaven. They were also uncertain because no one had seen that happen before.

The signpost for these instances was that Jesus is coming back. They each had a story of the unbelievable coming true. But they also had a basis for certainty, and that was the promises from Jesus' own mouth.

Father's Day can be a time of certainty. If your father gave you reason to trust him, then it's easy to remember this day fondly. But even if that wasn't your experience, you still have every reason to be certain about the love of a heavenly Father who always keeps His promises, including the promise of Jesus' return.

Lord, help me be certain when it comes
to You fulfilling all Your promises.

THE TOGETHER EFFECT

Come, let us worship and bow down; let us kneel before the LORD our Maker. For He is our God, and we are the people of His pasture, the sheep under His care.
PSALM 95:6–7 HCSB

The Christian life is so much better when you have the support of others who also believe in God's love and goodness. God encourages us to worship and honor Him with others, not just in our own personal "quiet time" (as important as that is).

It's always good to worship the God who cares for you, even when you think you already have it all together and know where you put it. *You don't.* You never will. *That's God's job.* It's always good to worship God by yourself—and with others.

You can and should choose to take heart with other Christians, even when it seems impractical to do so. God never intended for you to be a "Lone Ranger" Christian. On the contrary, He wants to share Himself with you and have you share yourself with Him—in the presence of other believers.

You can receive God's encouragement and strength—together with others.

. . . .

Lord, You want to encourage me and strengthen me as I take the time to worship and honor You. May I never neglect time alone with You. But also please remind me often of the importance of meeting with others so that we can celebrate Your goodness and love.

ENCOURAGED TO ENCOURAGE

*[The widow] said, As the Lord your God lives, I have not a loaf
baked but only a handful of meal in the jar and a little oil in
the bottle. See, I am gathering two sticks, that I may go in and
bake it for me and my son, that we may eat it—and die.*

1 KINGS 17:12 AMPC

Elijah was a wanted man. He was guilty of praying. Ahab was a king
whose legacy included some very bad public policy. God worked to
get his attention, but the king had no use for the Lord.

At God's direction, Elijah prayed that no rain would fall. No
gentle afternoon rain. No summer squall. The clouds left town. The
waterways dried up, and each passing day made weather spotters long
for precipitation.

King Ahab wasn't happy, but Elijah took heart in God's
promises—including His promise that Elijah would always be fed.
A widow in a nearby town was gathering what was needed to make
one last meal for her son and herself when Elijah showed up and
essentially said, "I understand you will take care of me."

God supplied the miracle that kept the widow, her son, and Elijah
healthy and fed. And He also used Elijah to give this dear woman
some desperately needed encouragement.

*I need to be encouraged so I can encourage others, Father.
May Your words give me the courage to tell others of Your goodness.*

THE BETTER TARGET

Reconsider your lives; change your direction.
ACTS 2:38 VOICE

Bad things can happen to a man who loses heart. It makes him cynical toward others, apathetic, or even angry with those closest to him. It will often lead him to compound the situation by making choices that fall into the *bad* category.

The bold, persistent, gentle encouragement to someone who seems to have lost heart is found in today's scripture verse: "Reconsider your lives" and "change your direction."

You can't force those who have lost heart to take a different direction, but you can suggest that choice in a way that shows real love. You can be an example to follow. You can be a friend who walks with them past the bullseye of discouragement on the way to the better target.

Too many people today are willing to "cancel" others because they don't conform to their way of thinking. Christians should be known for something different. The forgiveness you offer and the direction you identify for others to consider is an act of love. Don't write people off as if they have no hope and no future. Give them a reason to seek something better. Give them a reason to take heart.

I think of You as my best example, Lord. That's the right choice.
But help me take the responsibility seriously to follow Your
example so others can glimpse Your grace in my actions.

IMPRESSIVE VIEWS

*The heavens proclaim his righteousness,
and all peoples see his glory.*

PSALM 97:6 NIV

The three months of the summer season act as a siren calling people away from indoor hiding and toward outdoor adventure. Summer is a season that focuses on water and sunshine. People will sit on back porches and around residential fire pits enjoying the sounds of insects. It allows them to inspect a white-freckled night sky. There may be trips to the lake or banks of a nearby waterway. People will pause to see the last moment of a sunset.

Be encouraged. What you witness is a proclamation that God's glory shows up in His creation. He didn't have to make the evening sky beautiful, but it means something to you that He did. He didn't have to create fire, but it has many uses. He didn't have to create lakes, but every day someone will choose them as a destination to enjoy.

These are small things for God, but they continue to make a big difference for those who take the time to experience His wonder.

. . . .

I will praise You for the beauty of the earth, God. Let me take time this summer to enjoy what You consistently provide for me to enjoy. Someone who can do this is worth a second, third, and fourth thought. Keep my mind on You and my heart encouraged to keep remembering.

MICAIAH'S CHOICE

Micaiah replied, "If you return safely, it will mean that the LORD has not spoken through me!" Then he added to those standing around, "Everyone mark my words!"

1 KINGS 22:28 NLT

Micaiah was a true prophet, meaning he spoke what God told him to speak. But other men who were also called prophets were comfortable telling the king what he wanted to hear. They stopped listening to God. That left Micaiah as one small reef of truth in a sea of lies.

How hard would it be to stand when everyone else sits, go when everyone else stays, and tell the truth when everyone else is comfortable swapping lies? This is the world Micaiah lived in, the people he lived with, and the struggle to keep speaking God words when so many other voices wanted him to say something else.

You have faced this—or you will face it—and that's when you'll have to make the same choice Micaiah had to make. You can say what's easy, knowing it lacks God's truth, *or* you'll say something truthful, knowing that your words may be rejected and you could be ridiculed. Consider your choice—carefully.

· ·

May truth find a home in my heart and on my lips, Father.
Give me words to say and courage to say them. Give my heart
the space to hide Your words and a mind willing to retrieve what
the heart stores for use in each conversation I will ever have.

WHET THE APPETITE

Joseph, a Levite and a Cypriot by birth, the one the apostles called Barnabas, which is translated Son of Encouragement, sold a field he owned, brought the money, and laid it at the apostles' feet.
Acts 4:36–37 hcsb

Being called by what you are is impressive. Being called a Christian means you are someone who follows Christ. No fear. No embarrassment. No apologies. But how impressive would it be to have the nickname "Encourager"?

The apostles met Joseph and gave him a new name that connected what he was with what he was called. They chose the name Barnabas. That name told those he met that he would always be quick to offer some much-needed encouragement.

Some people can't encourage others very well because they have not been encouraged themselves. They can't model what they've never witnessed.

Most of us like spending time with someone who encourages us. If you're not used to that, it can feel like a cold drink on a hot day, a full plate of food after skipping a meal, or a breath of fresh air after an afternoon in a musty cave. We all need encouragement at times. It whets our appetite for more. It increases our thirst. It makes us desire more deep breaths. Take it all in. Send it back out.

I need to be encouraged, Lord. I need to encourage.
Send the first. Give me the courage to share the second.

THE WORSHIP OUTCOME

Let them confess and praise Your great name,
awesome and reverence inspiring! It is holy, and holy is He!
PSALM 99:3 AMPC

Worship is the natural result of taking heart. If you haven't taken heart, it is hard to see the good things God has already done. You can only concentrate on what you don't have that you want. You live in a place of discontent. Pessimism may be a perfect description of your emotional state.

You don't have to minimize the truth of your feelings to acknowledge that there might be a better response. God has already chosen to be near men with broken hearts and crushed spirits. He recognizes your struggle but still says that you should take heart. Why? You're trusting His response and the outcome He orchestrates. You're no longer looking at the outcome as something that can't be known. When God takes over, it will ultimately be good—even if that's not today.

Worship is the visual and audible expression that demonstrates you have/are taken/taking heart. It's a testament to the things God is doing to renew your mind, change your perspective, and your heart's response.

. . . .

Lord, You are good and I don't thank You enough for Your
goodness. I don't think enough about the wonder of who You are
because I spend too much time thinking of my personal struggle.
Alter my view, enlarge my heart, and change my mind.

BELIEVE. TRUST. WAIT. REPEAT.

Don't worry; all will be well.
2 KINGS 4:23 VOICE

Moms use variations of 2 Kings 4:23 all the time. It's a phrase designed to comfort children. It may even help the mom calm her own turbulent thoughts.

Elisha was a great prophet of God. His actions led to the words of the above verse being said. He told a woman that God would give her a son. She hadn't even asked, but it was clear to Elisha that she had longed for a son. She would become a mother—and she and her husband loved the boy. But one day the child complained of a headache, and it wasn't long before he died. When Elisha learned what had happened, he prayed and believed, and the boy's life returned. Everything would be all right.

The woman, whose heart had been shattered when her son died, responded with deep gratitude. "She fell to the floor before Elisha's feet, bowing to the ground, and she wept with happiness. She picked up her son and left the room with him" (v. 37 VOICE).

This kind of faith believes when it doesn't seem logical, trusts when emotions say it's a worthless pursuit, and waits when anguish is a bully. Believe. Trust. Wait. Repeat.

Heavenly Father, the Bible is full of accounts of You doing the impossible. Help me believe that the impossible is still possible with You. I don't need to worry. All will be well.

A DAILY CHOICE

I will sing of your love and justice;
to you, LORD, I will sing praise.
PSALM 101:1 NIV

David was a king, a poet, and a shepherd. He was a champion, a man after God's own heart, and a songwriter. His songs weren't about breakups, country living, or the latest trends. David's words were for and about God. What was David's motive? God's love, His justice, and the need to praise God for all He does.

Throughout his life, David was an example of a man who took heart, a man who needed to take heart, and a man who was grateful to God for the reward of taking heart.

Being heartened isn't necessarily an emotional response, but the result can be emotional. It is not a knee-jerk reaction, but it can cause you to spend time on your knees. It's not even a promise of a perfect answer, but God's answer will be perfect. If that sounds like a contradiction, you should know that God won't always answer your prayers the way you expect Him to, but the end result might just exceed your expectations.

You have decisions to make every day. Your choice could be despair or trust. It will always start with believing God is good, trustworthy, and strong.

I want to be encouraged, Lord, and I want to remember who encouraged me. Help my mouth form words of gratitude.

FED UP WITH GOD

The king showed up, accusing, "This trouble is directly from GOD! And what's next? I'm fed up with GOD!"
2 KINGS 6:33 MSG

Have you ever been so angry or frustrated that you begin to blame God for choices that someone else made? Second Kings 6 offers some harsh words from a human king who questions the integrity of the Lord: "I'm fed up with GOD!"

You may wonder where God is when it seems that the world is falling apart. You struggle when you see people hurting and facing extreme pressure. It could be people who have been evicted from their homes, who don't have enough food, or who can't find jobs. It could be a widespread issue, just like it was in 2 Kings 6. You may even demand that God step in and make things better. But trust shouldn't be replaced by anger, requests shouldn't be replaced with demands, and mercy can't be completely disposed of in favor of 24/7 justice.

When the king spoke those words of frustration, God was already at work and change was coming. God didn't make the mess the king and his people faced, but encouragement was on schedule and would be delivered soon. Don't give up—wait as long as God needs you to wait. Help is on the way.

*Help me with patience, God. I don't like to wait.
I need to remember Your answers are coming.*

A KIND OF DESPERATION

*[God] will pay attention to the prayer of the
destitute and will not despise their prayer.*
PSALM 102:17 HCSB

To be destitute means existing without the essentials for daily living, such as food or shelter. When you live in this kind of desperation, God isn't embarrassed by your situation, and He won't pretend He doesn't know you. He doesn't send a message telling you to quit bothering Him. Psalm 102 says God pays attention when you cry out for help. He won't act like your prayers annoy Him.

David wrote this psalm as one who was suffering and facing trouble. David frequently found himself in troubling situations, and his writings serve as reminders for those facing difficulties to check in with the God who wouldn't turn them away. David understood from firsthand experience that God comes close to those facing trouble.

You can be encouraged in the truth that you never have to fight to have God pay attention to you. He has had His attentive eyes on you from your beginning. You can be certain that the outcome of every bad situation can be a closer friendship with the God who can bring you through it.

*Heavenly Father, when I struggle and have less than I need,
remind me that You remain close and will not abandon me when I
need help the most. You stand with me when others find places to
hide. You care when others believe I'm getting what I deserve.*

THE LEARNING CURVE

Joash was seven years old when he became king.
2 KINGS 11:21 NLT

Most seven-year-olds are getting used to the idea of school and playing outside with their friends. One day, they will look back at this time in life as one when they didn't pay taxes and didn't need a job. They were free to be kids.

Joash didn't have this experience. Through a series of national events, he became king of Judah. If you're using the daily Bible reading program that comes with this book, you will read more about this king tomorrow. What may be important to remember is that if a seven-year-old is to be king and lead the people in a godly direction then he might face the steep learning curve of depending on the God who is wise enough, strong enough, and patient enough to encourage a young boy to be a good king.

You won't always get to choose when you reach certain milestones in life. They could come later—or sooner. They can be small milestones that test your faithfulness or big life events that help you witness God's faithfulness. There's no such thing as ageism with God. He welcomed children and encouraged those more mature. God is still working on you, and He's not finished.

. . . .

Lord, let me talk with You; help me to listen.
Teach what I need to learn. I want to be the
right kind of student—and the right kind of son.

NOT FOR SALE

*When Simon saw that the [Holy] Spirit was
imparted through the laying on of the apostles' hands,
he brought money and offered it to them.*

ACTS 8:18 AMPC

Simon was a street magician who saw that the crowd was impressed
with the miracles of the apostles. Simon's idea of success was pleasing
a crowd, and the apostles' miracles certainly accomplished that.

Simon made a logical (though ultimately very faulty) conclusion.
If he could simply offer a financial incentive to learn the tricks of
these new street performers, then he could gain a solid return on that
investment by doing what the apostles had been doing. *Wouldn't that
impress the crowd?*

Simon could not receive anything from God because this wasn't
a matter of true faith in Him but the desire to purchase a commodity
to leverage new income opportunities.

God didn't create the new life in Christ as a way to improve
personal income as much as He did to improve today and the future
for everyone who freely takes heart. God calls people to represent
Him well, and some do make a living from that work, but His gifts
have always been free. They will never be for sale.

*Lord, I don't want to try to buy what I can never afford.
You've offered gifts, so I will accept them as gifts and say thank
You with an improved heart response to You and Your plans for me.*

WHAT IT MEANS TO FEAR GOD

*For as the heaven is high above the earth, so great
is His mercy toward those who fear Him.*

PSALM 103:11 SKJV

If perfect love makes fear go away (1 John 4:18), then does it make sense that God can love us and make us afraid at the same time? If His mercy (kindness, love) is given to those who fear Him, maybe there's another definition for fear when it's used in Psalm 103:11. *There is.* To fear God this way means to show awe and reverence. It's a sign of respect and honor. It's important to the idea of worship.

This use of this kind of fear might be seen when seeing the Grand Canyon for the first time. You may not literally be afraid of the canyon, but it may take your breath away. The same is true for the first time you see the ocean or Niagara Falls. You're in awe because it's something you've never encountered and it's even more impressive than you imagined.

It is possible to actually fear God before you meet Him and then fear (stand in awe of) Him in a whole new way when you believe that His faithfulness can do new and amazing things in your life.

* * *

*You're welcome to impress me anytime, Father.
May I revere Your goodness, stand in awe of
Your rescue, and respect Your ability to help.*

NO LOST CAUSES

*For some days Saul was with the disciples who were at Damascus.
And immediately he preached Christ in the synagogues, that
He is the Son of God. But all who heard him were amazed
and said, "Is this not he who in Jerusalem destroyed those
who called on this name and has come here for that intent,
that he might bring them bound to the chief priests?"*

ACTS 9:19–21 SKJV

Imagine a winless NFL team becoming Super Bowl champions the
next season. Such a mammoth turnaround only scratches the surface
of the change God worked in Saul.

You know the story: a rabid opponent of Jesus attacks the fledgling
church. Then Jesus Himself overwhelms Saul with a heavenly light,
both physical and spiritual. . .and the persecutor becomes a preacher
of Christ. Going forward, Saul—now known by the Latin name
Paul—will suffer cheerfully for Jesus, start churches, write letters that
become books of the Bible, and change the world.

Who saw that coming?

Certainly God, for whom "all things are possible" (Mark 10:27
SKJV). He wanted Paul as His special envoy to the world—and
got him. The Lord's people, who had been under terrible pressure,
"had rest and were edified. And. . .were multiplied" (Acts 9:31 SKJV).
Things got better in God's mysterious way and timing.

In our own dark world, God still has that power. Remember—with
Him, there are no lost causes.

Lord, please change my world like You did Paul's.

END OF THE WORLD?

You placed the world on its foundation so it would never be moved. . . . You set a firm boundary for the seas, so they would never again cover the earth.

PSALM 104:5, 9 NLT

We hear dire predictions of our planet's demise due to climate change. Some of us, though, can remember terrifying ten- and twenty-year predictions that are now thirty or forty years old. . .and not even close to reality.

Human beings do have a God-given responsibility to care for the earth. Adam's obligation to "tend and watch over" Eden (Genesis 2:15 NLT) comes down to each of us, wherever we live. But if we believe God's Word, we can take heart in verses like today's—describing the earth's superintendence by God Himself.

And there are others. "As long as the earth remains," God said after the flood, "there will be planting and harvest, cold and heat, summer and winter, day and night" (Genesis 8:22 NLT). "Not a single sparrow," Jesus proclaimed, "can fall to the ground without your Father knowing it" (Matthew 10:29 NLT). Ultimately, "the earth is the LORD's, and everything in it" (Psalm 24:1 NLT).

Only God determines when our planet's time is up. "The present heavens and earth have been stored up for fire. They are being kept for the day of judgment, when ungodly people will be destroyed" (2 Peter 3:7 NLT).

Lord, may I be ready for that day. Use me to prepare others as well.

NO FEAR NECESSARY

*"Say to Hezekiah king of Judah: Do not let the god you
depend on deceive you when he says, 'Jerusalem will not be
given into the hands of the king of Assyria.' Surely you have
heard what the kings of Assyria have done to all the countries,
destroying them completely. And will you be delivered?"*

2 KINGS 19:10–11 NIV

Mockery toward God and His people is nothing new. Centuries
before Jesus' birth, the Assyrian king Sennacherib tried to dishearten
Hezekiah with a threatening letter ridiculing the Lord. "Did the gods
of the nations that were destroyed by my predecessors deliver them?"
Sennacherib asked (2 Kings 19:12 NIV). Then he listed ten people
groups wiped out by Assyria.

Sennacherib's boasting wasn't hot air. While praying to God,
Hezekiah admitted, "It is true, LORD, that the Assyrian kings have
laid waste these nations and their lands" (2 Kings 19:17 NIV). But as
king of God's people, Hezekiah recognized a truth that Sennacherib
missed. The reason the Assyrians had been so successful was that those
nations' gods "were not gods but only wood and stone, fashioned by
human hands" (v. 18 NIV). The one true God, who had spoken those
false gods' wood and stone into existence, had no reason to fear
Sennacherib's threats.

God saved Hezekiah and Judah from the Assyrian threat. He'll
protect us as well, even if that's by taking us home to Himself.

Lord God, with You on my side, I never need to fear.

DEPENDENCE DAY

*Here is the sea, vast and wide, teeming with creatures beyond
number—living things both large and small. . . . All of them
wait for You to give them their food at the right time.*

PSALM 104:25, 27 HCSB

On July 4, 1776, the thirteen American colonies declared their
independence from England. What if we as Christians allowed this
date to remind us of our *dependence* on God?

It's not just the sea creatures who wait for His provision. Jesus
said His Father also feeds the birds and clothes the flowers. And we
as human beings, who have the ability to "sow or reap or gather into
barns. . .labor or spin thread" (Matthew 6:26, 28 HCSB), only do those
things by God's grace. As Moses told the ancient Israelites, "Remember
the LORD your God, for it is he who gives you the ability to produce
wealth" (Deuteronomy 8:18 NIV).

Ultimately, human life itself is granted by God and under His
control. In His parable of the rich fool, Jesus described a farmer whose
abundant crops led him to build larger barns. Though the man thought
he would "take life easy; eat, drink and be merry" (Luke 12:19 NIV),
Jesus reported that God would say to him, "This very night your life
will be demanded from you" (v. 20 NIV).

Dependence is our true human condition. The sooner we
acknowledge God's supremacy, the happier and less stressed we'll be.

Father, I need You. Please be my everything.

YOU CAN BREAK THE PATTERN

Before him there was no king like him who turned to the LORD with all his heart and with all his soul and with all his might, according to all the law of Moses, nor did any like him arise after him.

2 KINGS 23:25 SKJV

Today's scripture summarizes the life of Judah's King Josiah. The accolade is even more impressive when you consider his family background.

Josiah's grandfather Manasseh was an atrocious king who ruled fifty-five years. Son of the wise and good Hezekiah, Manasseh took over at age twelve and basically thumbed his nose at God. He loved to worship false gods, and even sacrificed a son to them. Another son of Manasseh, Amon, was just as evil. After two years, his own servants conspired to assassinate him.

Then something remarkable happened. Amon's eight-year-old son Josiah became king and shattered the family pattern. "He did what was right in the sight of the LORD, and walked in all the ways of his father David, and did not turn aside to the right or to the left" (2 Kings 22:2 SKJV). Perhaps his mother, Jedidah, guided him into righteousness. Whatever spurred him on, Josiah turned his toxic genealogy on its head.

Not every family is like Josiah's, but even the best have their flaws. Happily, with God's help, no man is bound to fail. You can break the pattern.

Lord, I want to be a Josiah. May I never turn aside from Your path.

JUSTICE IS SERVED

Immediately, because Herod did not give praise to God, an angel of the Lord struck him down, and he was eaten by worms and died.
ACTS 12:23 NIV

Some scriptures just bring out a man's inner eight-year-old. *Eww, gross!* we think, with a gleam in our eyes. Death by flesh-eating worms is some of the nastiest imagery in the whole Bible. (Though 2 Kings 18:27 is right up there too.)

All joking aside, this account of Herod's demise should encourage us today. Strange as it may seem, it's a story of God's knowledge, power, and justice.

Herod Agrippa I, grandson of the Herod who tried to kill baby Jesus, persecuted the early church. He ordered the death of John's brother James, who became the first of the Twelve to be martyred. Herod then arrested Peter, with plans to kill him too. After Peter was miraculously sprung from prison, Herod had the hapless guards executed.

Then God said, "Enough."

As Herod made a lordly speech in the region of Tyre and Sidon, which depended on him for food, the people shouted, "This is the voice of a god, not of a man" (Acts 12:22 NIV). Apparently, Herod enjoyed that—for a split second. Then God dropped the hammer on him.

Nobody ultimately gets away with murder—literally or figuratively. God will make sure that justice is served.

. . . .

Lord God, the injustice of this world is appalling. May I trust You to make everything right, in Your perfect time.

GOD IS PATIENT

For about forty years he endured their conduct in the wilderness.
ACTS 13:18 NIV

The "he" in today's scripture is God. "Their" refers to the ancient Israelites who had just escaped slavery in Egypt. "Conduct" includes whining, complaining, and outright rebellion. God "endured" these provocations "for about forty years" because He had committed Himself to these people.

God is remarkably patient. He delays judgment on the earth, "not wanting anyone to perish, but everyone to come to repentance" (2 Peter 3:9 NIV). When we join His family by faith, He "does not treat us as our sins deserve or repay us according to our iniquities" (Psalm 103:10 NIV). In this age of grace, He views His children through the perfecting lens of Jesus, "who gave himself for our sins to rescue us from the present evil age, according to the will of our God and Father" (Galatians 1:4 NIV).

The faults and failures that characterize our lives, though troublesome to us, are no surprise to God. In His great patience, He is always ready to forgive and forget our sins, so always run *to* rather than *from* Him. The scriptures tell us, "Whoever conceals their sins does not prosper, but the one who confesses and renounces them finds mercy" (Proverbs 28:13 NIV).

If you are in Christ, God is fully, patiently committed to you. . . forever.

Father in heaven, I praise You for Your patient love.
May it spur me to an ever-greater commitment to You.

MAN'S PASSIONS, GOD'S HEART

These were all David's sons. . .
in addition to the sons by his concubines.
1 CHRONICLES 3:9 HCSB

David was a bundle of contradictions. The man who composed powerful worship psalms also collected women like so many pretty stones. The heroic slayer of Goliath also schemed against Uriah, a loyal soldier whose marriage David had violated. The figurative father of Jesus Christ was the literal father of nineteen named sons by seven named women, "in addition to the sons by his concubines." *This* is an example for Christian men today?

Well, yes. The apostle Paul taught, "Whatever was written in the past was written for our instruction" (Romans 15:4 HCSB), so what can we learn from David's life?

Certainly, we see the dangers of unrestrained sexual passion. But we also learn that our own struggles with sex are common (1 Corinthians 10:13)—even in as great a man as David. What saved him was exactly what saves us: the grace and mercy of God, received through faith.

Despite his flaws and failures, David loved God. Though he often acted rashly in the flesh, he responded humbly in the Spirit. David could say, with even greater passion than that with which he sinned, "God is my helper; . . .the sustainer of my life" (Psalm 54:4 HCSB).

That is being a man after God's own heart, the lesson we take from David's life.

Lord, please make my passion for You
greater than my physical passions.

YOU'VE BEEN WARNED

*We must go through many persecutions
as we enter the kingdom of God.*
ACTS 14:22 VOICE

Dishonest sellers have long used the "bait and switch," a technique that draws customers in with the promise of a great deal. Then they're either sold an inferior product or pressured to buy something more expensive. God never deals like that.

To be sure, He "advertises" an amazing offer—salvation from sin, membership in His family, eternity in glory with Him, all for free through faith in Jesus. But there are some terms alongside the deal, and God is very up front about them.

Paul and Barnabas spoke the hard truth of today's scripture to believers in Lystra, Iconium, and Antioch. Jesus Himself warned, "In this world, you will be plagued with times of trouble" (John 16:33 VOICE)—and His life certainly proved that. Peter wrote, "The Anointed One suffered for us and left us His example so that we could follow in His steps" (1 Peter 2:22 VOICE).

As a Bible-believing, self- and sin-denying Christian in today's culture, you'll be branded a weirdo at the least. But you've been warned. God has not tried to trick you in any way.

If He's so honest about the negative side of following Jesus, don't you think He's being truthful about the benefits?

*Lord God, You've said that following Jesus would be
difficult—but that You provide strength and protection.
Please keep me faithful no matter what.*

NEVER STOP AT ONE VERSE

"Unless you are circumcised, according to the custom taught by Moses, you cannot be saved."
ACTS 15:1 NIV

Does today's scripture "feel funny" to you? It should, as it contradicts the biblical message of salvation by grace alone.

The quote is 100 percent accurate but, when read by itself, misleading. The words were spoken by tradition-bound Jews who wanted the new Gentile Christians to obey the Old Testament's ceremonial laws. This demand brought the mission team of Paul and Barnabas "into sharp dispute and debate with them" (Acts 15:2 NIV). Later in the chapter, other church leaders also disagreed. "Why do you try to test God by putting on the necks of Gentiles a yoke that neither we nor our ancestors have been able to bear?" the apostle Peter asked. "No! We believe it is through the grace of our Lord Jesus that we are saved, just as they are" (Acts 15:10–11 NIV).

When you're reading scripture, never stop at one verse—the surrounding passage will always provide important context. And if you see Bible verses anywhere—on internet posts or T-shirts or even in devotional books like this—stop and ask yourself, "Is that being used correctly?" Then dig in to scripture to be sure.

The Bible can't tell us everything about God, but it does contain all we need to know for salvation and Christian living. Be sure to study and obey it.

Lord, guide me into an ever-deeper understanding of Your Word.

EVEN SO

Our ancestors in Egypt were not impressed by the LORD's miraculous deeds. They soon forgot his many acts of kindness to them. Instead, they rebelled against him at the Red Sea. Even so, he saved them— to defend the honor of his name and to demonstrate his mighty power.

PSALM 106:7–8 NLT

Have you ever overlooked God's incredible power? Forgotten His kindnesses to you? Even rebelled against Him? We all have.

Even so, God loves you.

If you have accepted His gift of salvation, your mistakes and outright disobedience are covered by Jesus' sacrifice on the cross. Because of Christ, God the Father saves you "to defend the honor of his name and to demonstrate his mighty power." This is how God shows His righteousness, "for he himself is fair and just, and he makes sinners right in his sight when they believe in Jesus" (Romans 3:26 NLT).

We're still human and prone to sinful behavior. Sometimes we'll stay quiet when we should speak up. Sometimes we'll pop off when we should zip our lips. Sometimes we'll let our minds or eyes or feet wander to places they shouldn't go. Even so, God loves us.

Nothing will separate us from His love through Jesus (Romans 8:39). That's not an excuse to live in sin. But when we do sin, it's an invitation to return to God's fellowship in repentance.

Father, I'm grateful for Your steadfast love. May it continually move me to greater obedience and service.

"BUT HIS FATHER. . ."

There was a disciple named Timothy, the son of a
believing Jewish woman, but his father was a Greek.
ACTS 16:1 HCSB

Here is Timothy's biblical debut. The man who would become the apostle Paul's "dearly loved and faithful son in the Lord" (1 Corinthians 4:17 HCSB), recipient of two letters that became books of our Bible, is introduced as the child of a believing Jewish woman. "But his father," the author of Acts tells us, "was a Greek."

Luke may have meant that Timothy's father was non-Jewish, from Greece, or both. The word *but*, however, seems to indicate a lack of Christian faith compared to Timothy's mom. That was no impediment, though, to Timothy's own acceptance of Christ and his growth in grace. The believers of his hometown of Lystra "spoke highly of him" (Acts 16:2 HCSB), as did Christians in Iconium, a day's journey away.

Timothy's experience can (and should) be true of all of us, whatever "but his father" realities we face: was not a Christian, worked too much, was abusive, never came to ball games, acted hypocritically. Even great human dads sometimes disappoint their sons, if only by causing pain when they die.

As Ezekiel 18 plainly teaches, each of us is responsible for choosing to obey God. And He will gladly give us that power as our hearts incline toward Him.

⋯⋯⋯⋯⋯⋯⋯⋯⋯⋯⋯⋯⋯⋯⋯⋯⋯⋯⋯⋯⋯⋯⋯⋯⋯⋯⋯⋯

Lord, I want to be a Timothy—respected for my present
goodness no matter what challenges dot my past.

TAKE A STAND

Then Phinehas took a stand and intervened,
so the plague was stopped.
PSALM 106:30 VOICE

Psalm 106 recounts a particularly grievous event in the history of ancient Israel.

Between the time prophet-for-hire Balaam blessed rather than cursed the Israelites (Numbers 22–24) and the people prepared to enter their Promised Land (Numbers 26–36), God sent a plague that killed twenty-four thousand of His own. Why? Because the Israelites, while camped near a place called Shittim, got sexually involved with pagan Moabites. The immorality and idolatry infuriated God, who sent a quick and severe punishment. But even as the people mourned their losses, one Israelite brazenly led a Moabite woman into his tent. A priest named Phinehas, grandson of Aaron, followed them into the tent and ran a spear through the couple. "That one act appeased God's anger and put an end to the death cascading through the Israelite camp" (Numbers 25:8 VOICE).

It's an awful story, all the way around—but it points to the importance of taking a stand against sin. Ask God for the wisdom to know when and how to act. And be strong in the strength that God Himself provides. Take heart and take a stand. You may help limit the consequences of sin and point others to salvation.

Lord, it's not easy to oppose this culture, but as much
as possible I want to head off sin's results for my
fellow man. Please give me courage to take a stand.

DOING VS. BEING

I, the Eternal One, will build a house for you,
instead of you building a house for Me.
1 CHRONICLES 17:10 VOICE

On the whole, men are doers. We like to accomplish things—for ourselves, our loved ones, our communities and churches. God made us to work like our ancestor Adam: "The Eternal God placed the newly made man in the garden of Eden in order to work the ground and care for it" (Genesis 2:15 VOICE). The work we do is honorable and necessary...though we must keep our *doing* in balance with our *being*.

When David was crowned ruler of all Israel, he prepared his own home in the capital of Jerusalem and—with great fanfare—brought the ark of the covenant into the city. He soon felt a nagging guilt, though: "I live in a sturdy house made of expensive, imported cedar, but the covenant chest of the Eternal lives in a temporary house made of curtains. This does not seem right" (1 Chronicles 17:1 VOICE). David wanted to erect a temple for God, who completely turned the tables on him, as you read above. The Lord would "build a house" for David, the eternal kingship of his descendant Jesus.

Let's *do* what God tells us but more importantly *be* who He says—humble, loyal, obedient, loving sons. And let's pray, as David did,

"You are pleased to bless the house of Your servant; may Your pleasure continue forever" (1 Chronicles 17:27 VOICE).

GOD WILL DO WHAT IS GOOD

*"Be strong, and let us fight bravely for our people and the cities
of our God. The LORD will do what is good in his sight."*

1 CHRONICLES 19:13 NIV

The unsaved world often describes Christianity as a crutch. . .in their view, faith is simply something that weak people use as a prop.

There is truth in the claim, since we as Christians *are* weak and need all the support we can get. (This is even more true of unbelievers, though that's a topic for another time.)

As followers of Jesus, we have come to believe in an all-knowing, all-powerful God who has our best interests at heart. Having reached that point of belief, we can live our lives according to His Word, then say as King David's military commander Joab did, "The LORD will do what is good in his sight." We don't need to stress over every potential outcome, since we know it is in our God's supremely capable hands.

Human as we are, we'll sometimes struggle with this off-loading of responsibility. As men, we're wired to figure things out and fix whatever's wrong. But many things are truly beyond our ability. Absolutely nothing is beyond God's. He'll do whatever is good in His sight, and we can rest easy.

If that's a crutch, so be it.

*Lord, life throws many challenges at me.
I'm grateful for Your knowledge and power
and the fact that You will do whatever is good.*

YOU'RE SURROUNDED!

One night the Lord spoke to Paul in a vision: "Do not
be afraid; keep on speaking, do not be silent. For I
am with you, and no one is going to attack and harm
you, because I have many people in this city."
ACTS 18:9–10 NIV

Ever feel like you're surrounded by troubled, troublesome people? In less charitable moments, you might say "lunatics."

Well, you are—that's the nature of our fallen world. But never think you're totally alone. Of course, Jesus promised, "Surely I am with you always, to the very end of the age" (Matthew 28:20 NIV). But He has also placed flesh-and-blood fellow believers in strategic places to help you on your way to heaven.

Remember Elijah? After defeating Baal's prophets at Mount Carmel, his life was threatened by the evil Jezebel. Suddenly terrified, he complained that he was the last remaining God worshipper. But the Lord told Elijah, "I reserve seven thousand in Israel—all whose knees have not bowed down to Baal" (1 Kings 19:18 NIV).

The apostle Paul referenced that story in his letter to the Romans (11:1–5). And Paul received a similar encouragement from God while facing harassment in Corinth: "I am with you, and no one is going to attack and harm you, because I have many people in this city."

God has many people, everywhere, available to encourage you. Keep an eye out—you're surrounded!

Lord, please send a fellow believer my way today—or vice versa.

MOVE ON

But some of them became obstinate; they refused to believe
and publicly maligned the Way. So Paul left them.

Acts 19:9 niv

No surprise here: Jesus was right when He said, "In this world you will have trouble" (John 16:33 niv). He took plenty of guff (and worse) from the religious leaders of His day. In the decades that followed, so did the apostle Paul.

But notice Paul's response when people in the Ephesus synagogue became difficult and abusive: he "left them." Paul moved his ministry to a nearby lecture hall, where he preached with great effect for the next two years.

The early church had done as Paul did, when he himself—as the rabid persecutor Saul—was trying to destroy Christianity: "All except the apostles were scattered throughout Judea and Samaria" (Acts 8:1 niv). Saul was undoubtedly angered to find that "those who had been scattered preached the word wherever they went" (v. 4 niv), though as Paul he would celebrate every advancement of God's kingdom.

"In case of great peril, the disciples of Christ may go out of the way of danger," the seventeenth-century Bible commentator Matthew Henry wrote, "though they must not go out of the way of duty." In our increasingly hostile culture, we may have reason and opportunity to move on from persecution. But let's be sure we still reflect Jesus wherever we land.

Lord Jesus, when my faith is under fire,
give me the wisdom I need to honor You.

TEAMWORK

Obil the Ishmaelite was in charge of the camels.
Jehdeiah the Meronothite was in charge of the donkeys.
1 CHRONICLES 27:30 NIV

Obil and Jehdeiah were King David's logistics directors. They oversaw the official "truck fleet" of ancient Israel, undoubtedly managing a large team of drivers. The two are among dozens named in 1 Chronicles 23–27 as leaders in David's realm, from priests and worship musicians to military commanders, vinedressers, and teachers. All of them contributed to the well-being of the kingdom.

The same is true for us. Some of us have "sacred" jobs in church or ministry settings. Some of us do "secular" things like repairing cars or originating loans. Whatever we do should be for God's glory (1 Corinthians 10:31) and the betterment of society.

One thing we must *not* do is envy or judge another person's role. Unless we're making our living through immoral means, all of our hard work is honorable in God's sight—and He will ultimately bless it. But if you ever feel like you need a change, talk to God about that. He may be prompting you toward duties more beneficial to yourself and others.

This section of 1 Chronicles is reminiscent of the apostle Paul's word picture of the body of Christ (1 Corinthians 12), in which everyone plays an important role. Today, your role is the job you have. Tomorrow? It may be something even better.

Lord, please guide me into the most appropriate,
fulfilling, and beneficial work.

UNEXPECTED

*"The LORD, the God of Israel, chose me from my whole family
to be king over Israel forever. He chose Judah as leader, and from
the tribe of Judah he chose my family, and from my father's sons
he was pleased to make me king over all Israel. Of all my sons—
and the LORD has given me many—he has chosen my son Solomon
to sit on the throne of the kingdom of the LORD over Israel."*

1 CHRONICLES 28:4–5 NIV

Here's a little Bible quiz for you: What is unusual about all of the leaders David mentions in today's scripture?

Answer: None of them were firstborn sons, breaking the custom of their time and place.

David himself was the last of eight sons of Jesse, yet he was the one God chose to be king of Israel (1 Samuel 16). David's tribe was God's choice for prominence in Israel, yet Judah had been the fourth of Jacob's twelve sons (Genesis 29). And David's God-ordained successor, Solomon, was at least the seventh of the king's sons (1 Chronicles 3).

God is never bound by conventional wisdom—He often turns human expectation on its head, choosing "the weak things of the world to shame the strong" (1 Corinthians 1:27 NIV). If you're not the most talented, smartest, wealthiest, best-looking—or even "most spiritual"—guy you know, that's okay. If you're simply willing, God can use you for good.

Lord, here I am. Live Your life through me!

"IF POSSIBLE"

*Paul had decided to sail past Ephesus so he would not
have to spend time in Asia, because he was hurrying to
be in Jerusalem, if possible, for the day of Pentecost.*
Acts 20:16 hcsb

Exactly where human decision-making and God's sovereignty intersect is a topic far beyond the scope of this devotional. It's enough to say that the two ideas exist side by side in God's Word.

The phrase "if possible" in today's scripture parallels a common interjection—"Lord willing"—that arises from the book of James: "Now listen, you who say, 'Today or tomorrow we will go to this or that city, spend a year there, carry on business and make money.' Why, you do not even know what will happen tomorrow. What is your life? You are a mist that appears for a little while and then vanishes. Instead, you ought to say, *'If it is the Lord's will*, we will live and do this or that'" (4:13–15 niv, emphasis added).

You are free to make your own plans, though it's wise to hold them loosely. Always add an "if possible" or "Lord willing," spoken or otherwise, to acknowledge God's higher authority in your life. He may overrule your pursuits for His own wise reasons. . .as a loving, all-knowing Father who has His son's best interests at heart.

*Lord, I ask You to oversee my plans, and overrule them
as necessary. I trust You to guide me into the best paths.*

GOD LEADS TO VICTORY

"Moab, my washbasin, will become my servant, and I will wipe my feet on Edom and shout in triumph over Philistia."
PSALM 108:9 NLT

In the New Living Translation of the Bible, 2 Samuel 8 is headlined "David's Military Victories." The eleventh and twelfth verses of this chapter indicate that Israel's greatest king had conquered the three nations mentioned in the verse above: he dedicated to God "silver and gold from the other nations he had defeated—from Edom, Moab, Ammon, Philistia, and Amalek."

The future tense of the verbs in Psalm 108:9 indicates God had not yet given David victory over these enemies, though some commentators speculate that Edom, Moab, and Philistia were rising again after previous military setbacks. Whatever the case may be, take special note of God's ultimate power to punish His enemies and preserve His own.

Three thousand years after David wrote these words, his descendants continue as a distinct people group, many of them in a prosperous modern nation named Israel. Christians, who trace their heritage through the biblical Jews, now number in the hundreds of millions, if not billions. Edomites, Moabites, and Philistines—their skeletons, at least—are found only in dusty archaeological digs.

Never doubt God's ability to see you through the hardships you face. The road may not be easy, but the Lord will fulfill His promises to you just as He did to David, Moab, Edom, and Philistia.

Lord, lead me to victory like You led David.

RESISTANCE IS FUTILE

When he would not yield to [our] persuading, we stopped
[urging and imploring him], saying, The Lord's will be done!
ACTS 21:14 AMPC

Kings or military leaders of history may have uttered the words
"resistance is futile," but today the phrase belongs to the Borg, a
frightful enemy from the fictional *Star Trek* universe. (Fans of British
sci-fi, meanwhile, claim the words were originally spoken to Dr. Who
by his nemesis, the Master.)

In pop culture, "resistance is futile" implies threat and danger:
some powerful force is exerting its will, and it's folly to fight back. In
real life, the phrase could be applied to God's will. The divine plan
is threatening and dangerous to those who oppose Him. But for
followers of Jesus, though God's will may at times be frightening, it's
always ultimately beneficial.

As the apostle Paul moved toward prophesied danger in Jerusalem,
his traveling companions and the believers of Caesarea pleaded
with him not to go. "What do you mean by weeping and breaking
my heart like this?" he asked. "For I hold myself in readiness not
only to be arrested and bound and imprisoned at Jerusalem, but also
[even] to die for the name of the Lord Jesus" (Acts 21:13 AMPC). At
that point, Paul's friends admitted that God's will took precedence
over their own.

That's a lesson we all must learn. Resistance to God's will is
futile—submission is the pathway to victory.

All-knowing, all-powerful God, I submit to Your will.

GOD'S NAME HELPS YOU

But you, Sovereign LORD, help me for your name's sake.
PSALM 109:21 NIV

Your literal name may be Luis, Tony, Mike, or Jerome. But your figurative name is the reputation by which people know you. This "name," if you've lived wisely, might be Honest, Generous, Helpful, Compassionate. . .or a combination of several. "A good name," according to Proverbs, "is more desirable than great riches" (22:1 NIV).

That's how God views His own name—and it's why He demands no one "misuse" it (Exodus 20:7 NIV). Certainly, to quote the old King James Version, taking God's name "in vain" includes making a curse word of it. But we also dishonor His name when we claim God as Father while living carelessly.

In spite of the ancient Israelites' extensive sin, God kept His promises "for the sake of my holy name" (Ezekiel 36:22 NIV). As Christian men, let's aspire to be more like David, author of today's scripture. He was far from perfect, as each of us is. But he knew where to find hope and help—and that was solely in God.

David recognized that the Lord is eager to bless His own for the sake of His name. When we consciously acknowledge our weakness and sin, the door to His blessing is unlocked. God's name is the key to help, in every aspect of life.

Lord, Your name is true and good and worthy of all praise. Please help me for Your name's sake!

4-D CHESS

Rehoboam turned a deaf ear to the people. God was behind all this, confirming the message that he had given to Jeroboam.
2 CHRONICLES 10:15 MSG

The act of thinking several steps ahead of an adversary, of considering every possible twist and turn of a contest so as to always come out on top, is described as "four-dimensional chess." Some people fancy themselves experts at this imaginary game, but God is the undisputed champion.

Only the infinite God can give humans free will while remaining sovereign over every outcome. Read the history of Rehoboam, Jeroboam, and the division of Israel in 2 Chronicles 10 and 2 Kings 11, and you'll see several examples of men making their own (often foolish) decisions, with God in the background mysteriously using those decisions for His own purposes.

The scripture above shows that Rehoboam's obnoxious treatment of his own people led to Jeroboam's rule over a breakaway Jewish nation. . .just as God had foreseen. Then, as Rehoboam prepared for civil war, a prophet brought a message of the Lord's sovereignty: "This is GOD's word: Don't march out; don't fight against your brothers the Israelites. Go back home, every last one of you; I'm in charge here" (2 Chronicles 11:4 MSG).

However things may look to us, God is always "in charge here." Consciously remind yourself that He is all-knowing and all-powerful—and leave the 4-D chess in His capable hands.

Lord, help me to trust in Your wisdom—and Your goodness.

OOPS. . .

Paul said to him, "God shall strike you, you whitewashed
wall! For do you sit to judge me according to the law
and command me to be struck contrary to the law?"

Acts 23:3 skjv

Ever spoken too quickly, too loudly, too angrily? Apart from Jesus, everyone has—even as great a man as the apostle Paul.

One beauty of God's Word is its absolute honesty. Scripture often shows when His chosen people failed. In Acts 23, Paul succumbed to an angry outburst, which he walked back just two verses later.

The high priest, object of Paul's ire, deserved a rebuke—he had just ordered Paul struck in the face for a simple comment he'd made. Ananias' behavior contradicted both scripture and every common-sense view of legal proceedings.

But when the kangaroo court accused Paul of breaking a biblical command (Exodus 22:28 [skjv]: "You shall not. . .curse the ruler of your people"), he immediately admitted his wrongdoing, no matter how unfair the treatment that preceded it.

There's plenty of unfair treatment in this world, and much of it will target us as Christians. Ideally, we'll be so sensitive to God's Spirit that He'll guide us through without a stumble. But if we fail, like even Paul did, God "knows our form; He remembers that we are dust" (Psalm 103:14 skjv). And "great is His mercy toward those who fear Him" (v. 11 skjv).

Lord, I want to do right—but I appreciate Your mercy when I fail.

THE PATHWAY TO WISDOM

The fear of the LORD is the beginning of wisdom.
PSALM 111:10 HCSB

Today's scripture will be familiar to many. These words are repeated verbatim in Proverbs 9:10, and similar statements occur throughout the Bible's wisdom books. Psalm 111, however, provides a practical guide to developing "the fear of the LORD" and getting on the pathway to wisdom.

It all begins with praise (v. 1), and praise comes by our recognition of what God has done—since that's a reflection of who He is. God performs great, delightful works that are worthy of study (v. 2). His "splendid and majestic" doings show an enduring righteousness (v. 3 HCSB). He helps people to remember such works, because He is "gracious and compassionate" (v. 4 HCSB). He provides for physical needs and honors His promises (v. 5). He is truthful, and His Word is established forever (vv. 7–8). The fact that He redeems people gives Him a "holy and awe-inspiring" name (v. 9 HCSB).

This was all true for the ancient Israelites, the first audience for Psalm 111. But it is also true for us, who possess not only the Old Testament scriptures but the Lord Jesus Himself through His Holy Spirit.

If you want to be wise, review God's works—in His written Word, the Bible, and in your own life. Delight in His goodness. Study His majesty. Trust His promises. You'll be well on your way.

. . . .

Lord, I want to be wise. Remind me of Your wonderful works.

ONLY WHAT GOD SAYS

*"There is one more man who could consult the LORD for us,
but I hate him. He never prophesies anything but trouble for me!"*
2 CHRONICLES 18:7 NLT

Ever known someone who always pushed you spiritually? Maybe it was your dad or grandpa, or a guy in your church. Human as we are, we sometimes bristle at being challenged. *Why*, we wonder, *can't he just be nice?*

"Christians should be nice" is a great misconception of the faith. Of course we should be kind, gentle, helpful, and generous—these are all biblical teachings. But if "nice" means we agree with everyone on everything, our theology has problems.

Israel's wicked King Ahab, who spoke the words of today's scripture, wanted a "nice" prophet—someone to tell him just what he wanted to hear. Micaiah, to his everlasting credit, was not that kind of guy.

When the messenger sent to summon Micaiah told him, "Look, all [Ahab's] prophets are promising victory for the king. Be sure that you agree with them and promise success" (2 Chronicles 18:12 NLT), this true prophet replied, "As surely as the LORD lives, I will say only what my God says" (v. 13 NLT).

That's the way it should be. Don't expect fellow believers always to affirm your attitudes, behaviors, or choices. And don't always affirm those "ABCs" of others. The ironclad rule must be "Only what God says."

Lord, give me wisdom and courage always to speak the truth, in love.

POLAR OPPOSITES

*Who is like the L*ORD *our God, the One who sits enthroned on
high, who stoops down to look on the heavens and the earth?
He raises the poor from the dust and lifts the needy from the ash
heap; he seats them with princes, with the princes of his people.*

PSALM 113:5–8 NIV

It's inevitable—sometimes you'll feel poor and needy. Maybe financially,
or perhaps emotionally, physically, relationally, or spiritually. Life in
this world has a way of humbling us, of occasionally showing how
utterly helpless we are.

Isn't it good to know that God is our polar opposite?

While we're choking in the dust of despair, He's watching from
His throne on high. While we wipe the ash of frustration and weariness
from our faces, God stoops down for a closer look at our pain. But
He doesn't stop there.

Not only does God observe our struggles, He steps in to help.
Notice the verbs in today's scripture reading: God "raises" and "lifts"
us. Then He "seats" us with the princes of His people.

When we can't do anything, God can do everything. When we
can barely raise our heads, He can raise us—every part of us, every
one of us—to glory. Our polar opposite is ready and eager to turn our
defeats into His victories. So "let the name of the LORD be praised,
both now and forevermore" (Psalm 113:2 NIV).

Lord, please raise me up and seat me with Your princes.

OF COURSE GOD CAN

*"Why should it be thought an incredible thing
with you that God should raise the dead?"*
ACTS 26:8 SKJV

Our perspective of God affects everything. If we see Him as distant, uninterested, and weak, why even pretend to worship Him? But if we view God as scripture does—the all-powerful, all-knowing, lavishly loving Creator who sent His Son as the sacrifice for sin—we can have total confidence in His plan for our lives.

The apostle Paul could cheerfully face the suffering and dangers of his mission since he saw God as far beyond any human trial. When his enemies ginned up false sedition charges against him, Paul appeared before two Roman governors—Felix and Festus—and the region's king, Agrippa. The words of today's scripture were spoken to the latter.

Paul's Jewish enemies hated the message of Jesus' resurrection. They didn't want to believe Jesus was the promised Messiah, so they discounted the truth of His return from the dead. But for people who accepted the Genesis account of creation—that a self-existent God had spoken the heavens and earth into existence—Paul argued that raising the dead was no "incredible thing."

Christians today serve the same powerful God. And we can enjoy the same powerful confidence of Paul. Whatever difficulty we face, God is able to—and will ultimately—make things right. Of course He can.

*Lord, please apply Your power to my trials. Make me
strong until the day You completely remove them.*

GOD > IDOLS (IT'S NOT EVEN CLOSE)

Not to us, O LORD, not to us,
but to your name goes all the glory.
PSALM 115:1 NLT

Contemporary Christian music fans of a certain age might recognize today's scripture as the inspiration for a song by the Imperials. The 1985 recording drew its refrain from a psalm that graphically portrays God's superiority to idols.

Unbelievers in the psalmist's day—as in ours—were asking, "Where is their God?" (Psalm 115:2 NLT). The answer was stark: "Our God is in the heavens, and he does as he wishes" (v. 3 NLT).

Some were bowing to so-called gods of precious metal, formed by human hands. The idols had mouths, but couldn't speak a single word; eyes, but couldn't see the midday sun; ears, but couldn't hear a dump truck driving through a nitroglycerin plant. "Those who make idols are just like them," the psalm writer declared, "as are all who trust in them" (Psalm 115:8 NLT). In other words, they were blind, deaf, and dumb, spiritually speaking.

Happily, we know the truth. The one true God is in heaven, overseeing the world He created. He is actively working for the benefit of those who put their faith in Jesus Christ. He surpasses any man-made "god" by orders of infinity. And that is why all glory goes to Him alone.

Heavenly Father, may I never glory in myself, my possessions,
or my achievements. May I always direct every bit of praise to You.

YOU ARE INVINCIBLE. . .

*Do not be frightened, Paul! It is necessary for
you to stand before Caesar; and behold, God has
given you all those who are sailing with you.*
Acts 27:24 AMPC

The three dots following today's title are "suspension points." They
indicate a thought that trails off. "You are invincible" is a nice idea,
but it's not complete unless you add, "until *God* says your life is over."

In Acts 27, Paul is a prisoner on a ship bound for Rome. There,
he is supposed to present his case (and the gospel) to the emperor.
But those plans are imperiled by a ferocious, two-week storm with
the monstrous name *Euroclydon* in the old King James Version.

Fellow missionary Luke recalled, "When neither sun nor stars
were visible for many days and no small tempest kept raging about
us, all hope of our being saved was finally abandoned" (Acts 27:20
AMPC).

Well, that was true for 275 of the passengers and crew. Number
276 was Paul, who received a visit from an angel bearing the message
of today's scripture. God had an assignment for Paul, and no storm
on earth could stop him.

That's true of us too. We have no need to fear terrorism, pandemics,
crime, nuclear war, or disease. As Christians, we are invincible. . .until
God determines we're done. And don't fear that day either—then
you'll simply enjoy His presence in heaven.

Lord, thank You for protection and provision. Please banish my fears.

CONNECTING FOR CHRIST

When we got to Rome, Paul was allowed to live by himself,
with a soldier to guard him. . . . For two whole years
Paul. . .welcomed all who came to see him. He proclaimed
the kingdom of God and taught about the Lord Jesus
Christ—with all boldness and without hindrance!
ACTS 28:16, 30–31 NIV

What must it have been like to be Paul's guard? You've been assigned to keep an eye on this wandering preacher. He doesn't seem dangerous, at least not physically, but there's something about him, something about this *gospel* he keeps harping on. You see for yourself how it gets under the skin of the religious bigwigs who visit him—if this carpenter of his bugs them that much, maybe there's something to it. And he treats you like a real person, with thoughts and feelings and experiences, which you're not used to. You're thinking you might just ask him about this Jesus.

Who has been assigned to you in this season of life—who is around you on a regular basis that sees your habits and words and behavior? How are you reflecting Jesus? How can you invest in these people the way Jesus invests in you? The story of how God has changed you might just be the difference maker for them. Don't pass up the opportunity.

Jesus, give me Your wisdom, Your heart, for those around me and let
me represent You well enough to make them curious about You.

PRECIOUS DEATH?

*The death of His faithful ones is
valuable in the LORD's sight.*
PSALM 116:15 HCSB

Psalm 116:15 is often quoted at funeral services, perhaps because it's usually interpreted to mean that God is glad that His saints are coming home to Him. After all, didn't Paul say to live is Christ, to die is gain? But is God really happy when His faithful ones die? Is that the message we want to send or receive as heartbroken spouses and grieving parents?

Some nuance is in order. The psalmist in the first part of Psalm 116 recounts how he cried out to God to save him from a near-death experience, and while he is grateful and exuberant in his praise, the experience itself was horrible. So, how is death "precious" or "valuable" in God's sight?

Jesus was fiercely angry when Lazarus died. He knew that this wasn't God's original plan, that death resulted from sin's corruption, not God's intention. So, He did something about it. And maybe that's the psalmist's point: God may not save us from dying, but He will save us from staying dead. Death is a tragic consequence of a broken world. But Jesus defeated death so that its sting is only temporary. He has the last word, and it is life for His faithful ones.

* * *

*Lord Jesus, thank You for conquering the grave
so that I won't be stuck there, apart from You,
for eternity. You bring life, now and forever.*

TEST-READY

*"Be strong and courageous! Don't be afraid or discouraged
because of the king of Assyria or his mighty army,
for there is a power far greater on our side!"*
2 CHRONICLES 32:7 NLT

Hezekiah, one of Judah's few good kings, cleaned up the temple, both literally and spiritually, and made God the center of life in Jerusalem again. God strengthened him to stand against mighty Assyria and gave him an astonishing victory and the regard of the surrounding nations. Second Chronicles 32:30 (NIV) says that Hezekiah "succeeded in everything he undertook."

But then something frightening happened: "God left him to test him and to know everything that was in his heart" (v. 31 NIV). Turns out Hezekiah had a pride issue—one that delayed his healing in one case and aided Babylon's ultimate conquest of Judah in another. God promises never to leave us nor forsake us, so His "leaving" of Hezekiah can only mean that He withdrew His immediate material blessings, to see if the king loved Him for who He is or only for what He gave him.

When God tests you, cling to the bottom-line truth: There "is a greater power with us than with [the world]" (2 Chronicles 32:7 NIV). Whatever God allows in your life He equips you to face. Stay faithful and you'll pass.

*Lord, Your tests are hard, but I trust that when You allow
one, You think I'm ready to go deeper into my relationship
with You. Be my strength and my portion, always.*

WORTH THE COST

*To those who by persistence in doing good seek glory,
honor and immortality, he will give eternal life.*

ROMANS 2:7 NIV

Relationships blindside us at times. A good one goes bad, or a hard one remains fruitless. It's normal, and sometimes necessary, to count the cost and decide if you should stick with it or get out. In Romans 2, Paul was writing about the work we do in response to God's saving grace through the gospel. God is paying attention to what we do as recipients of Christ's gift of salvation—how we work out being made more like Jesus.

Paul's point? Remember who you used to be, not to anchor yourself in guilt or shame, but so you won't return to looking at others the way you used to, through judgmental eyes. No one leads a perfect life, and no one can. But anyone can receive the good news by grace through faith. Your part is persistence; don't give up on what God can do.

When the people you're invested in don't respond to Jesus the way you want them to, take heart—God is still working, based on His bigger view of both your lives. His grace is enough for you and for them.

*God, my Father, Your grace means everything to me. Fill me
with Your Spirit so I can do the work You have for me today.
You never gave up on me; don't let me give up on hard people.*

ANCHORED TO TRUTH

What if some were unfaithful? Will their unfaithfulness
nullify God's faithfulness? Not at all! Let God
be true, and every human being a liar.
Romans 3:3–4 niv

We live in a time and culture where Jesus' prediction in Matthew 24:12 (niv) is partially fulfilled: "Because of the increase of wickedness, the love of most will grow cold." God's church is being tested and culled, and many are leaving their faith because they've been convinced that they are more capable of love and grace than God Himself.

When people reject the gospel, it doesn't mean something is wrong with God's good news. It just confirms what Romans 3:23 (hcsb) says: "All have sinned and fall short of the glory of God." We should stand on God's truth and call them up to His standard in as gentle and respectful a manner as possible, because verse 24 (hcsb) remains true too: "They are justified freely by His grace through the redemption that is in Christ Jesus."

If we stay true to God and His Word, we will be able to find ways to love the most challenging of people, including waffling brothers and sisters, without forsaking God's unchanging truth. He is your anchor if you will ground yourself in Him.

Lord God, be merciful to us, especially in Your church.
Help us seek what matters to You—unity in Christ, grace in
nonessentials, and sacrificial love for those who have gone astray.

THE SIZE OF YOUR GOD

*[Abraham's] faith in God's promise did not falter. In fact,
his faith grew as he gave glory to God because he was
supremely confident that God could deliver on His promise.*

ROMANS 4:20–21 VOICE

Paul draws on Abraham's example of faith to inspire us when doubts arise. Believing God's promise when he had no practical reason to is a hallmark of faith that anticipates the power of the gospel. Abraham had already left behind his homeland to answer God's call, and when God told him He was going to bless all the world's families through his currently nonexistent line, Abraham didn't doubt God's power.

Abraham's view of God was big. He believed that God was God, capable of doing whatever He decided to do and worthy of all his trust. Christians have seen this promise fulfilled in Christ—the work of a God big enough to save the world from sin.

When we think of God's work, we need to see it as finished—not just Jesus' work at the cross and His resurrection, but everything after it: our salvation, sanctification, and ultimate glory, all accomplished in God's eyes, all done *now*, even as we walk through it all. That kind of faith glorifies God and strengthens us to stand in hard times.

*God, when You say it is finished, it is—not just my
salvation but everything between now and Your eternal
kingdom. Strengthen my faith in Your good work.*

HOPE WON'T LET YOU DOWN

We can rejoice, too, when we run into problems and trials,
for we know that they help us develop endurance.

ROMANS 5:3 NLT

Even though the promise of the gospel is familiar, it's still underrated. Jesus freely gives us peace *with* God so that we can enjoy the peace *of* God. It's so beautifully simple—maybe that's why we complicate it with worry and doubt. Sure, both those responses to the world are normal, but we can't afford to let them bleed into the wonder of the freedom Christ purchased for us.

The path Jesus laid out for us starts with salvation, but it continues through the world's thorny, uphill road, a journey that challenges us again and again to trust God with all we are, think, and do. We don't thank God for the hardship but for His faithfulness while it lasts. He is doing something through each ordeal that He can't do any other way.

We need endurance to thrive in this life, and the gospel promises that—a progression that uses perseverance to develop character and character to grow hope. And hope fuels us to walk steadily with God. As Psalm 119:1 (MSG) says, "You're blessed when you stay on course, walking steadily on the road revealed by GOD."

Lord Jesus, help me stay the course with You. Be my
strength to face trials with courage, trusting that
You're shaping me more into Your image all the time.

FUELED UP, READY TO ROLL

*I have treasured Your word in my heart
so that I may not sin against You.*
PSALM 119:11 HCSB

How has knowing Jesus changed your life? Standard question, right? But your answer matters. You have your God story to tell, and because of the power of the gospel, your account of the difference He has made to you carries weight in the hearts of people you've never met.

Certainly, your actions should support your words—but you need the words. If you're not sure how to tell your story, use God's words. For example, Romans 6:4 (NIV) explains the power behind our new lives: "Just as Christ was raised from the dead through the glory of the Father, we too may live a new life."

You've often heard that you need to read the Bible regularly, daily even, and the analogy of putting gas in your car or charging your phone works well enough. On any given day, God will put people and opportunities in your path that only His Word can prepare you to meet. Like the writer of today's scripture verse, you will learn both the practical value of being fueled up and the joy of knowing God better. The power of your new life comes from Jesus, God's living Word.

. . . .

Jesus, my Lord and Savior, reconnect me with You through Your Word. Use it to keep me close to You and to prepare me each day for whatever You have in store for me.

SLIPPING SIN'S GRIP

*What a wretched man I am! Who will rescue me from
this body that is subject to death? Thanks be to God,
who delivers me through Jesus Christ our Lord!*
ROMANS 7:24–25 NIV

We all have moments, even as longtime believers in Christ, where our thoughts, words, or actions shock us. We can't believe what goes through our minds, what just comes out of our mouths, what we just did. And then, when the Spirit convicts us, our conscience and the devil dogpile on—*You call yourself a Christian? Jesus must be shaking His head.*

The good news is God is unshockable. He knows what a mess sin has made of our hearts and how it continues to battle for supremacy through our flesh. But that didn't stop Him from dying to save us, from serving notice on death and sin that, under the banner of His love, their hold is fleeting at best.

It sounds weird, but in a way, Jesus' blood has made you too slippery for sin to grip. Sin can trouble you, especially in unguarded moments, but it can't hold you anymore. Confess your dark moments and thoughts to Jesus, but then thank Him that you are His and nothing can separate the two of you.

*Lord Jesus, thank You for setting things right,
for sticking with me through all my ups and downs.
You won't quit on me till Your work in me is finished.*

HOLDING OUR BREATH

*The sufferings we endure now are not even worth comparing
to the glory that is coming and will be revealed in us.*

ROMANS 8:18 VOICE

No one looking at the world can deny that it's broken. People are divided, nature is rebelling, hope is fading. Can any of this ever be fixed? If God is there, when will He do something?

What's the answer? It's simple but not easy. When sin entered God's good creation in Eden, it didn't just bring death and decay to humans. All of creation suffers with us, ants to trees to quasars, innocent victims of Adam's choice (a choice any of us would have made as imperfect beings), all breaking down over time and awaiting God's redemption.

But just as a thorough and honest scientific study reveals design in the natural world, sin and decay point to a caring God at work. God's ultimate plan is to restore all the things He made and called good. Our rejection of God means we've invited His curse over His blessing, and He has allowed His curse to warp creation. But He has done so in hope. All of creation will receive the freedom Jesus purchased for humankind. Even now, He is making all things new.

. . . .

God, along with all creation, I eagerly await the day You will make things right, ending our suffering. As dark as these days are, the glory You have for us will outshine all our pain.

LIFE-PRESERVING WORDS

*Remember what you said to me, your servant—I hang
on to these words for dear life! These words hold me up
in bad times; yes, your promises rejuvenate me.*

Psalm 119:49–50 msg

Over and over, David ties his confidence in God's promises of
protection and provision to his own obedience of God's commands.
Just to clarify, this is not a matter of securing our salvation but our
only proper response to what God has done for us in Christ. We have
been liberated from our tendency to obey out of fear of reprisal; now,
we can do what God says because His love has freed us to love Him
for who He is. And we learn more about Him by reading His Word.

Paul's description of our triumph as believers in Romans 8:31,
33–35 (hcsb) is an example of words we can cling to for dear life:

> *If God is for us, who is against us? . . . Who can bring
> an accusation against God's elect? God is the One who
> justifies. Who is the one who condemns? Christ Jesus is the
> One who died, but even more, has been raised; He also is
> at the right hand of God and intercedes for us. Who can
> separate us from the love of Christ?*

Let God's life-giving words soak into your soul, and you can face
anything with grace and hope.

*Lord, I love the promises and power in Your
words. Knowing You better gives me life.*

FREE TO SUCCEED

I used to wander off until you disciplined me; but now I closely follow your word. . . . My suffering was good for me, for it taught me to pay attention to your decrees. Your instructions are more valuable to me than millions in gold and silver.

PSALM 119:67, 71–72 NLT

Most people have experienced imposter syndrome, the feeling that we've tricked everyone into believing we're competent. It hits especially when we've just had success—a promotion, a finished project, a relational breakthrough. Something in us calls us a fraud, and the doubt settles on us like a fog.

How do we overcome this tendency? By living with Christ at the center of our lives. Psalm 119:67 suggests that, until we learn to view hardship as God's method of maturing us, we will fall back on our worst tendencies to define us—perfectionism, the approval of people, the need to be liked.

You belong to Christ by grace alone, and so He has defined your worth: beyond measure. Embrace His love for you, His willingness to die to win you even while you were unredeemed. Let Him set you free. Then, when you pursue excellence, anxiety and fear can't get a grip on you. You are His, and His providence upholds you at every turn.

God, You are sovereign and faithful. You have set me free from all expectations but Yours, and You give me the power to love You as You deserve. Thank You.

RIGHT TOOL FOR THE JOB

*Even common laborers carrying building
materials did so while carrying a weapon.*
NEHEMIAH 4:17 VOICE

Sometimes our enemies are people who harass and oppose us, but at all times, our true enemies are spiritual, unseen, and just as real. When we see Nehemiah leading the wall builders, who had both work tools and weapons at the ready, we're reminded that all our battles exist on two levels. So, that's how we must fight them.

Think of the sacrifices we're willing to make for our job—laser-focusing on the task, putting in extra hours, balancing work tasks with home life so our family doesn't lose out. What if we treated our spiritual work as seriously—doing the necessary praying, Bible study, and service—with the same goal of excellence?

People do good all the time without glorifying God. To do the good works God has set aside for us, we must be walking as His light in the world. By equipping ourselves spiritually, we keep our work in the physical world in perspective. God's Word is the right tool for every job we do because it prepares us to see everything through the lens of what matters most to Him. We faithfully do the work God has given us to do—whether it's our job or ministry—and we trust Him with the outcomes.

*All-sufficient God, prepare me as I spend time with
You in Your Word for what today will bring.*

A LEADER WORTH FOLLOWING

Remember me with favor, my God,
for all I have done for these people.
NEHEMIAH 5:19 NIV

Nehemiah took care of his people. He trusted God for his security when his enemies slandered his name and plotted against his life. He honored God by carefully checking family records to make sure the priests assigned to minister were spiritually qualified. He stood up for his people when bureaucrats mortgaged them to the hilt. He refused the privileges of his position because his workers were bearing the cost. Going to bat for his people like that earned their trust and dedication to the work they were doing.

By keeping his focus on the Lord, his true leader, Nehemiah avoided the pitfalls of self-serving leadership—expedience, compromise, greed for power. God gave him a job, a hard one, and he leaned hard into God to get it done. More than once, he asked God to remember him favorably for all he had done for God's people.

What made Nehemiah a leader worth following? His dedication to God, which is the model for all effective leaders. God both confronts His children and empowers them, making His expectations clear and helping them grow in faith. When we lead ourselves and others as God leads us, we clear the way for greater success on every level.

Lord God, I will follow You, today and every day.
I know You will guide me as I strive to lead like You do.

UNCHANGING TRUTH

*Your words are so choice, so tasty; I prefer them
to the best home cooking. With your instruction,
I understand life; that's why I hate false propaganda.*
PSALM 119:103–104 MSG

How hard is it to find a trustworthy news source these days? Many outlets seem to favor falsehood over facts, politics ahead of people, and rage before relationships. Truth has become a fungible commodity, replaceable with whatever trends sweep the nation. But God's truth never changes. If we don't want to lose our way, we must filter everything we hear and read through His Word.

Most translations of Psalm 119:103 speak of God's words being sweeter than honey. The idea of scripture tasting better than our favorite home-cooked meal resonates—the simple comfort, the associations with good times, the people we've broken bread with—but too often we miss out on those connections. We see reading our Bibles as duty or covering our bases, instead of the way to cultivate our relationship with the living God who loves us dearly.

When we settle for the culture's junk food, we feed unhealthy thoughts, resulting in anxiety, frustration, and a growing sense of division from our neighbors. Comfort food settles our souls; God's Word will do the same when we value it as our true compass and anchor.

*Lord, Your Word is eternal, unchanging, true, and good—
just like You. Ground me in Your truth, grant me discernment,
and give me a growing hunger to know You more.*

DYING TO LIVE

Take your everyday, ordinary life—your sleeping, eating, going-to-work, and walking-around life—and place it before God as an offering. Embracing what God does for you is the best thing you can do for him.

ROMANS 12:1 MSG

Making yourself a living sacrifice is hard. The old way was easier: kill the animal, move on, do it again next week. But we must emulate the choice Jesus made at Gethsemane—*not my will but Yours be done, Father.* We don't do it at the level He did; He suffered the separation of hell so that we will never have to.

Still, we must commit ourselves to Him and His ways each day, sometimes minute by minute. We're crucifying our right to live as we choose—in many ways, there's nothing less American. But there is nothing more like Christ. It's a paradox of our faith: the more we surrender to God, the more freedom He gives us to be our best selves.

We don't have to like what He is asking; Jesus agonized at the thought of separation from the Father. But like Him, we believe. We trust Him, and if it feels a little like dying, take heart: it's only the dead part of you that's losing strength and control.

Lord God, I choose to worship You by doing what Psalm 119:112 (VOICE) says: "I have committed myself to do what You require forever and ever, to the very end."

REMEMBERING WHO'S IN CHARGE

Everyone must submit to governing authorities. For all authority comes from God, and those in positions of authority have been placed there by God. So anyone who rebels against authority is rebelling against what God has instituted, and they will be punished.

ROMANS 13:1–2 NLT

Paul raises a touchy issue in Romans 13: the call to submit to authorities. It's a call to trust God's sovereignty, that He knows who has the reins of the government and is still working all things together for good.

The matter goes deeper than political party. Paul wrote this when Rome, a government that would eventually sanction his decapitation, was in charge. His stance reminds us: Jesus didn't come to bring social or political reform. He upended expectations, saying we should give the government what belongs to it and give to God what belongs to Him.

Ultimate authority belongs to God. He has a history of moving despicable rulers into positions that accomplish His purposes. Our first responsibility is to Him. He wants us to be good citizens, unless compliance means disobeying His commands. If you must resist, make sure you're standing on solid ground biblically. Put on Jesus in every situation. His love fulfills the requirement of every good law.

* * *

Lord, I need Your wisdom and Your Word to help me submit where I can and stand up where I must. Let my words and deeds glorify You above all else.

SET FREE FROM JUDGMENT

None of us are permitted to insist on our own way in these matters. It's God we are answerable to—all the way from life to death and everything in between—not each other.

ROMANS 14:7–8 MSG

As a Christian, you are not your own, so how you live and die should bring glory to your Lord, Jesus Christ. You are subject to His lordship over every aspect of your life, and you will be subject to Him after you die.

For the nonbeliever, that's an ominous prospect. But for you, that's encouraging. Because your worth has been established by Jesus' death, and because you've been raised spiritually with Him, you are no longer bound by the punishing standards of yourself or the world.

Unredeemed, you can't help but make comparisons. It's the only way you can feel your worth, by finding ways to be superior to someone else in some way—*Yeah, I'm bad, but I'm not as bad as that guy.* But Jesus freed us from the pull of sitting in God's throne of judgment. You're free to love the way He loves you—as someone who truly needs to be saved and someone who is truly worth saving. He wants us to treat others the same way, opening His path of liberation to them.

Lord Jesus, You alone are worthy to judge our hearts. I will leave the judging to You and work on loving the way You do.

TRUST STRENGTHENS HOPE

*May the God of hope fill you with all joy
and peace as you trust in him.*
Romans 15:13 NIV

Romans 15 establishes reasons for our hope and confidence as Christians. In context, Paul was talking to Roman Jews about the validity of salvation in Christ for both Jews and Gentiles. His argument holds principles that impact how we are to live in this world: the humility of Christ, who went low to identify with us and bear our burdens; the reliability of scripture, God's words given and fulfilled through the ages to teach us to endure; and the power of the Holy Spirit filling us so that we can love others well, seeking their highest good just as Jesus seeks ours.

Verse 13 is the battery that charges our hope. Trusting God enough to humble ourselves brings the endurance we need to keep hoping for His kingdom to come. We have our role in God's bigger story, and when Jesus' attitude becomes ours—a work of the Spirit in us over time—we see the value of unity with other believers. We may not agree on some of the details of the Christian life, but if we are bound by the same core beliefs, we will glorify God in this hurting world.

*Jesus, You became God's servant to save the world and
bring unity with the Father. Fill me with Your Spirit
so I can do the same work in my corner of it.*

REWARDS OF OBEDIENCE

*I'm ecstatic over what you say, like one who strikes
it rich. . . . I follow your directions, abide by your
counsel; my life's an open book before you.*
PSALM 119:162, 168 MSG

When we feel threatened, our natural reaction is to be afraid. Even if we think we're up to the threat, doubt in our strength or wisdom pesters us. But that's only if we find our value in what the world thinks of us. David's joy came from his knowledge of God and God's Word—for him, it was a true treasure, unassailable by any enemy, even his own doubts and fears.

Scripture is more than a source of information; its value comes from the one who spoke it. God's guarantee is stamped all over His words—He will do what He says and accomplish all His goals. That's value beyond anything the world offers.

Like David's, our hope in God is tied to our obedience to His words and ways. Because He loved us, we love Him, and because we love Him, we'll do what He says. That trust in Him not only binds us to Him in love; it shows the world that we are His, glorifying Him further. The more we treasure God's Word, the easier it is to follow where He leads.

*God, Your Word lights my way and anchors my soul. Use it
to show me something about You and Your ways today.*

HEARING YOUR GOOD SHEPHERD

*Invigorate my soul so I can praise you well, use your decrees
to put iron in my soul. And should I wander off like a lost
sheep—seek me! I'll recognize the sound of your voice.*
PSALM 119:175–176 MSG

Sheep are notoriously stubborn, foolish, and fearful—not great to be compared to. And yet, in John 10:11, 14 (NIV), Jesus made it a point to call Himself the good shepherd, the one who "lays down his life for the sheep. . . . I know my sheep and my sheep know me." His character is good—noble, faithful, trustworthy, pure—and under His care, we are protected, guided, and nurtured away from our worst tendencies.

That's comforting because, as David reminds us, we tend to roam. Even when we belong to Jesus, we still wander off, sometimes when we're enticed by old habits, and other times, to our great surprise.

But when we get out among the wolves, Jesus comes looking for us. Our Shepherd doesn't leave us to the savageries of the world, the flesh, or the devil. He patiently endures our struggles, reminding us by His Spirit, His Word, and His faithful people that we are His. No longer bound by our sheeplike tendencies, we learn to hear His voice calling, and we can come home again.

*Jesus, my Good Shepherd, You are always
looking out for me, especially when I get off track.
Forgive me and restore me to Your good care.*

CONSTANT PROTECTOR

I lift my eyes toward the mountains. Where will my help come from? My help comes from the LORD, the Maker of heaven and earth. He will not allow your foot to slip; your Protector will not slumber. Indeed, the Protector of Israel does not slumber or sleep.

PSALM 121:1–4 HCSB

The Hebrew word for *help* here, *ezer*, carries the idea of a constant shield, of God's ongoing divine protection. God's care isn't passive. The Maker of heaven and earth doesn't sit back and watch His creation as if it were a theater production. He actively guides and protects His people, and He never falls asleep on the job.

In context, the psalmist was contrasting Yahweh with other deities in the Middle East, who were often depicted as sleeping—as good an explanation as any for the sneaky and self-serving behavior of the wicked. Nowadays, we hear of sleepless deities—commerce, news cycles, social media—and wonder when God will show Himself.

Psalm 121 assures us that we're not looking for Him pointlessly. We can't see Him personally, not yet, but everything in the Bible reveals that He is constantly attentive to us, deeply invested in our welfare, and able to help us in every struggle. God watches over us in this life, and He will never stop.

Lord God, I don't look to You in vain. You are my help, my constant protector. Keep me on Your path today.

WIRED FOR FELLOWSHIP

*[God] will also keep you firm to the end, so that you
will be blameless on the day of our Lord Jesus Christ.
God is faithful, who has called you into fellowship
with his Son, Jesus Christ our Lord.*

1 CORINTHIANS 1:8–9 NIV

The Corinthian church displayed many positive spiritual attributes, but their problem seemed to be their tendency to look at their attributes and praise themselves rather than God. The result was division, arguments over which leader to follow and leveraging the more prominent spiritual gifts into positions of power. Paul reminded them of the only solution: take their focus off themselves and put it squarely on Jesus.

God is the source of life, love, and right behavior. Every good gift comes from Him. Our old nature defaults to taking credit for good things—even those that clearly come from God's hand. He often teaches us that through our community at church.

The gift of God's fellowship compels us to take a higher view of our blessings, especially when they come unexpectedly through the hands and faces of those we tend to undervalue. Jesus is the only rock star in His church, but being His roadie remains a remarkable journey full of personal growth, good gifts, and joyful camaraderie.

*Jesus, Your church is full of people who represent different
aspects of who You are and what You want each of us
to learn. Thank You for giving me a part to play.*

SURROUNDED BY GRACE

*Just as the mountains surround Jerusalem, so the
LORD surrounds his people, both now and forever.*

PSALM 125:2 NLT

These days, in an age where freedom is considered the supreme goal, the idea of walls often stands for confinement or limitation. When we can't communicate well with others, we say it's because they've put up walls, defending themselves as islands of one rather than facing criticism or questions.

Our natural tendency is to self-protect, which is a God-given instinct in this broken world. But we've taken it and used it to create distance between us and our Maker. We either leave no room for God, or we filter the aspects of His character we're comfortable with—most often, His love and mercy over His holiness and righteousness. But His grace is bigger than our self-preservation, if we let it be.

When we allow ourselves a bigger view of God—embracing everything the Bible says of Him—we are liberated, not constrained. Being within God's walls means we're surrounded by His full knowledge of us (warts and all) but also His desire to preserve and protect us from whatever might separate us from Him. Trusting the Lord helps us face every challenge life presents with the confidence that we will grow in endurance and integrity.

*Lord God, keep my heart in tune with Yours so that
I value Your protective guidance and care above
my own resources. I'm only truly free in You.*

NOSE OFF THE GRINDSTONE

*Unless the LORD builds a house, the work of the builders is wasted.
. . . It is useless for you to work so hard from early morning
until late at night. . .for God gives rest to his loved ones.*
PSALM 127:1–2 NLT

The Bible consistently praises hard work. But it also offers reminders that we can make work an idol—a false marker of our value. Psalm 127 remarks on the vanity—the ultimate emptiness—of basing our worth on our work. It's a warning for those who overindulge in work and so neglect more important matters.

The workaholic might ask, "Why does God need to be involved in building a house? Surely, I can handle those details." But what if your dream of a house consumes you—your time, resources, and relationships? God's priorities get lost along the way—seeking His kingdom first and providing a secure, God-centered environment for your wife and kids.

Sometimes, we must burn the candle at both ends—but not as a way of life. *Rest* here means taking time for God and to recharge so we can be at our best for those we should value most. When we strive in His strength, not ours, we remind ourselves who God is and how much we need Him. That's worth taking a breath.

*Father, I will trust You with all I do, including my work.
Make Your priorities mine and grant me peace as I rest in You.*

PROCEED WITH CAUTION

*Judge nothing before the appointed time; wait until
the Lord comes. He will bring to light what is hidden
in darkness and will expose the motives of the heart.
At that time each will receive their praise from God.*

1 CORINTHIANS 4:5 NIV

Paul said in 1 Corinthians 4:4 (NLT), "My conscience is clear, but that doesn't prove I'm right. It is the Lord himself who will examine me and decide." That suggests that it's better to withhold judgment—either of ourselves as unfailingly aligned with God or others as out of step. God is the only one qualified to rightly judge what's in our hearts, and He knows more about our influences and motives than even we fully understand.

Above all, we want to please God, not to be nice to avoid offense or to be harsh in our truth-telling. The love required to do so can't be sentimental; it must commit to pursuing others' best interests, especially in telling hard-to-hear truths, which we must always do with respect, knowing we can't even rightly judge ourselves.

That said, there is a great deal of security in knowing that what God thinks is the most important measure of what we've done. When we think, speak, and act based on the reality that God knows all of it, it clarifies our priorities and purifies our motives.

*Lord, show me anything that is keeping me from
representing You well, so I can get right with You.*

REDIRECTING PAIN

"I have heard all this before. What miserable comforters you are! . . . I could say the same things if you were in my place. . . . But if it were me, I would encourage you. I would try to take away your grief."

JOB 16:2, 4–5 NLT

Sometimes, nothing anyone can say will comfort us. The pain is too recent, too raw for any words to help. That's when just being there counts the most—as Job's friends did when they first came to him in his grief and loss.

But comfort is more than commiseration. At some point, we must gently and firmly reconnect with the power of Christ's resurrection. His promises of seeing God face-to-face and death, sorrow, and suffering vanquished forever sustain us.

We seldom learn the reasons for the pain God allows. We learn to focus on Him and His promises of restoration, to give and receive grace. Go slow with someone who is hurting. Grieve with them, and be slow to weigh in, especially with opinions. Wait for them to speak; be ready to listen well. Ask God to equip you with what the person needs. It's not about fixing them but about finding some way to show them Jesus. He is our burden bearer, especially when we need to offer and receive comfort.

Jesus, You are the great healer of all hurts. Send me Your comfort in my pain, and help me comfort others by reminding them of You.

THE DIFFERENCE

*Some of you used to be like this. But you were washed,
you were sanctified, you were justified in the name of
the Lord Jesus Christ and by the Spirit of our God.*

1 CORINTHIANS 6:11 HCSB

We are not what we used to be, and Jesus is the reason why. In Him, we are new creations—no longer beholden to all the things that separated us from Him. You may have strongly identified with what you once were—but in fact, your sin defined you.

And yet, God pursued you, convicting you of the ways you chose yourself over your Maker. You started to see your need to be forgiven by someone who was perfect and just and good. You saw that God loved you more than you had ever imagined. Something pivoted in your heart, and Jesus became everything to you. What a glorious moment!

Since then, the Holy Spirit has redirected you back to Jesus when you've strayed, empowering you to behave as He did, and even giving you the desire to do so. The way you judged yourself and others belongs to a dead past, and you love this new life God has given you. He opens your heart—both to Him and to others.

*Lord Jesus, thank You for freeing me to be the man
You want me to be. Help me to extend Your love
and grace to those who need You as much as I do.*

HOPE FROM TRAGEDY

*"He knows where I am going. And when he
tests me, I will come out as pure as gold."*

JOB 23:10 NLT

Job was a good man who loved and honored God but was allowed by his Creator to be subjected to the worst losses a man can imagine: his children, the works of his hands, his health, and his reputation. It makes no sense—don't we expect God to bless us when we obey Him and do good? Job's story ends on a happier note, but it encompasses one of the main tensions of living the Christian life: God gives and takes away. Will we still honor Him under every circumstance He permits?

That's where hope comes in: Job's story is only the second most important account of suffering ever recorded. The story of Jesus is even more tragic—God Himself becoming human, subject to all our temptations and pains and sorrows, and yet perfect in His response to all of them. For that, we killed Him.

And yet, our hope is all the greater because dying for us was always His mission. He knew that when He rose, we could rise with Him. Everything God allows, He also uses for good. We're not trusting Him blindly but counting on a God who has always come through in the darkest hours.

*Almighty God, Your grace is sufficient for me. You give
and take away, but I will still bless Your name.*

WE NEED EACH OTHER

How wonderful, how beautiful,
when brothers and sisters get along!
Psalm 133:1 msg

In Psalm 133, David compares the blessing of fellowship to oil and dew. The oil represents God's anointing of His priests, the rich blessings of praising and serving Him. The dew stands for God's provision in parched lands, His generosity when life offers little to sustain us. God means to bless His people, but these blessings should be celebrated in community with other believers.

Christian fellowship isn't just sanctified hanging out—it's a commitment to go through life's ups and downs with our brothers and sisters, to seek God together and honor Him, to love each other as He has loved us.

The world and our flesh will test our unity with Christ, and God's model of community requires other believers to keep us aligned with Him. We need prayer and support in hard times and celebration in good ones. We need our rough edges honed, and we have experiences and traits that will help others know God better.

Family ties still matter to God, of course. But through different seasons of our lives, some short and others lifelong, He brings us into community with groups of like-minded people, assuring us that, despite our differences, He is a strong-enough common bond for all of us.

God, thank You for creating us to be in fellowship
with You and with Your other sons and daughters.

GOD'S ETERNAL TRUTH

Your name, O LORD, endures forever; your fame, O LORD,
is known to every generation. For the LORD will give justice
to his people and have compassion on his servants.
PSALM 135:13–14 NLT

Recent polls indicate that many who call themselves Christians are moving away from biblical truth. Significant percentages of churchgoers are saying that trusting Jesus isn't necessary for salvation, that hell doesn't exist, or that Jesus is not the only way to heaven. It happens most often as they drift from God's Word toward cultural trends.

However, truth is based on God Himself. He is eternal, unchanging, and all-powerful. His are the only words that can ever be fully trusted. God's truth can only be discovered, never invented. When we embrace it, it supersedes our biases and agendas, replacing them with a grounding in something bigger than ourselves, greater than the world and all its relentless reinvention of reality.

As the psalmist said, "I know the greatness of the LORD—that our Lord is greater than any other god" (Psalm 135:5 NLT). When we stick to Him, especially when the world says we're outdated and bigoted for doing so, we anchor ourselves to the only source of truth. God will vindicate and strengthen us when we remain loyal to Him.

God, You are truth. Anything that doesn't come from You is
a lie. Build my life on the rock of Your Word and Your ways.

GOD'S ENDURING LOVE

*Give thanks to the LORD, for he is good! His faithful
love endures forever. Give thanks to the God of gods.
His faithful love endures forever. Give thanks to the
Lord of lords. His faithful love endures forever.*

PSALM 136:1–3 NLT

Psalm 136 opens with words of gratitude to God for His goodness,
then goes on to proclaim, "His faithful love endures forever"—twenty-
six times. This psalm praises God as His people's miracle worker, their
Creator, their deliverer, and their sovereign Lord. But it reminds us
over and over of what is most important: His enduring love.

The Bible's overarching theme—from the first words of Genesis
onward—is that of God's love. Everything He did, every word He
spoke was with an eye toward pouring out His love on a needy but
undeserving world.

First John 4:8 tells us that God is love. That means that our
heavenly Father loves His people deeply and with an everlasting
love, simply because it is in His nature to do so. So dwell in His love
every day, spread that love to others, and make it part of your daily
communication with Him.

*Father in heaven, thank You for Your everlasting love.
May I dwell in Your love every minute of every
day. You are good—so good to me.*

DEFEATING TEMPTATION

No temptation has taken you but such as is common to man.
But God is faithful, who will not allow you to be tempted
above what you are able, but with the temptation will also
make a way of escape, that you may be able to bear it.

1 CORINTHIANS 10:13 SKJV

Sadly, many Christian men today take a fatalistic approach to sin and temptation. *I'm only human!* they think. *It's a given that I'm going to sin.* But while it is true that none of us will enjoy sinless perfection this side of heaven, it's a lie straight from the devil's mouth that it's inevitable that we will give in to temptation.

The Bible never promises us a life free of temptation. We all will be tempted at times and in different ways. But we who want to live a life pleasing to the Lord can take heart and be encouraged in the truth that God is for us and will give us a way out of temptation if we simply go to Him and ask for the help we need to get through it without stumbling or falling.

. . . .

Dear Lord, I often feel an almost overwhelming temptation
to do or say things I know are not pleasing to You.
When I face temptation—and I know I will—help me to
remember to turn first to You for a way out of it.

SETTING A GOOD EXAMPLE

Follow my example, as I follow the example of Christ.
1 CORINTHIANS 11:1 NIV

What do you think people see when they look at you? Do they see a man with a negative attitude toward others (your boss, your coworkers, your family, a man with a bad temper, a man given to using off-color language or telling dirty jokes)? Or do you think others see you as gentle, kind, loving, and patient?

As Christian men, we are all called to set examples of Christlike behavior, attitudes, and speech for others to see—what the apostle Paul would call "follow[ing] the example of Christ." Too many of us, however, know we haven't always been the example others need to see.

Your brothers in Christ, as well as the unsaved in your circle of influence, need to see in you a good example of what following and serving Jesus really looks like. You may have blown your witness in the past, but you can start anew today—and be the man of God people need to see.

. . . .

Lord Jesus, I want others to see Your light shine through me.
Forgive me for those times when I didn't represent You well, when I
don't follow Your example. Help me to do better starting today.

A GREAT GOD WHO SEES

Though the LORD is exalted, he looks kindly on the
lowly; though lofty, he sees them from afar.
PSALM 138:6 NIV

The God we serve, with whom we share an intimate love relationship, is a great and awesome God who occupies a lofty place in His eternal kingdom. He is exalted above anything and everything. And yet He looks at us from afar and cares for us, loves us, and watches over us day and night.

David felt overwhelmed at the thought of such an awesome God caring for mere human beings. David was a flawed man, but he was also a humble man—and that gave him confidence that the Lord was paying attention and that He would never fail to help him, encourage him, and strengthen him both in the relatively easy times and in times of difficulty and testing.

You can and should feel a sense of awe and wonder that such an awesome God watches over you, loves you, and cares for you from His throne in heaven—as long as you keep yourself humble before Him.

What an awesome God He is!

Father in heaven, You are a great and awesome God, but You still look from afar, from Your throne in heaven, to watch over and care for those willing to humble themselves before You. Help keep me humble so that I can feel the assurance of Your blessed presence.

HE KNOWS ALL ABOUT YOU

O LORD, you have examined my heart and know everything about me. You know when I sit down or stand up. You know my thoughts even when I'm far away. You see me when I travel and when I rest at home. You know everything I do.

PSALM 139:1–3 NLT

Most men are experts at hiding from others what they are truly like as well as their true thoughts and feelings. But we can never do that with our God—nor should we want to.

In today's scripture verses, David celebrates the truth that the Lord knows everything about him—what was on his heart, what he was thinking, what he was doing. The same is true for us today.

That sounds like the proverbial double-edged sword, doesn't it? On one hand, we can know the joy of enjoying a relationship with God so intimate that He knows absolutely *everything* about us. On the other hand, there are likely many things about us we'd rather He didn't know.

But when we consider God's love for us—despite all the "messy" stuff—we can feel encouraged and comforted in our relationship with Him. His love for us will never change.

Father in heaven, You know everything about me—everything I think, everything I do, everything I say. Though my sinful thoughts and actions can separate me from Your love, I want everything about me to be pleasing to You.

GOD THINKS ABOUT YOU

How precious are your thoughts about me, O God. They cannot be numbered! I can't even count them; they outnumber the grains of sand! And when I wake up, you are still with me!
PSALM 139:17–18 NLT

In Psalm 139, David marvels and praises God for knowing him so intimately, for knowing his thoughts and actions, and for being present for him at all times.

In the above scripture verses, David expresses his amazement that God would think of him so often. Those thoughts "cannot be numbered" and "outnumber the grains of sand."

God's thoughts of us are based in a love far too deep and far too wide for human understanding. And He thinks much about the object of that love.

God values you and His relationship with you. When you go to bed and when you wake up, He thinks about you and is there for you. He never stops thinking of you—or loving you with His deep, everlasting love.

Father in heaven, Your thoughts cannot be numbered, and yet Your every thought is precious. Yet with all that is on Your mind, You never forget me. I can go to sleep at night knowing that You are thinking of me, and when I wake up in the morning, You are still there for me.

SEARCH ME!

*Search me, God, and know my heart; test me and know
my anxious thoughts. See if there is any offensive way
in me, and lead me in the way everlasting.*

PSALM 139:23–24 NIV

In the first eighteen verses of Psalm 139, David praised his God
both for knowing him so intimately and for thinking about him so
constantly. It's obvious that David was absolutely basking in God's
love as he wrote this psalm.

Still. . .David wanted more.

In today's scripture verses, David welcomed God to know him
even better as he asked Him to "search me," "know my heart," "test
me and know my anxious thoughts," and "see if there is any offensive
way in me."

This was David asking the God with whom he shared an intimate,
loving relationship to search him and show him any lack of faith or
unknown sins. This was a man essentially saying, "Lord, I know You
love me, so I'm asking You to help me be the man You want me to be."

Today, God invites you to do the very same thing.

. . . .

*Heavenly Father, help me to be so secure in Your love for
me that I have the courage to boldly ask You to search
me and let me know where I may be falling short.*

HONOR AND OBEY HIM

That's the whole story. Here now is my final conclusion:
Fear God and obey his commands, for this is everyone's
duty. God will judge us for everything we do, including
every secret thing, whether good or bad.

ECCLESIASTES 12:13–14 NLT

The Bible called Solomon the wisest man in the world (see 1 Kings 4:29–34). At Solomon's very specific request, the Lord had gifted the young king with the wisdom he knew he'd need to lead the people of the then-great nation of Israel. For many years, Solomon used that wisdom to serve God and lead his people spectacularly. Sadly, though, he spent his latter years serving himself by chasing more wealth, more power, and more women—all while seemingly forgetting his God and his earlier vow to love and obey the Lord all the days of his life. The results were disastrous.

Many believe that Solomon wrote the book of Ecclesiastes near his life's end, as he looked back and recognized the folly of chasing after the wrong things, after anything but God's well-deserved glory. If that's true, then it gives even greater weight to his wise counsel that we should "fear God and obey his commands." As men who know Jesus as Lord and Savior, that is our duty—and our privilege.

Lord God, I want to glorify You in everything I do.
May I never forget to honor You, love You, and obey You.

THE RISEN CHRIST

*For if there is no resurrection of the dead, then Christ has
not been raised either. And if Christ has not been raised,
then all our preaching is useless, and your faith is useless.
. . . But in fact, Christ has been raised from the dead.
He is the first of a great harvest of all who have died.*
1 CORINTHIANS 15:13–14, 20 NLT

We Christians understand the importance of Jesus' death on the cross
as a sacrifice for our sins. But His death wasn't the end of the story.

Jesus' death was the moment when God took it on Himself
to provide the once-and-for-all sacrifice for our sin. But the above
scripture passage clearly states that Jesus rising from the dead is
absolutely essential to the Christian faith. In fact, the apostle Paul
wrote, "[Jesus] was delivered over to death for our sins and was raised
to life for our justification" (Romans 4:25 NIV).

Thank God every day that He sent His Son, Jesus, to die for your
sins. But also remember to thank Him for the empty tomb. Because
Jesus lives, you will live with Him in heaven forever.

*Father in heaven, thank You for sending Your Son
to earth to live as a man and die on a wooden cross
so that You could forgive my sins. Thank You also for
raising Jesus from the dead so that I can live forever.*

VICTORY OVER DEATH

"O death, where is your sting? O grave, where is your victory?"
The sting of death is sin, and the strength of sin is
the law. But thanks be to God, who gives us the
victory through our Lord Jesus Christ.

1 CORINTHIANS 15:55–57 SKJV

The thought of dying scares most men—even many Christian men. We don't like thinking about the truth that we'll all die one day. We also grieve when a loved one dies, knowing that we'll never see them again—at least in this life.

It may come as a surprise to most, but God never intended for us humans to taste death. Adam and Eve, the first humans, enjoyed perfect fellowship with their Creator in a beautiful garden where He intended for them to live forever; but when they chose disobedience, they brought death and destruction into the human experience.

But almost immediately after Adam and Eve sinned, God announced that He would send a Savior into the world to defeat sin and death once and for all. When Jesus died and was raised from the dead, He broke the power of sin and death and the law for everyone who would believe in Him. Now we can enjoy victory over death and eternal life in a forever home with Jesus in heaven.

Jesus, when You rose from the grave, You defeated
the curse of death forever. Though my body will
die one day, I know that I will be raised.

BRINGING YOUR WORRIES TO GOD

I cry out to the LORD; I plead for the LORD's mercy.
I pour out my complaints before him and tell him
all my troubles. When I am overwhelmed,
you alone know the way I should turn.

PSALM 142:1–3 NLT

David had plenty to be gravely concerned about when he wrote Psalm 142. He was holed up in a cave in a place called Adullam, hiding from the persecution of King Saul. From there, he brought his worries and concerns to the Lord.

Though David wrote in the above scripture passage, "I pour out my complaints before [the Lord]," he wasn't complaining against God about his present situation but bringing his troubles and concerns to the one he knew could and would calm his heart and mind and bring him relief.

When David brought his problems to the Lord, he set an example we should all follow, an example well summarized by the apostle Paul: "Do not be anxious about anything, but in every situation, by prayer and petition, with thanksgiving, present your requests to God" (Philippians 4:6 NIV).

Boldly take your problems, big and small, to your heavenly Father. He wants to hear from you!

Gracious Lord, may I never forget that You want me
to bring my worries, complaints, and concerns to You.
You know what I'm dealing with, but You want me to talk
to You about it and not hold anything back from You.

THE GOD OF ALL COMFORT

*Praise be to the God and Father of our Lord Jesus Christ,
the Father of compassion and the God of all comfort,
who comforts us in all our troubles, so that we can comfort those
in any trouble with the comfort we ourselves receive from God.*

2 CORINTHIANS 1:3–4 NIV

Just as a good parent comforts his child when it is suffering, our perfect heavenly Father is always ready to comfort His children when they are going through trials and difficulties.

Our God always knows what we need, and He always knows the best way to meet that need. Sometimes He comforts His people with just the calming assurance of His presence, and sometimes He sends human agents to speak words of comfort. Either way, He is the ultimate source of comfort.

Think of the times when God provided you much-needed comfort and encouragement. Then purpose in your heart to "pay it forward" and allow God to use you as a source of comfort to others around you.

. . . .

*Father, I can think of so many times when You encouraged and
strengthened me when I needed it—sometimes with Your mere
presence when I was going through dark and difficult times and
sometimes through the comforting words and actions of others.
I want You to use me as a source of comfort to others who need it.*

CLEANSED!

Then I said, "It's all over! I am doomed, for I am a sinful man.
I have filthy lips, and I live among a people with filthy lips.
Yet I have seen the King, the LORD of Heaven's Armies."

ISAIAH 6:5 NLT

When Isaiah entered God's temple, he was in awe as he saw the glory of the Lord. But he was also quite terrified, believing that he was about to die. But God had plans for Isaiah, and they didn't include him dying that day.

In today's scripture verse, Isaiah laments his own sinfulness and unworthiness to be in God's presence. But the Lord made a way for him: "Then one of the seraphim flew to me with a burning coal he had taken from the altar with a pair of tongs. He touched my lips with it and said, 'See, this coal has touched your lips. Now your guilt is removed, and your sins are forgiven'" (Isaiah 6:6–7 NLT).

Each of us should think about Isaiah's example when we're confronted with our own sinfulness in light of God's holiness. And, like Isaiah, God can and will cleanse us when we confess our sin (see 1 John 1:9).

Heavenly Father, I am by nature a miserable sinner who is unworthy to approach You in any way. Yet You have cleansed me—my mouth, my eyes, my heart. . .all of me—through Jesus Christ. Thank You for doing for me what I could never have done for myself.

THE MYSTERY OF GOD'S LOVE

O Lord, what are human beings that you should notice them,
mere mortals that you should think about them? For they are
like a breath of air; their days are like a passing shadow.
PSALM 144:3–4 NLT

As the king of a great nation, David was obviously a man of amazing accomplishment. Yet in the above scripture passage, he marvels that such a great God—*his* God—would even think about a mere mortal like him. . .or the rest of humanity.

It's not a bad thing for a man of God to marvel at the same thing today, is it?

God's love for His people is a mystery—a wondrous, unfathomable mystery. Nothing about us makes us worthy of even the notice of an all-holy God, yet He thinks about us and loves us more deeply than we can comprehend. And why? Simply because love is the essence of who He is.

When you wake up in the morning, it's not a bad idea to thank the Lord from your heart for allowing you to spend the coming day basking in His wonderful love.

Father in heaven, I'm filled with wonder and awe that You,
the most high God and Creator of all things, even notice me,
let alone love me more deeply than I can comprehend.
I am not worthy of Your love, but I thank You for it.

PROCLAIM HIS WONDERFUL NAME

"Give praise to the LORD, proclaim his name;
make known among the nations what he has done,
and proclaim that his name is exalted."

ISAIAH 12:4 NIV

Think about the wonderful things God has done for you, starting with saving you and setting you on a course that will take you to an eternity in heaven with Him. Then think about how He, through His Holy Spirit, has empowered you to live a life that pleases Him. Think about how He has filled your heart with the kind of joy only a truly saved man can experience.

The Lord has all those things for you—and still more.

It's good for a man of God to take stock of the great things God has done for him. But it's even better for him to open his mouth and speak words of praise and thanksgiving to the one who is his source of all good things.

We live in a world filled with people who desperately need to see and hear about God's goodness and love. So don't be shy. Instead, "proclaim his name" and "make known among the nations what he has done."

Wonderful Father, I confess that I don't open my mouth and proclaim and praise Your name as much as I should. Please forgive me. Encourage and empower me to speak of Your goodness and generosity toward me to those who most need to hear about You.

WHERE HAVE YOU PUT YOUR TRUST?

Don't put your confidence in powerful people; there is no help for you there. When they breathe their last, they return to the earth, and all their plans die with them. But joyful are those who have the God of Israel as their helper, whose hope is in the LORD their God.

PSALM 146:3–5 NLT

In what or in whom do you trust with your whole heart? In well-established government institutions? In a lifelong friend who has never let you down, who would literally give you the shirt off his back?

Today's scripture passage tells us that placing our full trust in anything or anyone other than the Lord is unwise. That's because even the most dependable worldly institutions or the most dependable friends are temporary—both will one day cease to exist. But eternally dependable help comes only from our eternal God. He alone is worthy of our praise and absolute trust.

God calls those who belong to Him to trust in Him with our whole hearts. No one or nothing is even close to Him when it comes to dependability and trustworthiness. Count on Him always.

. . . .

Lord God, this world's people and institutions may be of help to me, but only in the short-term. But You will never fail me or make Yourself unavailable to me. You are, and always will be, my unfailing source of help. I trust in You!

AN ETERNAL HOME

*For we know that if the earthly tent we live in is destroyed,
we have a building from God, an eternal house in heaven,
not built by human hands. Meanwhile we groan, longing
to be clothed instead with our heavenly dwelling, because
when we are clothed, we will not be found naked.*

2 CORINTHIANS 5:1–3 NIV

In the above scripture passage the apostle Paul likens our physical bodies to a tent. If you've ever slept outside in a tent, you know that it has severe limitations, especially when it comes to cold or stormy weather. Also, tents—even expensive, high-quality ones—are prone to wearing out relatively quickly.

Like literal tents, our physical bodies don't last forever—usually seventy to eighty years—before they wear out and cease function. But when that happens, Paul says, we will receive new bodies—eternal houses—that will never wear out, never grow old, and never die.

When you feel anxious about growing old, even dying one day, take heart. The body you live in now is only a preview of something infinitely better.

. . . .

Dear Lord, I know that as I grow older, my body will begin to wear down and wear out. Eventually, my earthly tent will die and my soul will leave this earth. Thank You for the new body You've prepared for me and for the place where I'll live forever with You.

AN ETERNAL PERSPECTIVE

Sorrowful, yet always rejoicing; poor,
yet making many rich; having nothing,
and yet possessing everything.
2 CORINTHIANS 6:10 NIV

Second Corinthians 6:3–10 is an extended list of the suffering and hardships the apostle Paul and his traveling companions endured as they worked day and night to take the message of salvation through Jesus Christ into the world around them. It's a list that can make you shake your head and say "wow!"

In the final verse of this passage, Paul concludes that despite his sorrows he was constantly filled with joy, despite his poverty he helped enrich many, and despite his lack of worldly possessions, he had everything. . .all simply because he had Jesus.

That's what an eternal perspective will do to a man.

Though it's very unlikely that you'll face suffering even remotely close to that of Paul, you will have your share of distress, hardships, and afflictions in this life. But you can take heart in knowing that God is more than able to get you through it victoriously. And when He does, you can point others to Him as the source of all peace, comfort, and empowerment.

. . . .

Father in heaven, I know You want me to have an eternal perspective,
much like Your servant Paul did while he ministered here on earth.
Remind me daily that whatever happens in this life, I can have lasting
inner peace and joy because I have eternal life through Jesus.

WILLING TO SPEAK THE TRUTH

*Even if I caused you sorrow by my letter, I do not regret it.
Though I did regret it—I see that my letter hurt you, but only
for a little while—yet now I am happy, not because you were
made sorry, but because your sorrow led you to repentance.*

2 CORINTHIANS 7:8–9 NIV

The church in Corinth was a mess, and the apostle Paul found himself in the unenviable position of having to write a letter of correction.

Many believe that Paul was referring in today's scripture verses to the letter that now appears in the Bible as 1 Corinthians. In that epistle, Paul spoke very direct correction to the church for not only tolerating but condoning the sinful actions of one of its members. As a result, the church stopped tolerating sin. Not only that, the man repented of his sin and got right with God.

If you've ever been in a situation where you knew a Christian brother needed reproof, then you know how Paul must have felt in writing his first letter to the Corinthian church. But Paul was willing to tell the hard truth. Are you willing to do as Paul did?

*Lord, speaking hard truth to an erring brother in Christ
isn't easy. Give me the courage to speak the truth and the
love to do it in a way that assures my brother that I care
about him and want him to receive Your very best.*

FOR YOUR SAKE

For you know the grace of our Lord Jesus Christ,
that though he was rich, yet for your sake he became poor,
so that you through his poverty might become rich.
2 CORINTHIANS 8:9 NIV

The apostle John wrote of Jesus: "In the beginning was the Word, and the Word was with God, and the Word was God. He was with God in the beginning. Through him all things were made; without him nothing was made that has been made" (John 1:1–3 NIV).

Jesus, the one and only Son of God, lived for all of eternity past in heaven with the Father and the Holy Spirit. And yet, at God's appointed time, Jesus left all the riches He enjoyed in heaven and was born into a world ravaged by sin and into a human race that was in full rebellion against a loving Creator.

Jesus' arrival into this world—where He lived, taught, performed miracles, and then died a grisly death—was the greatest act of love of all time. And God did it for you so that He could share with you His riches.

* *

Lord Jesus, You demonstrated Your love for me by humbling Yourself, leaving behind Your home in heaven for a time, and living a life of poverty here on earth so that You could save me from my sins and give me eternal life with You in heaven. Thank You!

WAITING FOR THE LORD

So the LORD must wait for you to come to him so he can
show you his love and compassion. For the LORD is a
faithful God. Blessed are those who wait for his help.

ISAIAH 30:18 NLT

The nation of Judah was in deep trouble. The powerful and ruthless Assyrian army was attacking Israel and Judah, and Israel would soon be conquered—then the Assyrians would set their sights on the southern kingdom of Judah. But instead of turning to the Lord for help, Judah looked to Egypt for protection.

The first half of Isaiah 30 was God's rebuke of Judah for looking to Egypt for help instead of the Lord. But in verse 18 (today's scripture verse), Isaiah calls on Judah to trust in God and His love, compassion, and faithfulness toward His people.

God's call in Isaiah's time to turn to Him first is as valid today as it was back then.

When you're faced with what seems like an impossible situation, turn with your whole heart to the Lord. He's waiting to hear from you, and He's more than willing and more than able to step into your situation and shower you with His love and compassion.

. . . .

Lord God, I will trust in You first when I need help or deliverance.
Thank You for Your love, compassion, and faithfulness.

WHEN YOU FEEL WEAK

Lord, be gracious to us; we long for you. Be our strength
every morning, our salvation in time of distress.
ISAIAH 33:2 NIV

After the rebuke of Judah, as well as the words of encouragement, in Isaiah 32, the people did exactly what they needed to do: cease looking to themselves or Egyptians for deliverance from a very real Assyrian threat and start looking to the Lord. Today's scripture verse is a prayer confessing Judah's longing for God and their plea for Him to be their strength and their salvation.

Many men have a difficult time confessing to any kind of weakness or neediness. We like to think of ourselves in terms of toughness and rugged individualism. But inside of every Christian man is a very real sense of weakness and need.

The Lord wants to hear from you when you feel spiritually weak, emotionally weak, even physically weak. And He wants to be your strength and the source of everything you so desperately need.

God is your strength and your source of encouragement, today and every day. So when you feel weak and overwhelmed, you can pray from your heart with Isaiah.

. . . .

Lord, be gracious to me; I long for You. Be my strength
every morning, my salvation in time of distress.

BE LIKE THE APOSTLE PAUL

*I have worked hard and long, enduring many
sleepless nights. I have been hungry and thirsty and
have often gone without food. I have shivered in the
cold, without enough clothing to keep me warm.*

2 CORINTHIANS 11:27 NLT

The apostle Paul understood well what suffering for the sake of Jesus and the gospel message really looked like. In today's scripture verse he lists many of the hardships he endured as God's instrument to take the gospel to the Gentile world. Then, of course, there were the accusations, the beatings, and other mistreatment at the hands of others.

Though Paul suffered much, he never lost sight of Jesus and what He had called him to do. Humanly speaking, Paul had every reason to pack up and go home. But he wouldn't—couldn't—do that. Instead, he remained firm in his faith.

It's extremely unlikely that you'll suffer the kinds of things Paul did. But you'll still have to endure difficulties and hardships. And when you do, you'll have a choice to make: Will you allow those things to distract you from your faith in Christ *or* will you cling even harder to Him, knowing that He has a purpose for everything you're enduring?

*Lord Jesus, thank You for being my everything. When I
am overwhelmed with problems here on earth, help me
to do what the apostle Paul did: keep myself focused on
You and what You have for me to do every day.*

THE THORN IN THE FLESH

So to keep me from becoming proud, I was given a thorn in my flesh, a messenger from Satan to torment me and keep me from becoming proud. Three different times I begged the Lord to take it away. Each time he said, "My grace is all you need. My power works best in weakness." So now I am glad to boast about my weaknesses, so that the power of Christ can work through me.

2 CORINTHIANS 12:7–9 NLT

One of the great mysteries in the Bible is the apostle Paul's "thorn in the flesh," which he also called "a messenger from Satan to torment me." It's not certain whether this thorn was a physical issue, a spiritual enemy, an emotional affliction—or something else. Whatever it was, Paul acknowledged that God used it to "keep me from becoming proud."

Paul's response to his "thorn" was perfect. He didn't complain—he simply asked God to remove it but submitted himself to the Lord's will. God didn't remove the thorn, and in the end, Paul could boast in his weaknesses and acknowledge that it allowed the power of Jesus to work through him.

Lord Jesus, when I pray for relief but You allow my "thorn in the flesh"—be it a physical problem, spiritual opposition, or other issues—remind me that You have a purpose for all things and that Your grace is sufficient for me and that You work best through my weaknesses.

OUR SOURCE OF WISDOM

For the LORD grants wisdom! From his mouth come knowledge and understanding. He grants a treasure of common sense to the honest. He is a shield to those who walk with integrity.
PROVERBS 2:6–7 NLT

It's safe to say that every Christian man has come up against life situations where he wasn't sure what to do or what path is right for him. He wants to please and glorify the Lord, but he wonders, *What is the wisest course for this situation?*

If you're wrestling with what choice would please and glorify God, take heart. The Bible instructs those who need wise direction: "If any of you lacks wisdom, you should ask God, who gives generously to all without finding fault, and it will be given to you. But when you ask, you must believe and not doubt, because the one who doubts is like a wave of the sea, blown and tossed by the wind" (James 1:5–6 NIV).

Our God gave us physical life as well as new life when we believed in the Lord Jesus Christ. He is also our source of perfect knowledge and wisdom—and He gives both generously.

Father in heaven, thank You for Your promise to grant wisdom to men of God who ask for it. I confess that I don't always know the best course of action to take. But I know I don't have to go it alone, for You freely offer me unlimited grace and wisdom.

STRENGTH TO FACE YOUR TROUBLES

"So do not fear, for I am with you; do not be dismayed,
for I am your God. I will strengthen you and help you;
I will uphold you with my righteous right hand."
ISAIAH 41:10 NIV

Ever wake up in the morning feeling overwhelmed and wanting to just go back to sleep? You might be facing daunting financial issues. Or marital/family problems. Or conflicts at work. Or physical illness. Or. . .

Life has a way of throwing any number of troubles and struggles in the path of even the godliest of men. It often fulfills this promise from Jesus (which, if we were completely honest with ourselves, we wish He hadn't made): "In this world you will have trouble" (John 16:33 NIV).

On those mornings when you feel like staying in bed, pull yourself up, get on your feet, and take heart. God is still bigger than any of your troubles. And He has promised never to let you face them alone but always to give you all the strength you need.

. . . .

Lord God , thank You that I don't have to face my troubles
and struggles alone and that I don't have to allow fear to
rule my life. Instead, I can live in peace and confidence
knowing that You have promised to be with me,
strengthen me, and hold me in Your right hand.

SINS FORGIVEN. . .AND FORGOTTEN

"I, even I, am He who blots out your transgressions for
My own sake and will not remember your sins."

ISAIAH 43:25 SKJV

The Bible repeatedly instructs brothers in the faith to forgive one another. For example, the apostle Paul enjoins believers to "be kind and compassionate to one another, forgiving each other, just as in Christ God forgave you" (Ephesians 4:32 NIV).

It's not always easy to "forgive and forget," but we must do just that if we want to maintain healthy relationships with others—at home, at work, at church. God wants to maintain and grow relationships between Himself and His people. Perhaps that's why He promises to blot out our transgressions and remember our sins no more.

In our limited mortal understanding, it's impossible for us to comprehend how an all-knowing Creator can simply choose to permanently put our wrongdoing out of His thoughts. Perhaps, then, it's best just to rejoice and take heart in the wonderful truth that when God forgives us, He also promises never to hold the past against us or bring up again what has been forgiven.

Lord Jesus, thank You for taking the punishment for my sin
on the cross so that the Father could keep His promise to
blot out my transgressions and remember my sins no more.
I don't deserve what You did for me; it's only because of
God's goodness and grace that I can stand forgiven.

DON'T FEAR FOR THE FUTURE

Have no fear of sudden disaster or of the ruin that overtakes the wicked, for the LORD will be at your side and will keep your foot from being snared.
PROVERBS 3:25–26 NIV

During His Sermon on the Mount, Jesus delivered some comforting, challenging teaching on the subject of worry (Matthew 6:25–34), concluding with this important question: "Can any one of you by worrying add a single hour to your life?" (v. 27 NIV).

The world today offers much that can be reasons for concern or worry. Will there be a big economic downturn in the near future? Will war break out, and will it affect the United States? When and where will the next devastating natural disaster strike? What about the next pandemic? And it doesn't help that so many modern-day "prophets" deliver almost-daily predictions of doom.

In today's scripture verses, Solomon offers some great wisdom for those given to worry about future events. Don't fear or worry about sudden calamities, for the Lord is in control of all things—including natural disasters. And even if what you see as a worst-case scenario becomes reality, you can take heart, knowing that God promises to be with you always.

Lord, sometimes I find myself worrying about what could happen in the future. Help me to rest always in the truth that You are in control of all things and that You love and care for me.

JESUS: THE ONLY WAY

*If the law could give us new life, we could be made right
with God by obeying it. But the Scriptures declare that
we are all prisoners of sin, so we receive God's promise
of freedom only by believing in Jesus Christ.*

GALATIANS 3:21–22 NLT

It might seem strange to think of it this way, but every man who has ever lived (except for Jesus) is born a prisoner. Not only that, we have no hope for freedom—in this life or in the life to come.

No hope, that is, except in the Lord Jesus Christ.

Paul stated in the above scripture verses that no one can be made right with God by obeying the law of Moses. That can only be done, he wrote, through faith in the one who came to earth not to abolish but to fulfill the law (Matthew 5:17).

Jesus once stated, "I am the Door; anyone who enters in through Me will be saved (will live). He will come in and he will go out [freely], and will find pasture" (John 10:9 AMPC). In light of Galatians 3:21–22, we might well see Jesus as the one-way door out of that prison of sin.

*Lord Jesus, thank You for freeing me from the prison
of sin. Help me to always cling to and proclaim that You
and only You can free men from that terrible prison.*

A HEAVENLY FATHER'S LOVE

And because we are his children, God has sent the
Spirit of his Son into our hearts, prompting us to call out,
"Abba, Father." Now you are no longer a slave but God's own
child. And since you are his child, God has made you his heir.
GALATIANS 4:6–7 NLT

Sadly, many men go through most of their lives with what are commonly called "father wounds"—the sometimes-severe negative emotional consequences of growing up with a physically or emotionally distant/absent father. Such a man may later have difficulty bonding emotionally with others—and he may also find it hard to think of God as a loving heavenly Father.

Perhaps you can identify with that scenario.

Galatians 4:6–7 offers great encouragement to any Christian man, especially the one who grew up in a home with an absent or distant father. This passage defines God as a personal, loving Father who wants His people to address Him as "Abba"—*Daddy*.

Whether or not you had an emotionally available earthly father, you have a Father in heaven who loves you—deeply and perfectly—and wants a spiritually/emotionally intimate, affectionate Father-son relationship with you.

Loving heavenly Father, thank You for Your love
and for adopting me into Your eternal family.
Thank You for giving me the privilege of addressing
You as my own Father—as "Daddy."

YOUR SALVATION PLEASES GOD

*Yet it pleased the LORD to bruise Him. He has
put Him to grief. When You make His soul an
offering for sin, He shall see His offspring.*

Isaiah 53:10 skjv

Your salvation is as solid as the Rock of Gibraltar. Even more so, coming from the God who created the Rock of Gibraltar.

When Isaiah prophesied of God's "righteous Servant" (53:11 skjv), he knew only a fraction of what we do today. By inspiration, the great prophet described a Messiah who would suffer terribly before enjoying the fruit of His work. We look back on the birth, life, death, and resurrection of Jesus Christ and understand exactly what Isaiah saw only in a distant vision: God the Father "bruised" His own Son on the cross. Jesus was "put. . .to grief" to pay the penalty for sin. His soul was an "offering," the perfect and final example of the old sacrificial system. But Jesus would return to life and "see His offspring," the hundreds of millions, if not billions, of people who would put their faith in Him for salvation.

All of this was by God's plan, His "determinate counsel and foreknowledge," to quote Peter's sermon at Pentecost (Acts 2:23 skjv). Nothing could have kept Jesus from going to the cross. Nothing will stop Him from seeing your salvation through eternity. This pleases the all-knowing, all-powerful creator God we serve.

* * *

*Heavenly Father, I'm so glad for Your pleasure
in my salvation. May I please You in return.*

BE YOURSELF*

*It is for freedom that Christ has set us free. Stand firm, then,
and do not let yourselves be burdened again by a yoke of slavery.*
GALATIANS 5:1 NIV

Why the asterisk with this devotional's title? Because that "be yourself"
phrase requires some explanation.

God made billions of human beings, each with similarities, yet
no two exactly alike. Everyone has specific interests and abilities that
contribute to God's plan, so you should "be yourself." You are free in
Christ to become the very best *you* you can be.

But about that asterisk. . . Though our freedom is broad, it does
have limits. The apostle Paul, who wrote today's scripture, also described
believers as slaves to obedience and righteousness (Romans 6:16, 18).

Christians are not bound by the Old Testament's ceremonial
and civil rules—Galatians 5 argues that no believer should try to
supplement faith in Jesus with circumcision. But God's moral laws
do still apply. . .hence the "slavery" of Romans 6.

Within Christianity, "be yourself" means you can choose to be a
businessman, an artist, a deep-sea diver—whatever interests you and
honors God—without anyone's interference. But you can't steal from
your neighbor, either his money or his wife.

Imagine yourself as a kid on a vast, incredible playground. You're
free to do whatever you please. . .just don't jump the fence. It's dangerous
outside.

*Lord, I'm thankful for the freedom and opportunity
You offer. Help me to be my best self, within Your will.*

SEXUAL SATISFACTION

Here's what you should do to be satisfied: go home and drink in the pleasures of your own cistern, your wife; enjoy the sweet, fresh water that has been there all along, flowing from your own well.

PROVERBS 5:15 VOICE

In a world where sexual inhibitions are rapidly disappearing, does it seem like people are happier? Or have increasing sexual freedoms been accompanied by a tidal wave of anger, confusion, and depression?

Christian men are not immune to the overwhelming messages of culture: *Give in to your desires. Do whatever feels good. Follow your heart.*

But any honest reading of God's Word yields a singular rule: sex is to be experienced between one man and one woman, in a faithful, lifelong marriage.

Is that limiting? Yes. And no.

By keeping sex within God's marital framework, all other partners and forms of expression are out. (So too are the disappointments, fears, embarrassments, and even physical diseases that go with unbridled sexual activity.)

According to the Proverbs, the gain of following God's rules is the satisfaction of a truly committed marriage relationship—drinking in the joys of your own loving wife. Your marriage becomes a place not only of physical pleasure but of emotional safety and support.

In a world gone crazy, take heart and guard your heart. Whether you're married now or hope to be someday, God has the better way.

Lord, help me to understand Your wise way for sex. Keep me pure and true in Your care.

REALLY HELPFUL PRAYER

*I keep asking that the God of our Lord Jesus Christ, the glorious
Father, may give you the Spirit of wisdom and revelation, so that
you may know him better. I pray that the eyes of your heart may
be enlightened in order that you may know the hope to which he
has called you, the riches of his glorious inheritance in his holy
people, and his incomparably great power for us who believe.*

EPHESIANS 1:17–19 NIV

Praying for physical health needs is good. So are prayers for financial
challenges, relationship issues, job situations, and any of a million
other practical concerns.

But one category of request goes far deeper than these day-to-
day needs, to the very bedrock of our faith. The apostle Paul provides
the example in his ongoing prayer for the Ephesians, that they would
know God better.

When we receive the requested "Spirit of wisdom and revelation,"
much of our daily confusion is resolved. When we know God
more deeply, as well as "the hope to which he has called" us, our
spiritual struggles diminish. When we recognize and trust in God's
"incomparably great power," miracles can happen.

This kind of prayer—for ourselves and others—can truly change
lives. Certainly, keep praying for all those other needs. But don't
forget to address the deepest need of every human being: a living,
growing knowledge of the God who made, keeps, and redeems us.

Father, I echo Paul's prayer—for myself and for others.

BRAINPOWER AND MORE

*Take a lesson from the ants, you lazybones. Learn from
their ways and become wise! Though they have no prince
or governor or ruler to make them work, they labor
hard all summer, gathering food for the winter.*

PROVERBS 6:6–8 NLT

This is scripture's famed passage on laziness. But it also offers encouragement for those times we feel lost and confused.

How big can an ant's brain be? And yet the little guy knows exactly what to do, when. God has made the ant wise enough to work hard now to prepare for his future time of need. Our lives are certainly more complicated than an ant's, but we also have vastly more brainpower. . .and a direct connection to our Creator, who made us in His own image.

When we're struggling, we can ask Him for wisdom (James 1:5). Jesus Himself has taught us to ask His Father for "our daily bread" (Matthew 6:11). We know that God cares for the birds and that we as human beings are much more valuable to Him (Matthew 6:26; Luke 12:24).

So, if you're a lazybones, take a lesson from the ants. And if you ever feel overwhelmed by life, do the same. Those tiny creatures do what God created them to do, and they succeed. So can we. It's all a matter of prayer and obedience.

*Lord God, thank You for giving me a strong mind—
may I always direct it toward Your ultimate wisdom.*

IT'S ALL GOOD

*"Look! I am creating new heavens and a new earth,
and no one will even think about the old ones anymore."*

ISAIAH 65:17 NLT

What are your fondest memories? Of leading (or simply cheering) your team to a championship? Of a certain vacation, a business achievement, the acquisition of some long-desired object? Of meeting your girl, getting married, having kids?

How about your *worst* memories? A bad diagnosis, an accident, a house fire? A breakup, betrayal, or bankruptcy?

Life is an ongoing roller-coaster ride. We exult in the peaks and hold on for dear life as we careen into the valleys. But no matter how exciting or depressing our experiences on this earth, a day is coming when none of it will matter.

God's promise through Isaiah indicates that our worst experiences will one day be completely erased from our minds. The Christian's eternity with God will be so good that "no one will even think about" what went before.

On the other hand, even our *best* experiences will pale in comparison. As the apostle Paul wrote, referring to another passage from Isaiah, "That is what the Scriptures mean when they say, 'No eye has seen, no ear has heard, and no mind has imagined what God has prepared for those who love him'" (1 Corinthians 2:9 NLT; see also Isaiah 64:4).

Eternity is coming. And it's all good.

Lord, thank You for the promise of perfect peace and rest. I need it!

ANGER MANAGEMENT

Let all bitterness and wrath and anger and clamor and
evil speaking be put away from you, with all malice.
EPHESIANS 4:31 SKJV

Anger is a tricky issue for Christian men. Chances are we get angry. . . some of us often. Many of us fear that our angry reactions are sinful, and we're often disappointed with ourselves—perhaps to the point of questioning our salvation.

But reread today's scripture. As a command, it implies that anger, in all its various forms, will sometimes arise in our hearts. The key is to "put [it] away," in a conscious act of obedience. And don't overlook the imperative a few verses earlier, in Ephesians 4:26 (SKJV): "Be angry and do not sin. Don't let the sun go down on your wrath." The apostle Paul clearly states that there is an anger that's not sinful—consider, for example, Jesus' cleansing of the temple. Of course, we are not Jesus, so we must deal with our own "wrath" by day's end. There's that conscious act of obedience again.

It seems that anger is much like any temptation—a regular visitor at the door of our hearts, not necessarily sin itself but something that must be turned away quickly. When we allow it in to stay, trouble will follow. As the Proverbs say, "A furious man abounds in transgression" (29:22 SKJV).

Lord God, please help me to control my anger.
Give me Jesus' anger toward sin, but may I never sin in it.

USE THE RIGHT NAME

For you were once darkness,
but now you are light in the Lord.
Ephesians 5:8 hcsb

It's a paradox of the Christian life: the more we grow in our relationship to God, the more we recognize our own sinfulness.

That's not all bad. We should be amazed at God's grace, His willingness to save rebellious human beings through faith in Jesus. But once we are saved—once we're much-loved sons of God by the work of *the* Son of God—let's not obsess over our failings. When we sin, let's just confess to God, ask His forgiveness, and move on in His grace. The backward look is a poor use of our time and energy.

Famed nineteenth-century preacher Charles Spurgeon found encouragement in the fifth verse of Genesis (hcsb): "God called the light 'day,' and He called the darkness 'night.' Evening came and then morning: the first day." Both darkness and light, Spurgeon noted, were called "by the name that is given to the light alone!" Though we find both darkness and light in ourselves, we shouldn't think of ourselves as sinners but as saints—because we possess some degree of God's holiness.

Saints on earth still have darkness inside, but the day will come when we are completely light in God's presence. Until that time, emphasize the grace He's given you. Call yourself by the right name: "Light in the Lord."

Thank You for saving me, Lord.
Increase Your light in my life every day.

GOD'S PARAMETERS

"Why aren't you in awe before me? Yes, me, who made the shorelines to contain the ocean waters. I drew a line in the sand that cannot be crossed. Waves roll in but cannot get through; breakers crash but that's the end of them."

JEREMIAH 5:22 MSG

With the exception of the great flood of Genesis, the seas have kept to their God-ordained limits since the third day of creation. That's when the Lord decreed, "Let the water under the sky be gathered into one place, and let the dry land appear" (Genesis 1:9 HCSB). If God sets parameters for His creation, they'll be obeyed.

The physical world follows God's orders without complaint. Only human beings, made in God's image but possessing free will, resist His good and wise direction.

Even at that, God still sets protective limits. "A king's heart is like streams of water in the LORD's hand," the Proverbs say. "He directs it wherever He chooses" (21:1 HCSB). "The nations rage like the raging of many waters," Isaiah wrote. "He rebukes them, and they flee far away" (17:13 HCSB).

When it seems like the world is spinning out of control, it isn't. . .God is completely aware of everything that happens and superintending it. We may not understand or even like what we see. But we can trust that even as circumstances crash like breakers, they will never go beyond God's parameters.

. . . .

*Lord, thank You for protecting me with
Your wise and powerful boundaries.*

WISDOM IS CALLING

Does not wisdom call out?
Does not understanding raise her voice?
PROVERBS 8:1 NIV

Proverbs 8 personifies Wisdom, describing a woman who stands in public places, shouting for attention, offering instruction, promising a better life to anyone who will listen.

It's a compelling image. But in today's world, we see countless people completely missing her. Faces buried in screens, they never look up to notice her beckoning. Ear buds filling their heads with noise, they never hear her cries.

"Choose my instruction instead of silver, knowledge rather than choice gold," she calls out, "for wisdom is more precious than rubies, and nothing you desire can compare with her" (Proverbs 8:10–11 NIV). Christian men, though prone to the distractions of this world, know that Wisdom's call is true. We are taught by God's Spirit within us that she is a genuine friend.

And real friends always point us to God. "The LORD brought me forth as the first of his works, before his deeds of old. I was formed long ages ago, at the very beginning, when the world came to be," she says. "I was constantly at his side. I was filled with delight day after day, rejoicing always in his presence, rejoicing in his whole world and delighting in mankind" (Proverbs 8:22–23, 30–31 NIV).

This knowledge of God, this true delight, is ours for the taking. Wisdom is calling. Heed her words in your own Bible.

Lord, please grant me Your wisdom today.

VICTORY IS COMING

Stand united, singular in vision, contending for people's trust in the Message, the good news, not flinching or dodging in the slightest before the opposition. Your courage and unity will show them what they're up against: defeat for them, victory for you—and both because of God.
PHILIPPIANS 1:27–28 MSG

When Paul wrote his letter to believers in Philippi, he did it from prison. But he certainly wasn't languishing there—Paul was praising God, witnessing to guards, and encouraging others with his quill and ink.

The great missionary to the Gentiles, the "chief of sinners" (1 Timothy 1:15) whose life was turned upside down by Christ, was living out Jesus' promise of "hard suffering" in his calling (Acts 9:16 MSG). But Paul never complained, and he urged other believers—those of the first century and every one of us since—to follow in his footsteps.

Christians must know that opposition will come. And we must never cower. Standing firm in the faith, always true to our Lord, proves the reality of God's work in our lives.

By pulling together as a group, we gain strength individually. Our persecutors will recognize their losing hand, and perhaps even change teams (Philippians 1:13). Corporate faithfulness enables us to rise above our daily hardships, to be confirmed in our belief in ultimate victory. And this is all to God's praise and glory.

Lord God, I thank You for victory—success in the daily battles and ultimate triumph in the war.

GOD IS SUPREME

None at all is like You, O Lord; You are great, and Your name is great in might. Who would not fear You, O King of the nations? For it is fitting to You and Your due! For among all the wise [men or gods] of the nations and in all their kingdoms, there is none like You.

JEREMIAH 10:6–7 AMPC

If we accept the Bible's account of origins, we should recognize the absolute supremacy of the God we serve. He predated and created the physical universe we inhabit. His wisdom and power brought matter and life into being where none had existed before. He simply spoke to produce vast, star-filled galaxies and one particular planet, perfectly suited for life, that enjoys His special attention. What other "god" or theory or superstition can even vaguely compete with the I AM?

We as Christian men know this mind-boggling God personally. In a limited way, of course—but He has allowed us to understand enough of His majesty to recognize Him as our source of life and hope. With a God like this for us, who can be against us (Romans 8:31)? Why would we ever fear any person or idea or circumstance that arises in opposition?

Life is difficult. But our God is supreme. When we follow Him by faith, we can trust that He has every situation in hand, for our ultimate benefit and His ultimate glory.

I praise You, Lord, for Your wisdom and power.

PRIORITY

I now realize that all I gained and thought was important was nothing but yesterday's garbage compared to knowing the Anointed Jesus my Lord. For Him I have thrown everything aside—it's nothing but a pile of waste—so that I may gain Him.
PHILIPPIANS 3:8 VOICE

Even the most ambitious, aggressive men find that worldly success is elusive or unfulfilling. Average guys often learn that lesson early on.

Scripturally speaking, though, every worldly achievement is nothing—"yesterday's garbage" and "a pile of waste" in the words of The Voice Bible, "loss" and "dung" in the language of the old King James.

What truly matters—what rises above all other things in importance—is knowing the Lord Jesus Christ. And, happily, that's achievable by the ambitious and the average alike. Whether you're riding high as the CEO of a Fortune 500 company or you're a retired laborer in an assisted living facility, if you desire and pursue more of the Lord, He will allow you—like the apostle Paul—to "gain Him."

Bible reading, prayer, meditation, church attendance, fellowship, service. . .whatever God the Father allows you to do, to whatever level, will lead you to have more of His Son, Jesus Christ, and the Holy Spirit in your life.

Anything that came earlier, whether good or bad, is history. Only Jesus Christ matters going forward. This is our priority.

Heavenly Father, grant me Your Spirit so I can better know Your Son. May Jesus Himself be my priority.

BEHIND ENEMY LINES

All God's people here send you greetings,
especially those who belong to Caesar's household.

<small>PHILIPPIANS 4:22 NIV</small>

The apostle Paul wrote his letter to the Philippians three centuries before the Roman empire officially adopted Christianity. But the faith was already planted in "Caesar's household."

Rome, with its pagan beliefs and emperor worship, was no friend—and often a powerful enemy—of Christianity. Paul wrote Philippians while imprisoned in the city, awaiting trial before the emperor. Many believe that was the infamous Nero, who ultimately had the apostle beheaded.

But during his stay in Rome, "what has happened to me has actually served to advance the gospel," Paul wrote. "As a result, it has become clear throughout the whole palace guard and to everyone else that I am in chains for Christ" (Philippians 1:12–13 NIV). By his cheerful submission to unfair treatment from Jesus' enemies, Paul had a powerful effect behind enemy lines.

The same can be true of us. In a world so clearly darkened by Satan, the light of Christ in our lives should shine all the brighter. If we're "always giving thanks to God the Father for everything, in the name of our Lord Jesus Christ" (Ephesians 5:20 NIV), we'll have opportunities—like Paul—to point a member of Caesar's household or a Philippian jailer (Acts 16) to the Lord.

God is working in all times and places. Let's be sure we join Him.

Here I am, Lord. . .use me behind enemy lines.

THEN AND NOW

*Although you at one time were estranged and alienated from Him
and were of hostile attitude of mind in your wicked activities,
yet now has [Christ, the Messiah] reconciled [you to God] in the
body of His flesh through death, in order to present you holy and
faultless and irreproachable in His [the Father's] presence.*
COLOSSIANS 1:21–22 AMPC

"Then and Now" features are popular internet clickbait. That gorgeous actress we all dreamed of in the 80s is now a middle-aged grandma. The leading man of '93, who all the girls thought was just hunky, is now—dare we say it?—just chunky.

In the physical world, then-and-now signifies decline. In the spiritual realm, it's the opposite.

The apostle Paul describes our "then"—life before Christ—as estrangement and alienation from God, hostility and wickedness toward Him. But thanks to the Father's grace and the Son's obedience, we "now" enjoy reconciliation, holiness, faultlessness, and irreproachability. The change is entirely due to the goodness of God, who has "drawn us to Himself out of the control and the dominion of darkness and has transferred us into the kingdom of the Son of His love, in Whom we have our redemption through His blood, [which means] the forgiveness of our sins" (Colossians 1:13–14 AMPC).

Then-and-now may be rough on your body, but it works wonders in your soul.

*Heavenly Father, thank You for reconciling me to Yourself
through Jesus Christ. May I always respond in obedience and love.*

A MAN OF INTEGRITY

*People with integrity walk safely, but those
who follow crooked paths will be exposed.*
PROVERBS 10:9 NLT

Liars' lives get complicated fast. They have to remember every falsehood they tell, to whom, when, and why. . .and try to keep every detail straight when they're inevitably challenged.

It's much the same for adulterers, embezzlers, plagiarists, tax cheats, and any of a thousand other kinds of lawbreakers. "Those who follow crooked paths" bring stress and strain into their own lives . . .since they know, deep down, that they'll ultimately be exposed.

How much better it is to walk with integrity, to follow Jesus' Golden Rule, to obey God's commandments regarding people, money, and things. Sure, even as Christians we'll occasionally mess up—but part of integrity is quickly confessing our failures to God and the folks we've offended. Then we can pick up again with walking in safety.

Why are we tempted to lie, cheat, and steal anyway? Isn't the problem a lack of trust in God's provision and protection? If that's true of you, maybe it would help to memorize Psalm 37:28 (NLT): "The LORD loves justice, and he will never abandon the godly. He will keep them safe forever."

. . . .

*Heavenly Father, remind me to trust in Your perfect goodness
so I can avoid any and every temptation to cheat. Please
make me a man of integrity who always walks safely.*

LET THE WIND BLOW

*When the storm has swept by, the wicked are
gone, but the righteous stand firm forever.*
PROVERBS 10:25 NIV

We as Christians may wonder why God allows storms in our lives. But today's scripture indicates that everyone—righteous and wicked alike—experiences rough weather. The difference is who's still standing when the tempest is past.

Believers build their lives on the firm foundation of Jesus—and however hard the wind blows, their house is unmoved (Matthew 7:24–25). Through the worst of storms, Jesus goes with us, awaiting the proper moment to calm the wind and waves (Mark 4:35–41). God directs hail- and snowstorms to His own purposes, "for times of trouble, for days of war and battle" (Job 38:23 NIV). Whether literal or figurative, the tempests of life are simply one of God's methods for dealing with humanity.

Since He wants "everyone to come to repentance" (2 Peter 3:9 NIV), God may use the terror of storms to draw the unsaved to Himself. In believers' lives, He might allow a storm for His greater, unseen purposes—as He did with Job. In ultimate terms, God will use the storm to sweep away His enemies, all the while strengthening and protecting His own children.

We won't always understand the storms. But we can be sure that God does and is using every one of them for His wise design.

*Lord, help me to accept storms as part of
Your plan—and keep me standing strong.*

CHANGE IS POSSIBLE

*Put on your new nature, and be renewed as you learn
to know your Creator and become like him.*

COLOSSIANS 3:10 NLT

"Change the world!" people shout. Yet, if we're honest, most of us struggle to change our own thoughts, emotions, and behaviors. Is positive change really possible?

In a book themed on Jesus' encouragement to "take heart," it's no surprise to see an answer of yes. The bigger issue is *how*.

In Colossians, the apostle Paul shows the way. It's not terribly complicated, but it does require effort.

Notice the commands, either stated or implied, leading up to today's scripture. Colossians 3:1 tells us to set our sights on heaven. Verse 2 reiterates the idea: *think* about heavenly things. Consider yourself dead to sin, anticipating the day you're made like Jesus (vv. 3–4).

"Put to death" and "get rid of" the sins that drag you down (vv. 5–9 NLT). If that sounds impossible, note that it helps if you've followed the previous commands.

Having done all that, you can obey verse 10: "Put on your new nature, and be renewed as you learn to know your Creator and become like him."

The key to everything is God's Word, described elsewhere as "alive and powerful" (Hebrews 4:12 NLT). You've made a good start with this devotional. . .now dig deeper, on your own, and commit to living out what you learn.

*Lord, I'm glad that change is possible.
Help me to learn and apply Your Word.*

BE A GOOD FIG

The LORD said to me, "What do you see, Jeremiah?"
And I said, "Figs, the good figs, very good. And the evil,
very evil, that cannot be eaten, they are so evil."
JEREMIAH 24:3 SKJV

Throughout scripture, committed followers of God are compared to sheep, trees, eagles, and. . .figs? Specifically, good figs. There are also inedible, "evil" figs that have no place in God's perfect plan.

Jeremiah is called "the weeping prophet" for his agonizing reaction to the Babylonian conquest of Judah and Jerusalem. After generations of Jews had sinned and resisted God's efforts to turn them around, He finally appointed the pagan king Nebuchadnezzar as His divine disciplinarian. Babylonians ransacked Jerusalem, destroying the temple and carrying off residents in waves of deportation.

In the midst of this, Jeremiah saw a vision of two baskets, each holding a very different type of fig. God explained that the good figs were those people exiled first, sent away for their benefit, people who would worship God when He restored them to their own land (Jeremiah 24:5–7). The bad figs were fellow Jews who would never return to God, whose exile would destroy them (vv. 8–10).

Though the people's trauma was universal, God would help certain ones through it. He knew which individuals were "good figs," and He planned for their ultimate blessing.

Perhaps a similar scenario is unfolding in our day. Be ready. Be a good fig.

Lord, please make and keep me good.

PRAYED OVER

We always thank God for all of you in our prayers. Your actions on behalf of the true faith, your tireless toil of love, and your unfailing, unwavering, unending hope in our Lord Jesus the Anointed before God our Father have put you consistently at the forefront of our thoughts.

1 THESSALONIANS 1:2–3 VOICE

Imagine being on the apostle Paul's prayer list—and not only his, but those of other early church leaders like Silas and Timothy.

Today's scripture shows Paul and Company praying specifically for the believers of first-century Thessalonica. Perhaps they even looked forward from that time and place, praying for yet unborn people to be blessed by the Thessalonians' faith. Looking backward from the early 1900s, Scottish evangelist Oswald Chambers thought his ministry might be "the answer to someone's prayer, prayed perhaps centuries ago."

One great figure of Christian history *definitely* prayed for you—and those prayers were undoubtedly heard by God the Father. In John 17, Jesus Himself looked ahead to your life, praying for your spiritual well-being as a beneficiary of His disciples' work: "Father, may they all be one as You are in Me and I am in You; may they be in Us, for by this unity the world will believe that You sent Me" (v. 21 VOICE).

Be encouraged: you've been prayed over by the best. And according to Romans 8:34, He's still interceding today.

Lord Jesus, I appreciate Your prayers—I need them!

GUARANTEED RETURNS

One person gives freely, yet gains even more; another withholds unduly, but comes to poverty. A generous person will prosper; whoever refreshes others will be refreshed.

PROVERBS 11:24–25 NIV

From *A Christmas Carol*'s Scrooge to *SpongeBob SquarePants*' Mr. Krabs, misers are seen as greedy and heartless. (Though, to be fair, Scrooge ultimately came around, and Mr. Krabs is just funny.)

What's not funny is a cheapskate Christian. God, who gives lavishly, calls His children to similar generosity.

And if you ever worry about "giving too much," don't. . .worry, that is. If your contributions are properly motivated—to honor God and help others—the Proverbs indicate you'll "[gain] even more," you'll "prosper" and "be refreshed."

The apostle Paul warned that "the love of money is a root of all kinds of evil" (1 Timothy 6:10 NIV), so don't emphasize the return on your giving. The truth of today's scripture may be more like Jesus' words in Matthew 19:29 (NIV): "Everyone who has left houses or brothers or sisters or father or mother or wife or children or fields for my sake will receive a hundred times as much. . ." The implication: your extended Christian family will be so large and generous that anything you give up for Jesus will be amply resupplied.

And don't miss the end of Jesus' promise: ". . .and will inherit eternal life" (Matthew 19:29 NIV).

Lord, everything I have comes from You. Help me to share it freely, trusting that You will supply my needs.

LIFE AFTER DEATH

*I do not want you to be ignorant, brothers, concerning those
who are asleep, lest you sorrow as others who have no hope.
For if we believe that Jesus died and rose again, even so
God will bring with Him those who sleep in Jesus.*

1 THESSALONIANS 4:13–14 SKJV

Of all great promises in scripture, here is one of the greatest.

We Christians know that this world is not everything. Death is
not the end. Life, now such a strange mixture of joy and sorrow, will
one day be completely good. Our Christian family and friends who
have died on earth are fully alive in heaven, awaiting the day they
return with Jesus, when He comes back to make everything right.

All of these things are based on the reality of Jesus' resurrection.
We believe that He died a real death on a real cross in a real time and
place. And we believe that He really came back to life to demonstrate
His infinite power. Death and Satan have no hold on Jesus, and He
promises the same protection and victory to those of us who trust
in Him.

We do not "sorrow as others who have no hope." The Christian's
sorrow points toward an ultimate joy. So the apostle Paul says, "Comfort
one another with these words" (1 Thessalonians 4:18 SKJV).

*Lord Jesus, You showed the way by Your death and resurrection.
Thank You for promising me life after death—with You, forever!*

BEST REST

Just then I woke up and looked around—
what a pleasant and satisfying sleep!
JEREMIAH 31:26 MSG

Where do you fall on the sleep spectrum? Some guys can't wait to lie down. Others think they're missing something when they rest. As with so much of life, there's a balance to be found—a certain amount of rest is essential to our health and well-being. Too much or too little can be harmful.

Ideally, we find the proper amount of sleep for our age, health, and personality, then regularly get that. Even better if the sleep is, like Jeremiah's, "pleasant and satisfying."

Remember that he lived during the decline and ultimate devastation of his nation of Judah. But God gave Jeremiah promises of better days to come, of the restoration of his people and nation. And that made for sweet, restful sleep, even in the midst of difficult days.

We as Christians live in similarly troubled times, and we've been given similar promises. Even better promises, really, since God "has blessed us in the heavenly realms with every spiritual blessing in Christ" (Ephesians 1:3 NIV). Those blessings include adoption into God's family, the forgiveness of sins, knowledge of His will, and the understanding that all things will be ultimately renewed in and through Jesus (vv. 4–10).

If that doesn't lead to better sleep, what will?

Thank You, Lord, for providing rest. Remind me of Your
great promises so my sleep will be pleasant and satisfying.

HONESTY IS THE BEST POLICY

*Truthful lips shall be established forever, but a
lying tongue is [credited] but for a moment.*
PROVERBS 12:19 AMPC

An old story describes a woman and her young son walking through a cemetery. When the boy sees a tombstone reading "Here lies a lawyer and an honest man," he asks his mother, "Why did they bury two people in that one grave?"

Okay, let's not be too hard on the lawyers. . .a Gallup survey from 2022 found that of sixteen major American institutions, television news and Congress were the least trusted—and a perception of dishonesty must certainly play a role in their historically low ratings.

Certainly, some who lie get ahead in this world. But don't breeze past that final phrase: "in this world." The Proverbs say that lying tongues prevail "but for a moment." The honest man (hopefully everyone reading this devotional) will have his lips "established forever." And if your lips are eternally secure with God, you can be certain the rest of you will be there too.

It's not easy to be 100 percent truthful. We're often tempted to exaggerate, fabricate, fib, fudge—let's be honest, to *lie*—to gain an advantage or get ourselves out of trouble. But God has promised to protect and provide for us, so don't derail His good work with dishonesty. Lying gains are temporary. Obedient honesty pays off forever.

*Lord, give me the wisdom and courage
to be truthful—every time, everywhere.*

PEACE, MAN

*Now may the Lord of peace himself give you
peace at all times and in every way.*
2 THESSALONIANS 3:16 NIV

Had the apostle Paul lived in modern America, Second Thessalonians might have been Second Chicagoans, Second Angelenos, or Second New Yorkers. As it is, his first-century letter still speaks powerfully to Christians everywhere.

The Macedonian believers who originally received Paul's message were suffering from persecution and trials (1:4), false teaching (2:2), and the misbehavior of fellow Christians (3:6). Some in the congregation had become lazy and disruptive, to the point of mooching food off of others. "Such people we command and urge in the Lord Jesus Christ," Paul wrote, "to settle down and earn the food they eat" (3:12 NIV).

All of these things contributed to the Thessalonians' suffering for God's sake. If we're committed to living godly lives in our culture, we'll suffer too.

But Paul offered hope in the form of God's peace. Notice how extensive it is: this peace comes from God Himself, "the Lord of peace," and it's available "at all times and in every way." Whatever frustrates and troubles us is more than offset by the peace of God—which, Paul said elsewhere, "transcends all understanding [and] will guard your hearts and your minds in Christ Jesus" (Philippians 4:7 NIV). All you have to do is ask.

*Heavenly Father, there are more than enough troubling
things in life. Please control my reactions and give me peace.*

THE BIBLE STANDS

After the king burned the scroll containing the words that
Baruch had written at Jeremiah's dictation, the word
of the LORD came to Jeremiah: "Take another scroll and
write on it all the words that were on the first scroll."

JEREMIAH 36:27–28 NIV

No wonder the southern Jewish kingdom of Judah was in trouble. Its king was burning God's Word.

Judah's northern neighbor, Israel, had already fallen to Assyria. Now Jeremiah warned Judah of a looming Babylonian threat. "Perhaps when the people of Judah hear about every disaster I plan to inflict on them," God told His prophet, "they will each turn from their wicked ways" (Jeremiah 36:3 NIV).

King Jehoiakim, however, resented Jeremiah's message. "Why did you write on it," he asked, "that the king of Babylon would certainly come and destroy this land?" (Jeremiah 36:29 NIV). As the prophet's scroll was read, the king cut off strips that he tossed into the fire.

Jehoiakim got rid of Jeremiah's scroll, but he could never destroy God's Word. Nor could any other king or nation. Why? Because the Word of God is "alive and active" (Hebrews 4:12 NIV). Though people are like withering grass, God's Word "endures forever" (Isaiah 40:8 NIV). In the words of an old hymn, "The Bible stands though the hills may tumble / It will firmly stand when the earth shall crumble; / I will plant my feet on its firm foundation, / For the Bible stands."

Lord, thank You for Your enduring Word.

IN DEFENSE OF DISAPPOINTMENT

Unrelenting disappointment leaves you heartsick.
PROVERBS 13:12 MSG

A guy wants his career to be exciting and lucrative. . .his favorite team to win it all. . .his wife to be strong, capable, and gorgeous. . . his muscles firm and his joints flexible. . .his kids to be successful. . . his car to go from zero to sixty in three seconds.

But jobs can disappear. Favorite teams fall short. Marriages struggle and sometimes implode. Bodies age and ache. Kids may jump the rails. Some cars hit sixty only if they go over a cliff.

Disappointment is common. But that's not a bad thing.

Consider: If you always got what you wanted, how much would you pray? Think God might use disappointments to draw you closer to Himself?

The psalm-writing sons of Korah recognized these truths—even when the disappointment included God's silence. "My tears have been my food day and night," they wrote. "I say to God my Rock, 'Why have you forgotten me?'" (Psalm 42:3, 9 NIV).

But Psalm 42 also suggests a practical solution: the conscious recognition of God's worth. "Why, my soul, are you downcast? Why so disturbed within me? Put your hope in God, for I will yet praise him, my Savior and my God" (vv. 5, 11 NIV).

Let today's disappointments push you to God, who promises a perfect forever.

. . . .

Father, many of my hopes have been frustrated.
May I find true satisfaction in You.

WALK WITH THE WISE

One who walks with the wise becomes wise, but whoever keeps company with fools only hurts himself.
PROVERBS 13:20 VOICE

Some biblical principles are easier to live by than others. Today's scripture is one of them.

While God will always provide the strength we need to do what He says, certain duties require a lot of faith. Shadrach, Meshach, and Abednego couldn't have stood tall in that crowd of prostrate Babylonians without some serious commitment to their Lord.

But walking with the wise? That's easy.

If you want to be wise, just make sure you're hanging out with the right crowd. Look for other Christian guys who have a clear passion for the Lord and His Word. In this world, they'll be pretty obvious . . .and because they are wise, they'll be happy to include you in their lives. True Christianity is never an exclusive club.

As you walk with the wise, the proverbs say you'll become wise. Then you can pass your wisdom along to other Christian guys, who will in turn do that for others. On and on the cycle goes until Jesus returns.

Really, it's a pretty ingenious system. But wouldn't you expect that from our all-wise God?

Heavenly Father, I want to be wise. Please lead me to wise men with whom I can walk. . .then help me to pass along the wisdom I gain to others.

GOD PROVIDES SO YOU CAN

*Anyone who does not provide for their relatives,
and especially for their own household, has denied
the faith and is worse than an unbeliever.*

1 TIMOTHY 5:8 NIV

With three kids—including a teenage boy eating truckloads of food—Eddie found that his salary barely covered his expenses. He sought out odd jobs, and even picked up flattened aluminum cans and returnable beverage containers on his morning walks. The kids were embarrassed, but hey—even a few extra bucks helped. As they say, "You do what you have to do."

When the apostle Paul wrote Timothy about providing for relatives, he was referencing poor widows. Some people, neglecting their own families, expected the church to step in with resources. Paul had strong words for them, as you read above. That was a specific issue in a particular time and place—but the fact that it's in our Bible highlights a principle for us.

Like Eddie, maybe you're scraping up random dollars for your family's needs. Or perhaps you have plenty of money—the issue is the time and attention you give to your own. Either way, God calls you to provide for your household.

Ask Him if there's anything more you should do. Then trust Him to provide the resources with His answer. Never forget that God's commands are accomplished in His strength.

Father, I need Your help to provide for my household. Please give me wisdom, energy, and resources to honor them and You.

CHANGE YOUR EXPECTATIONS

"Do you seek great things for yourself? Stop seeking!
For I am about to bring disaster on every living
creature'—this is the Lord's declaration."
JEREMIAH 45:5 HCSB

Sometimes life doesn't go as we expected. Whether we'd set goals and made plans to achieve them, or just had a feeling that we'd own, do, or be something by a certain age, we find ourselves disappointed.

It's not a new problem. Some twenty-six hundred years ago, Jeremiah's scribe wrestled with similar frustrations. Baruch wrote down the messages God gave to Jeremiah, and occasionally even spoke for the prophet. Apparently, Baruch had personal expectations that weren't playing out. In a very short chapter of a very long book, God had a specific message for him, the words of today's scripture.

God also said, "What I have built I am about to demolish, and what I have planted I am about to uproot—the whole land!" (Jeremiah 45:4 HCSB). That ominous promise was fulfilled in spades when Babylon invaded Judah and overran Jerusalem.

But there was good news, of a sort. Jeremiah 45:5 ends with the promise, "I will grant you your life like the spoils of war wherever you go" (HCSB). No matter how bad things got, God still had His eye and His hand on Baruch. That's also true for you today.

. . . .

Lord God, You never promised ease and pleasure
in this life. That comes in eternity! Please keep me
faithful until the day You make everything right.

WHEN GOOD OVERCOMES EVIL

Evil people will bow before good people;
the wicked will bow at the gates of the godly.
PROVERBS 14:19 NLT

As a kid at Halloween, did you ever dress up as a construction worker? Or maybe a baseball player or firefighter or robot? These days, it feels as if ax murderers are more in vogue.

Our culture seems to idolize evil. Popular movies and podcasts highlight the depraved lives of serial killers. The warped sexual activities of celebrities are splashed across magazine covers and websites. Leaders' lies and evasions are commended if they achieve some desired political goal—rarely one that's biblical. Committed Christians are increasingly mocked, insulted, and scapegoated.

That's the bad news. But, as Jesus commanded in John 16:33, "take heart." The day is coming when you—as a serious, obedient, self-sacrificing Christian—will be completely vindicated. Jesus will separate His beloved sheep from the wicked goats and send each one to its righteous reward, either heaven or hell (Matthew 25:31–46). Those who have steadfastly resisted God will finally get what they wanted: His total absence from their lives. We who have honestly followed Jesus, however imperfectly, will enjoy the intimate presence of the Trinity for all eternity.

For now, as you swim in a sea of evil, keep doing good. You have God's promise that you will ultimately overcome.

. . . .

Lord God, this is a hard, evil world. Please help me to
do good—Your good—consistently and cheerfully.

SPEAK UP—SPEAK OUT

*[God said,] Tell the nations of the world; announce
it to them all. Raise a flag—get their attention—
tell them! Hold nothing back; tell them, . . .*
JEREMIAH 50:2 VOICE

The verse you just read reads like a battle cry. It is a movement—with a purpose. A message—with a promise. It's inspiration—with a platform. The new life you lead is the result of a God who has a purpose and plan. People won't know about any of it if you keep silent.

The life you live as a Christian is not part of the secret service. You don't operate under cover. It's not a secret society that only a few can join. It is open to all. Christ's message is for everyone.

God wanted to rescue lawbreakers when He spoke these words in the above verse, and those who listened to His thoughts operated with stone-cold hearts. But God wanted this message to be heard before He put His restructuring plan into effect. He's doing the same thing today. People need to have every chance possible to be rescued and to take heart. *Tell them.* Proclaim God. Draw attention to good news. Don't hold back. Speak up. Take the message to people who might need to hear it again—or for the first time ever.

*Lord, I don't know why I hesitate to tell people that You have
a plan. If I believe it, then it's important for me to share it.*

UNCHANGEABLY TRUE

All Scripture is God-breathed and is useful for teaching, rebuking,
correcting and training in righteousness, so that the servant
of God may be thoroughly equipped for every good work.
2 TIMOTHY 3:16–17 NIV

What if only some of what God said in the Bible was absolute truth? How would you know what to believe? Who could tell you the difference between truth and rules that no longer apply? This issue can erect a barrier, with truth on one side and doubt on the other. You'll need to take a side, and if the Bible does not contain God's truth, then doubt is the side you'll consider most acceptable.

How do you take heart in something you suspect might not be 100 percent true? Paul wrote about the issue, saying that God inspired everything you read in the Bible and that every part of the Bible is useful to teach, correct, and train people who follow Jesus.

You can't be equipped to do the right thing if you can't be sure what the right thing actually is. God isn't interested in confusing you, so His Word takes the stance that it's unchangeably true.

Be encouraged by the very thing you should find most reliable. Spend time reading what God said so you'll be able to do what He asks.

. . . .

When I believe, Lord, You help me also believe what You've said.
I'm grateful that while so many things change, You never do.

A SATURATED LIFE

Knowledge flows like spring water from the wise;
fools are leaky faucets, dripping nonsense.
PROVERBS 15:2 MSG

If you find that you feel a little off today and that you may, in fact, be dripping a little nonsense, just know that you may only be temporarily suffering from a time change that happened overnight as you fully embrace shorter days. The upside might be that at least the time change gave you a chance for a little more sleep last night, but even that can be confusing to eyes that seem convinced that the time they see on the clock is wrong.

While you might be able to get used to this twice-a-year change in time, wisdom is something that's available to you every day of the year. Each day is reset with opportunities to learn. What you learn can be shared. What you share can be refreshing. If you don't embrace God's wisdom, then you will leak broken thoughts that don't reflect His wisdom. It simply leaves a mess that needs to be cleaned up, creating a disappointing case of nonsense drizzle.

Recognizing God's encouragement is a key bit of wisdom that can saturate your life and then refresh those who hear God's Word—from your mouth.

. . . .

I want Your wisdom to refresh me, Father. Make Your
wisdom refreshing to others. If I'm going to share,
may the words come from what You teach me.

TIME-OUT

My groans are many, and I am sick at heart.
LAMENTATIONS 1:22 HCSB

It was a nation in disarray. The worst-case scenario had become headline news. The people had ignored God's public service campaign. The people could have a change of heart or they would go into captivity. The people faced a national time-out, but this exile would end.

Jeremiah was the prophet who had been part of the campaign begging the people to turn their back on wickedness to seek God. Jeremiah could envision what the future would be like, but his words fell on deaf ears. In the end, this prophet put a pen to paper and wrote the book of Lamentations.

To lament is to be passionate about expressing deep grief over regrettable circumstances. You can imagine this prophet sitting in nearly empty streets, missing the faces of men and women who had laughed when he told them the truth. His groans were many. His heart was sick.

This was not what Jeremiah had wanted, and God had waited a long time before He acted. Perhaps Jeremiah thought it could have been avoided altogether. But this disarray would be the birthplace of men and women who learned to take heart in a God who could bring them away from the brink of their own foolishness.

Make me willing to recall that kindness leads to a change in heart, Lord. Help me remember that justice can be used to achieve the same change. I will still pray for kindness, mercy, and grace.

THE OFFICE HOLDER

The grace of God has been revealed,
bringing salvation to all people.
TITUS 2:11 NLT

Election day has arrived. You have the opportunity to choose between candidates, parties, and positions. The votes will be tallied, and many results will be known tomorrow. It can leave an individual unsettled and tied up in knots. You may stay up late hoping for the results. You may feel there is more riding on the results than some people think. Personal opinions will vary. Outcomes will be cheered and jeered. Some will be happy and some may sing a song of lament.

No matter what happens, you can take heart for one very specific reason—God's grace exists and His rescue is never dependent on who fills an elected office.

So until more is known about the outcome of the affairs of men, you can make the better choice to pray for those elected and then take heart in the God who wasn't taken by surprise and will not allow His plan to be thwarted based on the name and choices of those who are elected.

You have the privilege of trusting God every day of the year. Today should be an especially potent reminder of that truth.

. . . .

You used men and women who made good and bad choices, God.
Your grace is much more powerful than who led or failed to lead.
May I choose to rely more on You with each passing moment.

MORE THAN ONCE

*One who listens to life-giving rebukes
will be at home among the wise.*
PROVERBS 15:31 HCSB

Are you teachable, or do you secretly think you know it all? When someone asks for an opinion, do you assume it's *your* opinion that person is seeking out? Being the smartest man in the room can work . . .as long as you are, in fact, the smartest man in the room. But there will come a time when you encounter someone with more knowledge and understanding.

God's wisdom suggests that you should spend more time learning and listening than you do sharing your own opinions.

You are on your way to wisdom when you understand that there is always more to learn. And for everything you learn, there's even more to explore about what you have discovered. This is why reading through the Bible is an excellent idea and reading through it more than once is an even better idea. Each reading allows you to see things you may have missed before. That is how you gain more and more understanding of the truths of God's written Word.

Wake up excited that this is a day when you can learn more, share more, and do more because you've chosen to follow God on this most wonderful adventure of gaining knowledge and understanding.

. . . .

*Keep teaching while You help me learn, Father.
There will always be something more to discover because
You always have more to teach me. Make me teachable.*

THE PERSPECTIVE PIRATES

[God said,] Listen to what I tell you, son of man.
Do not follow their rebellious ways.
EZEKIEL 2:8 VOICE

Finding people who don't follow God is far from an impossible task—and those who aren't invested in following Him may find it odd that you want to. This can lead to ridicule and encouragement in paths that move you away from the Lord. Some may even give you an ultimatum: "Stop talking about God or I'm out." If you accept this ultimatum, it will be much easier to leave God out of future conversations with others.

Keeping your commitment to the Lord means being careful not to follow rebels in their path away from God. Your spiritual enemy, the devil, has no problem using people who don't love God to move you away from a friendship with the rescuer of mankind.

God warned that bad company will cause you to drift away from Him (1 Corinthians 15:33). Following God is infinitely harder when you embrace friendships with those who don't understand the benefits of knowing and following Him.

If you take your relationship with God seriously, then it's a great idea to be careful when it comes to human relationships.

. . . .

I want to share You with everyone, Lord. Teach me to be careful of those who would be happier seeing me fail to be faithful. Your Son spent time with everyone, but He didn't let it change His mission.

GOOD OR BEST

We must pay the most careful attention, therefore,
to what we have heard, so that we do not drift away.

HEBREWS 2:1 NIV

It can be easy to drift away from God, especially when you begin thinking you can slow your pursuit of Him, or when you somehow believe—even in the smallest recesses of your mind—that you can alter what you believe to make it fit in with the world around you. This can leave you in a place of having a divided heart—with one part trying to please God and the other trying to pursue your own desires. That can leave you in a place of lingering awkwardness.

If you can somehow keep yourself busy in the name of *good*, then you may miss God's *best*. Some of the things you can pursue in this world are actually good in and of themselves—or at least not bad or hurtful. . .to you or to others. But these things can be a big distraction when they distract you from pursuing God's very best—from God Himself.

Don't sacrifice God's best for what's only good. *Good* may seem admirable and worthwhile, but it is not God's best for you. So pay attention. Stop the drift.

. . . .

Lord God, You're better and more important
than even the very best things I can pursue in
this world. Give the wisdom to choose Your best.

POWER AND POSITION

Moderation is better than muscle,
self-control better than political power.
PROVERBS 16:32 MSG

You aren't the physically strongest or most politically influential man alive, but God has saved you and will put you in position to serve Him and to influence others for His kingdom.

Many men believe that it's best for them to pursue physical strength and political power. With strong muscles, they can do difficult jobs, and with political power they can influence the direction of a city, state, or nation. But the Bible suggests that a man doesn't need to be mayor, governor, or president to influence the world around him.

God has always looked at the heart of a man before his physical strength or position (see 1 Samuel 16:7). He's not opposed to physical strength or financial or political power, but He sees those things as temporary. You may not be impressive in the world's eyes, but you are important to God, and He has a purpose for your life—a purpose with eternal meaning.

That in itself is a great reason to feel God's encouragement as you live and serve in His power and strength.

· ·

Heavenly Father, I may not have impressive physical prowess
or great financial or political power, but I have You—and You
have a purpose for my life. Help me to lead a life that pleases
You and that helps people see You in everything I do and say.

MUTUAL ENCOURAGEMENT

Encourage each other daily, while it is still called today,
so that none of you is hardened by sin's deception.
HEBREWS 3:13 HCSB

There's a cliché that says "Seven days without God makes one weak." It touches on the corners of cute and clever, and it might cause some to groan a bit. But that doesn't make it less true.

You'll never get stronger by keeping your distance from God. You'll not become wiser, more loving, or more faithful without spending time with Him. Not only that, you can actually lose gains made in your journey with God when you fail to pursue Him with all your heart.

Hebrews 3:13 is a reminder that our relationships with other believers are incredibly valuable—both because others can encourage you and you can encourage others in your faith journey. On the other hand, when this mutual encouragement is lacking, deception can step in and make sin and rebellion seem more palatable.

Today's scripture verse even points to the urgency of encouragement. So don't wait for what seems like the perfect moment to encourage or seek encouragement. Those kinds of moments are rare and fleeting and disappear before you can catch them. So encourage and be encouraged—today and every day.

Lord God, I've been in weak spots. I've faltered in my walk with You. I've been deceived. Bring me more of what I need every day. That's You, and the encouragement You send. I don't want to be weak or deceived ever again.

ACHIEVE A GOAL—TOGETHER

Love prospers when a fault is forgiven,
but dwelling on it separates close friends.
PROVERBS 17:9 NLT

Mutual sacrifice is the driving force behind the phrase "band of brothers." It's easy to think of this phrase today—Veterans Day. This day commemorates and honors soldiers who fought for a cause and sacrificed together. At some point, each soldier was discharged from duty, but he never forgets the men he served with. Veterans took courage together, shared life together, and then later remember their service together.

This couldn't happen if there was no forgiveness or understanding. The life of a soldier isn't easy, and words can be said that cause seasons of regret. While this could separate friends, it is the common goal that insists they forgive and move on together.

Maybe it's easier to forgive when you're on a path to the same destination, but don't let forgiveness only be for people you like. Sometimes great friendships begin when one of two former adversaries forgives the other. Friends walk together—forgiven. Work together— rejoicing. Are kind together—for a cause.

I live because You first loved, God. I forgive because I'm forgiven. I serve because You've given me the encouragement of friends. You've given me Your encouragement. Let that change me. May my journey be filled with friends who are going Your way, so we can move forward—together.

FRESH STEPS

*[God said,] So will I break down the wall that you have daubed
with whitewash and bring it down to the ground. . . . And you
will know (understand and realize) that I am the Lord.*

Ezekiel 13:14 ampc

Ezekiel 13 is a tough passage. It's a complete view of justice that
came after long-term mercy. The people had failed, kept failing, and
indicated that they had no intention of seeking God. The people would
occasionally do something that suggested they would follow God,
but it was whitewash applied to internal decay. The people needed
to stop pretending, go through the process of redemption, and really
believe He was God.

The scripture verse above is packed away in what seemed like
very bad news. Yet it makes sense that this verse told the people they
should take heart because, in spite of their choices being exposed
as the worst possible rebellion, they could exit this difficult season
knowing, understanding, and realizing that God was in control.
They would realize the error of their poor choice and the value of
obedience.

Maybe you need a reminder that any whitewashed wall allowed
to stand will need to come down on the way to the encouragement
found in taking fresh steps with a good God.

. . . .

*Father, when I recognize I'm only existing in a time of poor
personal choice, help me remember that You will be known.
Take the walls down now. I need to know You better.*

HE'S NOT LIKE YOU

It is only fitting that we should have a High Priest who is devoted to God, blameless, pure, compassionate toward but separate from sinners, and exalted by God to the highest place of honor.
HEBREWS 7:26 VOICE

You can't rescue yourself no matter how hard you try—and if God were like you, then He couldn't rescue you either.

We should all feel a profound sense of appreciation that God isn't like us. He is separated from sinners yet compassionate toward them at the same time. He did for each of us what we could never do for ourselves. If you had to do it on your own, you would certainly fail.

How could you look forward to a future God created for you if He's no different from you? How could you expect unconditional love from God if you can't give unconditional love to others? How could you look forward to forgiveness from God if you can't forgive others? He does what you can't so you can learn how. Jesus, your example, lives and loves to show you how to do those things you can't possibly do on your own.

Lord, I don't want You to be just like me, but I want to be more like You. Thanks for being different enough to give me the example I need to move forward with the new life You've given me.

A HOPE EMBRACED

[God said,] "I the LORD have spoken, and I will do it."
EZEKIEL 17:24 NIV

If God never breaks a promise (*He won't*)—and if He gives a promise (*He has*)—and if you read His promises (*you can*), then how is it possible for you not to take heart?

What if this news touches your mind and misses your heart? You might think, *Yes, I understand that God's a promise keeper.* These thoughts might come when you've heard the news before. Yet somehow, today it lacks the deep impression it once made. You don't have to let this be the final word.

God made promises in the book of Ezekiel, and at the very end of chapter 17 He puts an exclamation point on His own proclamation: "I have spoken, and I will do it."

Even if God had promised justice and not mercy, there's still reason to be encouraged. The end of God's promises are good. The result is restoration, new perspective, and a hope embraced.

You've been promised a future. You've been offered forgiveness. God has promised a plan. He has spoken it and will do what you can't.

Now? Revisit that deep impression of a good God. There's much to look forward to.

Impress my mind, Lord God. Impress my heart. Remind me
that You have kept impressive promises and that You still are.
Help this thought give me the courage to believe You'll do it again.

IMPRESSIVE FAITHFULNESS

God's name is a place of protection—
good people can run there and be safe.
PROVERBS 18:10 MSG

If you're looking for very good news, then consider the message of today's scripture verse. You face dangers every day. Some you recognize and some you're protected from long before they ever show up. That protection comes from God, and that means He is more than worthy of your complete trust. Run to Him and find safety. Take heart and discover gratitude. Trust and discover the most impressive faithfulness you'll ever know.

The whole idea of avoiding God might make sense if you feel guilty, but He wants you to come to Him—even when you have sinned. You can't find forgiveness without Him, so waiting isn't a wise use of time. You won't find unconditional love without Him, so waiting often means spiritual bruising. You can't discover perfect faithfulness with anyone else, so any delay will only leave you disappointed.

When asked if you will take heart, you can frame the question around what you're learning about God. It can make it much easier to say yes.

. . . .

I want to take heart, Father. I need to take heart. I don't want to delay
or even attempt to manage on my own. I'm no good without You,
and I'm tired of trying to be. Give me strength—give me heart. Your
encouragement is satisfying. Protect me from my own bad choices.

HOLDING ON TO GOD'S PROMISE

Let us hold on to the confession of our hope without
wavering, for He who promised is faithful.
HEBREWS 10:23 HCSB

Use a firm grip and hold on to the life God describes as real. Observe His faithfulness and take heart. The struggles you endure in this life are not in vain. There is good coming. You may not see it today, this week, or this month; but when you look back at your life in Him, you can find the strength and the encouragement you need to hold fast to the hope and assurance that He will keep the promise He has made to those who belong to Him through Jesus.

Be bold without making demands. Be courageous without being rude. Be strong because God gave you the strength. This promise-keeping God is faithful beyond your wildest dreams. No one else will ever be as faithful in keeping His promises as He is. Better yet, you can take heart because this God loves you—endlessly, deeply, and faithfully.

. . . .

I don't want to second-guess You, Lord, because You are 100
percent faithful. I don't want to think for one single moment that
this life here on earth—which is a gift from You—doesn't have
meaning and purpose. Help me use a firm grip to hold on to
the life You have given me through Your Son, Jesus Christ.

OBEDIENCE REASONING

To acquire wisdom is to love yourself;
people who cherish understanding will prosper.
PROVERBS 19:8 NLT

The wisdom God offers is a game changer. Not only does it alter perspective, but it helps you understand some of the *why* behind God's laws. His prohibitions aren't designed to make life boring, but rather to keep you in good position to receive His best.

The choice between obedience and disobedience is yours. If you choose disobedience, then God can still work through the consequences you face to produce good outcomes—because He's God. The reason for obedience has to do with trusting God enough with your decisions that saying no doesn't seem like a hardship.

You can take heart in doing good because wisdom set up shop in your heart and has shown you that it's absolutely the best choice. Get wisdom. Cherish it.

Life on this big blue marble is relatively short, and the outcomes of your decisions either move you closer to God or place a wall between the two of you. You don't have to settle for the School of Hard Knocks. God loves to give wisdom and empowers you to be encouraged every single day.

You give wisdom, God. You even tell me I should ask, so I'm asking. Give me the understanding to do what You ask so I can be who You made me to be. I don't need to learn from my mistakes to discover the value in doing what You ask.

PERFECT ARRIVAL

Now faith is the assurance (the confirmation, the title deed) of the things [we] hope for, being the proof of things [we] do not see and the conviction of their reality [faith perceiving as real fact what is not revealed to the senses].

HEBREWS 11:1 AMPC

It can be hard to accept anything as trustworthy without proof. You don't feel confident when someone wants to sell you a car but they can't find the title. You don't buy a house without a deed. You shouldn't listen when someone tells you something they have no idea is true.

Faith in God asks you to do something you wouldn't normally do—believe, even when you have no proof. God's ways are referred to as mysterious, and He's considered the author of truth, life, and rescue. If there's anyone you can trust without holding back, it's Him. He assures delivery of what you need most and does work that you can't see with your eyes. Still? *Take heart.* His proof shows up in both astonishing and very simple ways. It may arrive all at once or in strategic deliveries.

Don't let what you don't know about God stop you from trusting Him. There's beauty in the mystery that is God. It's a time-released life of discovery, and each arrival is perfect.

Give me the wisdom to believe, Father. Trusting in what I can't see may be the exact response that leads me to the next place of discovery.

DECISION-MAKING

*The impulses of the human heart may run wild,
but the Eternal's plan will prevail.*
PROVERBS 19:21 VOICE

If every plan you conceived were without risk, you would never need to second-guess anything. If you knew that business deals would succeed every time, then you'd be rich. If you could buy a car that never failed, then you would never need another car. If every friendship lasted forever, no one would need to feel alone. But the human heart coexists with chaos. Sometimes there are risks without rewards—not every business deal works out, every car will fail, and friends leave.

God's plans are exactly what you want your plans to be. He knows how His plans will turn out. Yet you skirt around His plan to try plans that keep proving to be failures. They keep you chasing the pot of gold that's nothing more than an impressive mirage.

You can find the encouragement you need when you realize that you don't have to live with a never-ending cycle of failed decision-making. God never wanted that for you, but He gives you the choice to decide in favor of foolishness. This decision never leads to encouragement—unless it leads back to His choice.

* * *

*I need to get it out of my head that You want me to
do all I can before I ask You for help, Lord. Let me
seek Your plan before I make my next guess.*

OPPOSITION'S SECOND CHANCE

*Consider him who endured such opposition from sinners,
so that you will not grow weary and lose heart.*
HEBREWS 12:3 NIV

Not everything has worked out perfectly for you, right? You've endured enough disappointments to fill a book—maybe two. You've considered taking your show on the road and hitting the talk show circuit, where you can lament the circumstances that led you here. Maybe your story will be the cautionary tale others need—or maybe it only serves to feed the pain that's consuming you.

Jesus lived through more pain and punishment than you'll ever experience. Sinners opposed Him rather than running to Him. But He endured. He didn't grow weary. He didn't lose heart. Jesus didn't dwell on what was happening to Him, because He was thinking about what would happen when the sinners who opposed Him would finally recognize who He really was—when they would spend time rearranging their life choices. *Follow Him.*

If you can begin to understand all Jesus did as He took the pain and the penalty God required for your sin, then you'll also accept His gift of eternal salvation.

Your Son did an unthinkable and perfect thing, God. He loved me with everything He had and then wanted me to know that with Him I have every reason to stand strong and zero reason to lose heart.

SEEKING COUNSEL

Form your purpose by asking for counsel,
then carry it out using all the help you can get.
PROVERBS 20:18 MSG

Relationships with other Christian men are important because they can be useful in providing feedback on the choices you're thinking of making. They are no substitute for God Himself, but He can use the counsel of other godly men to help you sort things out so you can make a sound decision.

Once you've chosen the path you'll take, these friends can step in to shoulder some of the burden of the choice you'd struggle to do alone. They can stand with you as you seek God's best, and tell you the truth even when they believe you may be making a bad choice.

Purpose is finding what God made you to do and then doing that thing to the best of your ability—and with God's help. He didn't put you on earth for your own amusement or just to take up space. He created you on purpose and with a purpose. Discovering purpose is important when you make the decision to do what He wants you to do. Christian brothers can be a solid connection between your desires and God choices.

. . . .

It's more comfortable to stand alone, Father. I don't have
to feel accountable and there are no others to tell me no.
I want to be wise enough to spend time with godly men.

THE SHOW-AND-TELL EVENT

Your life should be free from the love of money.
Be satisfied with what you have, for He Himself
has said, I will never leave you or forsake you.

HEBREWS 13:5 HCSB

What if you could be satisfied with what you already have? That would be the show-and-tell event of the year! This is called contentment, and it can be hard to hold on to.

Advertising doesn't help, because it introduces the idea that somehow life would be better if you would simply buy whatever is being sold. What advertisements usually sell, however, is discontentment. What you take in can convince you that you don't have enough, that you deserve more, and that you've simply been settling instead of obtaining a better life.

Will *things* make your life better? God says no. You can't take things with you when you die, the things you do buy will eventually wear out or break, and you'll always get tired of the new thing you were certain you needed to own.

God doesn't leave, abandon, or deny knowing you—and you *own* that. Anything more is simply seasoning to this impressive God feast.

. . . .

It's easy to be convinced that I need more things when I
already have all of You, Lord. Help me be dissatisfied
in those things that keep me from You—and satisfied
with everything that leads me back to You.

A TWO-SIDED COIN

The Lord's light penetrates the human spirit,
exposing every hidden motive.
PROVERBS 20:27 NLT

You live with the choices you make—and with the repercussions of those choices. It could be a career choice guided by the expectation of a family member or a choice made because you're good at doing something you don't particularly like. You can make a choice based on your chance at a promotion or raise. On this side of the coin, there's pressure applied to each of your decisions because they affect others.

The other side of the coin includes choices made for purely selfish reasons. You keep those motives to yourself, but it's a game where you position circumstances to eventually fall in your favor and leave you better off because of it. This side of the coin doesn't consider the effect of this long series of choices on anyone else.

God looks deep into your motives—the visible and invisible ones—and He encourages choices that don't rely on the selfish side of the coin. The choices you make could lead you to do something that impacts eternity and not your next paycheck. It'll be a choice that helps others even when some sacrifice is required on your part.

Lord God, I'm confronted with another layer within the choices I
make. Help me seek You when I'd rather manipulate. Give me the
wisdom I need to make the right choice for the right reasons.

STOP FLYING UNDER THE RADAR

Has not God chosen those who are poor in the eyes of the world to be rich in faith and in their position as believers and to inherit the kingdom which He has promised to those who love Him?

JAMES 2:5 AMPC

You may have concluded you're a nobody, just a no-name flying under the radar that can do nothing because you are nothing. You believe you're "poor in the eyes of the world." You can't deny it, so you live in a place of ongoing despair. Old Testament men would demonstrate this kind of crushed soul by ripping their clothes and throwing ashes in their hair.

This depressed thinking features all kinds of inaccuracies. The conclusion is not only faulty—it's entirely wrong. God chose people just like you to do amazing things. You're a candidate for the title "Rich in Faith," a man who will inherit God's eternal kingdom. That's because when you accept His rescue, you're adopted as one of His sons.

There's no reason to lose heart unless you refuse to embrace God's reality. Being poor in the eyes of the world means nothing to the God who's preparing a place for your eternal home. Popularity contests are not important to the God who chooses you.

Father, please give me an accurate picture of who I am to You. I want to find lasting satisfaction, and I can't find that by chasing the approval of others. Help me find encouragement in following You.

POSITIVE OUTCOME
OF A NEGATIVE CHOICE

A naive person wises up when he sees a mocker punished.
A wise person becomes even wiser just by being instructed.
PROVERBS 21:11 VOICE

God can use cause and effect to help you learn some important lessons. You can be a young Christian who learns from the mistakes of other believers. Those teachable moments allow you to learn wisdom while being sympathetic to those living through the consequences of poor choices. When you don't know the right answer, watch how one choice negatively affects other Christians. Make a spiritual note that this is something you should avoid in your own future.

The negative consequences people face aren't just a corrective action; they are also visible witness to the importance of making right choices. God can use these things to teach, instruct, and correct faulty thinking.

The next step in this journey is to pay attention to instructions. Don't just wait to observe something. Learn from what God has already said about all kinds of issues. Pay attention to God and what He's doing in the world. Both steps lead closer to Him, and they mean something important when you engage with what He's teaching.

Father, I don't need to make bad choices to know that there are consequences for bad things I do. Help me pay attention to what happens around me so I can avoid what will never be good for me. Show me in Your Word things to avoid.

GET CLOSE

Come near to God and he will come near to you. Wash your hands,
you sinners, and purify your hearts, you double-minded. . . .
Humble yourselves before the Lord, and he will lift you up.

JAMES 4:8, 10 NIV

God walks with you. When you are distant from Him, it's never because He left. When you realize that you have drifted and turn back to Him, He welcomes you back with open arms.

When you return to Him, it's likely because you're tired of your own failed personal choices. You know that your heart needs to be cleansed, and you also know that God is faithful and that He will forgive and restore you when you humbly approach Him and confess your sin. God knows the truth about you, but He will never turn you away when you return to Him.

The story of the prodigal son demonstrates this process. It starts with a son who rebels. He demands what he's not owed and leaves with no visible signs of remorse. The father didn't leave the son—the son left the father. When the young man comes to his senses, he humbles himself and states his willingness to be a servant. The father runs to meet his son and welcomes him home. He could have been angry. He wasn't.

Get close to God. He's been waiting to welcome you back.

Thank You for never leaving me even when I walk away,
God. Thank You for welcoming me back.

SMALL GIFTS, BIG BLESSINGS

*Sinners are always wanting what they don't have;
the God-loyal are always giving what they do have.*
PROVERBS 21:26 MSG

God not only meets your needs—He exceeds your expectations. It's possible for Christians to give what they're not sure they can afford and still have enough to meet their own needs. God will always do a better job with your finances than you can. His math never needs to look like yours to prove accurate. You can trust Him with what you have, and He can do amazing things with your willingness to give. He doesn't need your money, but He wants your trust.

Even small gifts can do big things. There's satisfaction in allowing God to use your willingness to meet a need. His storehouse of blessing others may be in your bank account.

Those who aren't satisfied won't look for God's plan to bless others through the skills He's given to earn an income. He wants you to trust Him with what you have, not become frustrated because you aren't making more. Show that you can be faithful in small things first.

*You give and I accept, Father. Help me learn to give too.
What You've given is more than I could have dreamed
of, but there are times when I hold too tightly to
Your gifts as if they are only meant for me.*

LOUD, LONG, AND LIVING

Praise the God and Father of our Lord Jesus Christ.
According to His great mercy, He has given us a new birth
into a living hope through the resurrection of Jesus Christ
from the dead and into an inheritance that is imperishable,
uncorrupted, and unfading, kept in heaven for you.

1 Peter 1:3–4 HCSB

Let the celebration begin. Let it be loud, long, and living. This is a day to celebrate the collection of memories that inspire gratitude and praise for the God who blesses His beloved people with all good things.

God is good and merciful. He's given you new life through Jesus. He offers an inheritance to the rescued, love for the hurting, and hope for the disillusioned. His future can't be destroyed, corrupted, or face an expiration date. He keeps all His promises and knows the moment and the means for their fulfillment. His delays are not denials. He waits, but His promises are still sure. *So be it.*

Keep on the road to new life and soul-cleansing hope. This is just one more way on a day that encourages gratitude by saying, "This is the God I serve, and He has big plans for me."

. . . .

There's no end to Your goodness, Lord, no beginning to Your wisdom,
and no middle ground in Your love. Today, I rejoice and want my
heart to tell my voice to speak the language of thanksgiving.

EVERY DAY A SCHOOL DAY

I am teaching you today—yes, you—
so you will trust in the LORD.
PROVERBS 22:19 NLT

It's the day after Thanksgiving. Some shopped today, and others avoided the Black Friday crowds altogether. Yet God can use any setting to teach. With God, every day is a school day. There's no holiday in His timeline for instruction. The Old Testament festivals were often associated with God's goodness and included things that can teach us about God and what He wants us to know about Him.

God teaches, but why is that important? When you learn about the things God has done, you can see the many examples of His trustworthiness. Belief becomes stronger the closer you get to God, and you get closer to God by walking with Him consistently. That leads to change within you, and that change will allow what you learn to impact your family first, then your friends, your neighbors, and anyone in the world that will listen to some impressively good news.

Take the time today to look around you and see how God might use you. Read words that encourage you, and spend time talking to the God who loves you.

Dear Lord, I don't mind dipping my toes in Your goodness, but it's a little harder to be all in. Give me the courage to do that. Help me learn ways to let You lead me today.

YOU EXIST FOR A PURPOSE

*Once you were not a people [at all], but now you
are God's people. . .and have received mercy.*
1 PETER 2:10 AMPC

You were once the No Name, the Forgotten, the Undiscovered. You were the Wretched, Blind, and Embarrassed. You had nowhere to go, no one to love you, and no future to look forward to. You simply existed, and you often wondered why existing seemed so purposeless.

You may remember feeling that way. If not, you probably still know someone who feels/felt that way. It can seem a bit like a dystopian nightmare where people fight for the smallest things to survive and wonder why the effort was so important.

With God, all choices are important and all obedience is rewarded. In Him, you're not (and never have been) a No Name, Forgotten, or Undiscovered. God knew you before you were born, loved you even before that, and your name is as familiar as the thing He remembers most.

You are a member of God's family, and mercy is an everyday gift. Don't embrace the lie that you exist without purpose. You may not have found it yet, but God is more than willing to reveal it to you. Keep searching—keep walking with the Lord.

*You once called me a masterpiece, Father. Help me believe
that You created me for something more than I think
in this moment. Give me the courage to walk with You
and away from this place where I simply. . .exist.*

SECURE IN HIS PROMISES

*You were lost sheep with no idea who you were
or where you were going. Now you're named and
kept for good by the Shepherd of your souls.*

1 PETER 2:25 MSG

The Christian life is an invitation into suffering for a higher cause. Just as Jesus died to secure our eternal future in glory with Him, we must live our lives with His higher purposes in mind. Peter lays out what that looks like, particularly when we are suffering because of what we believe. That could be persecution for our faith, but it could also be our struggles against the pull of the world and our own flesh.

Peter gives a step-by-step account of Jesus' behavior that we are trying to emulate—silence in the face of mockery, taking abuse for doing good—and how He was able to do it: He was determined to let God vindicate Him.

Happiness isn't the be all/end all of your life. Pleasing God is. But when you please Him, you'll find that the momentary delights and narcissistic goals of this broken world no longer satisfy you. And that's good, because the mind-blowing future God has promised you will put this world's fake promises of meaning and pleasure to shame.

. . . .

*Jesus, You have given me my true identity, direction,
purpose. I know You will keep me secure and
guide me in living a life that pleases You.*

LEAN INTO IT

If you are suffering in a manner that pleases God,
keep on doing what is right, and trust your lives to
the God who created you, for he will never fail you.

1 PETER 4:19 NLT

God corrects His children in this life. That's hard to hear, but Peter makes it clear: Christians are subject to God's discipline. It's not judgment for our sin—Jesus took care of that on the cross. But God intends to shape us into Christ's character and ways, and that takes a grain rougher than our coarse edges: hardship and suffering.

Even if we know we should be asking what God is doing through trials and not why He is permitting it, the *why* still matters. God's right as our Lord and Savior is to mean more than anything else to us. It's natural to avoid suffering whenever we can, but spiritually, it leads to independence from God, which we can't afford. The *why*, then, is to increase our dependence on Him.

Peter's warning reinforces the hope we have that we are seldom more like Jesus than when we endure suffering well. God uses it all for His greater purposes, and He is always right there with us in the dark hours. Because He is faithful when He tests us, we can move past the *why* and lean into the *what*.

Lord God, grant me the faith to endure the
suffering You allow with grace and hope.

HIS HAND IS ON YOU

*Do not let your heart envy sinners, but be in the
fear of the LORD all the day long. For surely there
is an end, and your hope shall not be cut off.*

PROVERBS 23:17–18 SKJV

Trouble is always knocking. It's normal to ask if it wouldn't be easier
to be like people who don't care about God; they deal with trouble in
the most practical way possible. Without God, though, there is only
short-lived relief, and the ultimate result of eternal separation isn't
worth the expedience.

All the time and effort you spend caring about God and His
ways will be rewarded—that's the "end" Solomon mentions. An *end*
is a final outcome or goal, something you hope for and work toward.
The idea is that your future with God is secure, despite life's ongoing
trials.

First Peter 5:6–7 (MSG) offers assurance: "Be content with who
you are, and don't put on airs. God's strong hand is on you; he'll
promote you at the right time. Live carefree before God; he is most
careful with you."

Live today in the confidence that you are in God's hand. He will
allow hardship to test your faith, but His overall care and protection
will ensure that the outcome is the best possible, most Christlike
version of you.

*Strengthen me, Father, to choose Your ways above all else.
The more I obey You, the more I'll learn to love and trust You.*

YOU'VE GOT WHAT IT TAKES

His divine power has given us everything we need
for a godly life through our knowledge of him who
called us by his own glory and goodness.

2 PETER 1:3 NIV

One of sin's last strongholds in our flesh is self-sufficiency. While working hard and pursuing dreams matters, trusting God with everything we do matters more. Salvation is more than fire insurance; it's the beginning of the most important relationship in our lives. Continued reliance on ourselves leads to resenting God because He wants all of us. But if He is truly our Lord and Savior, we belong to Him now.

In Christ, Peter says, we can live the life God wants us to live. But first, we must let go of our rights and give Him His due. Full surrender takes time, but it's a process that gets more rewarding as it goes. Being God's son is as good as it gets.

Peter reminds us that we have access to God's promises and a full knowledge of who He is and how He operates. As a result, we are no longer bound to the corrupting, decaying priorities of the world. Our old, sinful habits are no longer our boss, Jesus is. That's liberation! Because Jesus has set you free, you have everything you need to follow Him successfully.

Jesus, thank You for bringing me into Your family. I trust
You to give me everything I need to bring You glory.

FOR HIS GLORY ALONE

Daniel answered the king, "Keep your gifts or give them to someone else, but I will tell you what the writing means."
DANIEL 5:17 NLT

Most men have dreamed of being a rock star or a record-setting athlete, an influential billionaire or a renowned doctor. In some cases, God allows those dreams to happen, but even then, the question remains: Whose glory are we seeking?

Popularity and power are self-made traps. When we're torn between honoring God and staying cool in men's eyes, God gets our worst. And when we fall, we'll make God's name look bad. If we end up seeking our glory and pleasure first, the writing is on the wall: we'll be weighed and found wanting.

Daniel walked that line for decades without falling into pride's snare. How? True faith, the result of constant, daily prayer, of listening to God and then obeying Him no matter what it meant for his reputation.

You were made for a life of meaning, but who you let determine that meaning will define you. At the bottom of every satisfactory composition, Bach wrote the letters *SDG*—*Soli Deo Gloria*, "For the glory of God alone." When that's your goal, you'll stay focused on the only one whose opinion matters in the end—and He will give you the wisdom and insight you need to represent Him well in all you do.

Lord Jesus, let everything I do be for Your glory, and Yours alone.

CALM, COOL, AND COLLECTED

*When Daniel learned that the decree had been signed and
posted, he continued to pray just as he had always done.*
DANIEL 6:10 MSG

While Daniel was in with the lions, who got stressed? The king. The mighty ruler whose word meant life or death couldn't get a wink that night, because he knew he had done a godly man wrong. Daniel, for his part, slept peacefully, kept calm in God's care through a situation that, from the world's viewpoint, offered no reason for rational hope.

But Daniel was less concerned about living or dying than he was doing whatever God wanted. How did he hold that line? Practice. Years and years of seeking God, of trusting Him when there was no reason to, other than God deserving that level of loyalty.

Daniel's prayer life must have been something special—but more than anything else, it must have been real. He didn't pray out of duty or go through a daily selection of rote recitations. He talked to God, praising Him, petitioning Him, and then listening to Him. He developed a genuine relationship with the Lord of the universe by being humble and obedient, maintaining his awe of God and forging an unbreakable bond of trust. When prayer becomes real to us, we can stay calm, cool, and collected, like Daniel.

*Father God, teach me how to pray, honor You, keep it
real, and develop a bond like Daniel had with You.*

PRINCIPLES OF FOLLOWING

I applied my heart to what I observed
and learned a lesson from what I saw.
PROVERBS 24:32 NIV

God's wisdom, which comes through a mixture of trusting His Spirit, book learning, and experience, instructs us. The key to Solomon's wisdom was his guiding principle: "I applied my heart to what I observed."

God uses both heart and head to guide and inform us, and we must be open to His leading on both fronts. To know His will, we must know His Word. Scripture is both decoder and decider for everything we face in life—telling us what matters to Him and thus, what we should prioritize when deciding. Sometimes, after praying, a rational weighing of pros and cons helps us choose. Other times, the Spirit speaks to us, often in the still, quiet voice of an inclination to go one way over another.

Trusting God with our plans will sometimes lead us down an unexpected path, one that makes no sense to anyone who isn't following Him. But when your relationship with God fills your heart and your head, you'll be satisfied following where He leads.

. . . .

God, guide me today however seems best to You.
Open my heart to hear and see You moving,
and give me courage to go where You lead.

STICK TO THE TRUTH

*You must remain faithful to what you have been taught
from the beginning. If you do, you will remain in
fellowship with the Son and with the Father. And in this
fellowship we enjoy the eternal life he promised us.*

1 JOHN 2:24–25 NLT

John warned believers to stick to what they had been taught from the beginning: the gospel. He emphasized the good news of Jesus Christ repeatedly because false teachers were already twisting that essential truth. A false teacher preaches any other way of salvation aside from Christ alone. John even called them antichrists—anyone who denies that Jesus is God, rejecting His place in the Trinity or claiming He wasn't fully God and fully human.

We have a reward for abiding in the gospel truth: fellowship with God through Jesus. False teachers sneeze at this unity, but it's one of Jesus' primary objectives, detailed in His prayer in John 17. He came and died and rose again so that we could be reunited with God, the way God intended it back in Eden. Because Jesus rose to new life, we rise with Him. We'll enjoy eternity with Him, but we also have His life in us now—the power to overcome the lies of the world and live to please our Lord and Savior.

*Lord Jesus, You died to bring me into fellowship with
God. Give me discernment to detect anything that
threatens my view of You or Your gospel.*

HE CALLS YOU FRIEND

*What we know is that when Christ is openly revealed,
we'll see him—and in seeing him, become like him.*

1 JOHN 3:2 MSG

If you need a confidence boost, remember this: you know God personally. Through Jesus, you know who He is and what He is doing in His people and in the world—a movement of redemption and restoration that will culminate when He returns and completes the good work He has begun in you. Jesus is your hope, now and in the future, and you are assured that you will be like Him.

You are a child of God. Soak it in. God Almighty has adopted you as a coheir with His Son. Jesus is your big brother, and He always has your back. Because He is your Lord, you effectively belong to Him; however, He doesn't call you a slave but a friend. And if you ever doubt it, the Holy Spirit confirms that you are His son, bearing witness in your spirit.

It was enough just for Jesus to save you from your sin, but He has more for you than you would ever dare hope for. One day, the world will know it too and bow before Him—so enjoy your head start!

. . . .

*Lord Jesus, I am so grateful that You call me a brother
and friend. Help me to love others the way You
love me, to show that I am Yours. Come soon!*

CONFIDENT IN HIS LOVE

Let's not merely say that we love each other; let us show the truth by our actions. Our actions will show that we belong to the truth, so we will be confident when we stand before God.

1 JOHN 3:18–19 NLT

Jesus is God's love on display: a sinless life lived for God's glory; a sacrificial death; a wondrous resurrection, breaking sin's hold on any who trust in Him. Once we've done that, we need to follow Jesus' example and put His love into action, just as He did.

Loving others is God's commandment to His children. It's hard, though—we either can't move past our fears and feelings to help people, or when we do, they're hard to love. Either way, though, 1 John 3:20 (NLT) assures us that "God is greater than our feelings, and he knows everything."

God loved us first, though in our broken, sinful state, we would never have reached out to Him. Jesus set things up so even our own hearts can't condemn us. Once we're His, we're His for good. He knows how hard it is for us to love like He does and, from His own experience, what it takes to make things right. That means we can go to Him and serve others with courage and confidence.

Father, You know everything about me and still love me. Fill me with Your Spirit so I can love others the way Jesus loves me.

DON'T STOP BELIEVIN'

Every child of God defeats this evil world, and we achieve this victory through our faith. And who can win this battle against the world? Only those who believe that Jesus is the Son of God.

1 JOHN 5:4–5 NLT

God's promises steady you when the world tries to undo you. Because you embraced the truth about Jesus Christ—that He is the Son of God, come in the flesh to defeat sin and death—His victory is yours. Faith is your trust that God is who He says He is—and that you are who He says you are: born again as a holy, blameless, righteous son of God, coheir with Christ to glory in eternity and a deep-seated, revitalized life now.

God controls all outcomes, including victory over your flesh and the world. Just keep believing. When His healing or provision doesn't come right away, keep believing. You believed in Jesus to save you from hell—believe Him now when He promises He will never leave you or forsake you, that He will provide for your needs.

In Matthew 9:29 (NIV), Jesus said, "According to your faith let it be done to you." Do you believe Jesus can make the difference you're looking for? Lean into His resurrection power. He will strengthen you to overcome suffering.

. . . .

Jesus, You are the difference maker. Make Your resurrection power known to me today. I trust You today for wisdom and guidance.

STAYING THE COURSE

"Sow righteousness for yourselves, reap the fruit of unfailing love, and break up your unplowed ground; for it is time to seek the LORD, until he comes and showers his righteousness on you."

HOSEA 10:12 NIV

Hosea addressed Israel's hard hearts toward God. They were acting religious but letting anxiety and fear drive their actions, instead of trusting the God who swore to protect and provide for them if they would just love Him enough to obey His commands.

We blame the division we see today on the influence of godless people, but their rampant individualism and selfishness has also infected the church. We're losing our saltiness—forsaking the power of the gospel to fit in with the culture. We show love without truth or truth without love. Neither approach honors Jesus, who always managed both in every situation He faced.

And there's our hope. Jesus' power, His Spirit, is in us; and if we go back to basics—love God with all we are and love others as ourselves—we can stand for Him in these troubled times. Let's heed Hosea's call to break up the hard soil of our hearts and seek God first in all situations. He will fill us with His righteousness and unfailing love, and we will once again impact the people around us for His glory.

Father God, show me anything in my heart that's keeping me from loving and obeying You as You deserve.

JESUS GETS THE LAST WORD

"Should I ransom them from the grave? Should I redeem them from death? O death, bring on your terrors! O grave, bring on your plagues! For I will not take pity on them."

HOSEA 13:14 NLT

Death still hurts, even when we know our fellow believer has gone to be with Jesus. Like Jesus when He wept in indignation at Lazarus' tomb, we know death is not God's original plan for earth or us. Death is a corruption of what God made and called good. Only because this life is harsh and broken can we ever consider death to be a mercy.

But death won't last forever.

Before Jesus came, God's plan to end death was clear. God asked in Hosea 13:14 if He should redeem His people from the grave. *Should* foreshadows what Jesus *did* at Calvary—what Paul celebrated in 1 Corinthians 15:55 (MSG), when he applied Hosea to the certain resurrection of the Christian: "Who got the last word, oh, Death? Oh, Death, who's afraid of you now?"

Satan has been winning since Eden, but as Jesus breathed His last at the cross, Satan's head—his long-standing power in this world—was crushed, just as God promised in Genesis 3:15. Sin, death, and guilt are all defeated, because Jesus gets the last word.

Jesus, Lord and Savior, thank You not only for Your victory over death but for sharing Your win with me. Help me live for You today.

FRIENDSHIP'S EDGE

In the same way that iron sharpens iron,
a person sharpens the character of his friend.
PROVERBS 27:17 VOICE

A true friend will share at least one common trait with you—a thriving relationship with Jesus. A friend like that will bring some aspect of Jesus into your life, and you into his, with this mutual benefit: you will sharpen each other's character.

A friend improves your character with his wisdom, his work ethic, his commitment to God and his family. He shoots straight about his own challenges and respectfully recognizes yours. Most importantly, a friend consistently points you back to God, reminding you of your commitment to Him and encouraging you with His Word and its truths and promises.

That friend needs you to do the same for him. This is where the knife-sharpening analogy comes in: a blunt knife is useless, and only another metal edge can sharpen it. Spiritual and mental sharpness are related. You can't be sharp for someone if your mind and heart are dull, which is what results from plowing through life without cultivating a relationship with God.

When God's Word tries to cut through your excuses or self-preservational instincts, let it. That's how you learn to follow Jesus' example in godliness, humility, and service. That's the power of iron sharpening iron.

Father, help me to be a good friend and to appreciate
that a good friend sharpens my character too.

WHAT REMAINS WHEN TROUBLE COMES

Be sure you know the condition of your flocks, give careful attention to your herds; for riches do not endure forever, and a crown is not secure for all generations.

PROVERBS 27:23–24 NIV

You've worked hard to make a good life, to provide for your family. And you've probably seen firsthand how fleeting everything you've worked for can be.

How you grew up comes front and center when trouble arises. If you grew up cared for physically and emotionally, trained up spiritually, you'll bring that atmosphere into your home. When things go sideways, though, you can find yourself frustrated that, despite your good behavior, you've somehow lost your blessings.

If you grew up around conflict and chaos, the only thing you may have learned was how not to run a household. The danger of hardship is that you may unwittingly default to what you took in growing up.

Trials press us to lean into God in a deeper way. Following Christ guarantees your suffering in this world—but also your security when it comes. Own that double-edged truth, and when trouble comes, you'll have a steady heart and wisdom to lead your family. Let God build Christ's character into your very core, and you will walk steady and guide your family through hard times.

Lord Jesus, You are bigger than any hardship I face. I trust You to strengthen me to keep standing for You, no matter what life brings.

BOLD AS LIONS

The wicked flee when no man pursues,
but the righteous are bold as a lion.
PROVERBS 28:1 SKJV

Righteousness is one of God's key attributes. It means doing the right thing, a standard that God embodies. The gift of Christ is that His righteousness gets passed on to us—attributed to us through no merit of our own, so that when God looks at us, He sees His perfectly right-acting Son.

When righteousness becomes anything less than that perfect standard, we get in trouble. Truth and even reality become relative, and our feelings become the arbiter of good and bad, right and wrong. The result, as Isaiah 64:6 (NLT) tells us, is human-based righteous deeds that are "nothing but filthy rags."

But when God is the source of our ethical behavior, our good works take on the character of His gift: we don't do the right thing because we feel superior but because we love God as our source of life. Righteousness results when we obey Jesus' command to love God and others sacrificially and humbly.

Through Jesus, God has allowed you into His presence, so you can embrace the moment you're in. No need to put on a show, be defensive, or scheme to get ahead. Your confidence is in your righteous God; be bold, knowing you're in His hands.

God, Your righteousness humbles and inspires me to live confidently,
knowing my fear of You has freed me from the fear of man.

NEVER GIVE UP

*Seek (inquire for and require) good and
not evil that you may live, and so the Lord,
the God of hosts, will be with you.*
AMOS 5:14 AMPC

Today's headlines are deflating—wars and rumors of wars, plagues and famine, birth pangs of the end times—but it's for such a time we are here, to cling to God and hold fast to the hope only He offers.

A fascinating parallel runs between Amos' admonition to seek good and Jesus' promise in Revelation 3:8 (NLT): "I know all the things you do, and I have opened a door for you that no one can close. You have little strength, yet you obeyed my word and did not deny me." Whatever we can do to love people well, we should do, because God augments our limited clout with His unlimited power.

The day is coming when, as Amos 5:24 (AMPC) says, "justice [will] run down like waters and righteousness as a mighty and ever-flowing stream." Just as these dark days point to the end of days, so we can stand for justice and righteousness as a precursor to Jesus' reign.

Take courage; God sees our efforts on behalf of the lost and oppressed, and when He opens a door of opportunity, no one can close it.

. . . .

Almighty God, You are my strength in these crazy days. Let Your Spirit lift mine so I can continue to stand for what matters to You.

BE A TRUTH SPEAKER

Amos stood up to Amaziah: "I never set up to be a preacher,
never had plans to be a preacher. I raised cattle and I
pruned trees. Then GOD took me off the farm and said,
'Go preach to my people Israel.' So listen to GOD's Word."
AMOS 7:14–16 MSG

There's some debate over whether the gift of prophecy exists in modern times. Prophets in the Bible served as God's messengers, His mouthpieces and agents of restoration. They literally spoke His words, which He gave to them directly.

In this current age of false prophets and teachers with selfish agendas, we can still rely on the Bible as God's Word. In fact, we must rely on scripture; otherwise, we'll go astray, even with the best of intentions. In one sense, to be a prophet today isn't to pass on new information from God but to speak the messages He has already given.

Amos' story encourages us in that regard. He wasn't a prophet by trade or upbringing. He was a farmer, but he knew God and loved His words, so when God called him to speak to Israel, Amos stepped up. He got cut down by the professional priests and prophets who didn't want this shepherd horning in on their business, but he stayed true to God and delivered God's truth. Our call today is no different.

* * *

God, give me a passion for Your Word
and the courage to speak Your truth.

BEING CONTENT

A grasping person stirs up trouble, but trust
in GOD brings a sense of well-being.
PROVERBS 28:25 MSG

The idea of a grasping person is someone with a greedy heart. The Hebrew phrase literally translates to "a proud heart" or "a large heart." But this isn't a heart enlarged by godly wisdom and knowledge or filled with affection and love, seeking others' highest good in Jesus. This is a narcissistic core, engorged with self-increase and hardened with self-preservation. A person like that is always stirring up trouble, fighting with neighbors and coworkers, because if he doesn't stand up for himself, who will?

God, however, looks out for those who trust Him. When He provides our core identity—sons of God, coheirs of glory with Christ—we escape the trap of self-reliance, of the fear of missing out, of letting materialistic standards shape us. When He fills our hearts with His love and truth, paranoia vanishes and keeping up with the Joneses loses its appeal.

The wealth God guarantees His children is the peace that, whether we have a lot or a little materially, God will always give us what we need. When God goes beyond our expectations, we greet those blessings with humility and a sense of purpose. He blesses us to bless others, and it's exciting to be part of His work.

* * *

Father, You are my source of peace and contentment.
Everything I truly need, You have provided.
Thank You for Your generous heart.

THE BREAKER

*The Breaker [the Messiah] will go up before them. They will
break through, pass in through the gate and go out through it,
and their King will pass on before them, the Lord at their head.*

Micah 2:13 ampc

The stunning scope of God's plan of salvation and judgment is on full
display in Micah 2:13. There's the familiar historical pattern of His
relationship with Israel: because God is holy, He must punish His
people for their rebellion, but when they repent, He redeems them
and brings them home. Folded into that is the greater prediction of
the Messiah, who will do the same for the entire world.

The Hebrew word for *breaker* carries the full implications of the
word, especially when applied to Jesus: one who bursts through the
world's lies, breaks down walls and fortresses, breaks away from old
habits, presses against our defenses and expectations, and spreads
through our hearts and so to the world around us.

Nothing in the world can keep Jesus at bay. Old sins may have
consequences, but He even breaks through the standard expectations of
the fear of punishment because He redeemed His unjust punishment
into a freedom the world can't give or take away. Praise Him today
for His breakthroughs in your life.

*Jesus, You are the Breaker, the one who has forged
ahead to save me and lead me into a bigger view
of life. Lead me in the way I should go.*

THE ROOT OF TRUE LEADERSHIP

*Leadership gains authority and respect
when the voiceless poor are treated fairly.*

PROVERBS 29:14 MSG

Solomon's observation in Proverbs 29:14 has prophetic meaning: The throne of a king who judges the poor fairly will last forever. It's true because such a king—such a leader—emulates God Himself. Before God, we are all poor, dead in spirit, our greatest achievements dwarfed by His most infinitesimal deeds.

Only those who see their true state before God—their desperate, powerless need for help—can appreciate the weight of what He has done in Christ. The idea of a leader as someone God specially selects for their inherent qualities is overrated. The Bible makes it clear that God is the only leader worth following without reservation, and the best leaders among us are those who reflect Jesus' style of leadership—servant hearted, humble, and God honoring.

To lead properly, we must see ourselves as God does: much worse off than we'd ever thought but much more loved than we'd ever hoped. From there, we can lead others. If vision comes to us naturally, we must submit our plans to God. If it doesn't, we must trust His leading and counsel to forge ahead. When we are for our people the way God is for us, we'll be on the right track, wherever He leads.

. . . .

*Lord God, grant me the wisdom and compassion to
lead in ways that honor what matters most to You.*

STRENGTH FOR THOSE WHO TRUST

The LORD is good, a stronghold in a day of distress;
He cares for those who take refuge in Him.
NAHUM 1:7 HCSB

The verses surrounding Nahum 1:7 are a declaration of God's power and righteous wrath. Verse 7 is a beam of sunlight piercing a tornado-dark cloud bank—a shot of relief and hope when trouble looms. But it's also light that illuminates areas where we aren't fully trusting Him.

God's justice and wrath are not His most popular attributes. We prefer His grace, mercy, and love—and rightly so. No one loves like God does, relentlessly and always with our best interests in mind. But the reason His kindness is so striking is because He is holy and just. As Jesus reminds us in Mark 10:18 (NLT), "Only God is truly good." All His attributes ultimately produce a positive impact—if we surrender our hearts to Him.

Anything less sets you against Him. Does that sound extreme or narrow-minded? Only if Jesus doesn't sit on the throne of your heart. When He does, you can see through any pretense that gets between you and His heart. Your sense of worth comes from Him, not popular opinion or wealth or being a good person. God is a refuge because He sees you for who you are and still loves you.

Lord God, I surrender anything in my heart keeping me from
fully trusting You. Be my strength and my stronghold today.

GOD'S CALLING CARD

"The revelation awaits an appointed time; it speaks of the end and will not prove false. Though it linger, wait for it; it will certainly come and will not delay. See, the enemy is puffed up; his desires are not upright—but the righteous person will live by his faithfulness."

HABAKKUK 2:3–4 NIV

Prophecy is God's calling card. In Deuteronomy 18:22 He told Moses the gold standard for a prophet: a 100 percent perfect track record. Miss one and you're out. God's tried-and-true record of calling His shots is perfect and, so, unmatched.

It's been estimated that the Bible contains about 2,500 prophecies. So far, 2,000 of them have been fulfilled—no runs, drips, or errors. The odds of that can be calculated, but it's one of those numbers that's so huge it doesn't make sense. What's fascinating about Habakkuk 2 is the proximity of a statement about the surety of God's prophetic words—a historical phenomenon—and a deeply personal declaration about how a righteous person lives by faith.

God knows how it all turns out, which is astonishing. But even more impressive is that He cares about you and knows the details of your life. Prophecy and provision are two of the most compelling reasons we have to trust Him.

. . . .

Almighty, all-knowing God, everything is in Your hands, from the greatest details of past, present, and future to the smallest, most personal matters. You care about it all. Thank You.

HE DELIGHTS IN YOU

"The LORD your God is living among you. He is a mighty savior.
He will take delight in you with gladness. With his love, he will
calm all your fears. He will rejoice over you with joyful songs."
ZEPHANIAH 3:17 NLT

At Christmas, we make a concentrated effort to rejoice in Christ's coming, to break through the busyness of the season and be reminded that God came to save us. We think of shepherds praising God as angels gathered en masse, proclaiming God's glory, the wonder of Immanuel, God with us.

And while it's good and right that we should sing His praises every day, it's humbling and heartwarming to think of Jesus singing over us. Zephaniah reminds us that God's plan was always that He should come live among us, because He wants to. He doesn't just tolerate us—He delights in us!

Jesus chose you, redeemed you, called you to be His. He gave you His righteousness, His power to live and hope and overcome. These are not the actions of a passive deity, removed from the cares of His worshippers. God pursued you when you were lost because you mean the world to Him. When you gave yourself to Him, He shouted for joy—"Yes! My son is home!" Today is a great day to celebrate the God who celebrates you.

Lord Jesus, when I sing Your praises today,
I will remember that You also rejoice over me.

WORK HARD AND LOOK FOR HIS COMING

Be strong, alert, and courageous, all you people
of the land, says the Lord, and work! For I
am with you, says the Lord of hosts.

HAGGAI 2:4 AMPC

God sent Haggai to His people at a critical moment in their history. After the return from exile, the task of rebuilding Jerusalem's walls and temple was proving daunting. The challenges were both physical and spiritual, and Haggai showed up to encourage them that God was with them.

In Haggai 2:9 (NLT), God said that while this new temple didn't have the splendor of Solomon's temple, the "future glory of this Temple [would] be greater than its past glory. . . . And in this place I will bring peace." If they were bold and courageous, they would finish the work, providing an example of hope that will be ultimately fulfilled when Jesus returns and rules the earth from Jerusalem.

Many of the prophecies Jesus fulfilled when He came include a further promise of His second coming, when He will restore the earth to God's original plan of peace, glory, and communion with Him. Christmas shows us that God will do what He promises, on scales both immediate and long-term. Our part is to trust and obey Him, and He will manage the outcomes, which will be far greater than we can even imagine.

God, strengthen me with the hope of Christ,
as I celebrate His coming and await His return.

UNDER HIS PROTECTION

*The Angel of the LORD spoke to those standing
before Him, "Take off his filthy clothes!" Then He
said to him, "See, I have removed your guilt from you,
and I will clothe you with splendid robes."*

ZECHARIAH 3:4 HCSB

Zechariah 3 depicts Satan showing up and accusing God's chosen ones, revealing the reality of spiritual warfare and the protection God provides. Revelation 12:10 (SKJV) calls Satan "the accuser of our brothers, who accused them before our God day and night"—and then says he has been "cast down." You are under God's protection.

God's cleansing of Jeshua, the high priest at the time, points to the ultimate spiritual cleansing that would happen when God's *Yeshua*—that is, *Jesus*—purified mankind at the cross. Zechariah 3:8–9 (NLT) reveals this stunning prediction: "Soon I am going to bring my servant, the Branch. . . . And I will remove the sins of this land in a single day."

Zechariah 2:8 (NLT) offers assurance as God says, "Anyone who harms you harms my most precious possession." Other translations say we're "the apple of His eye," a phrase showing special affection and attention. God makes us His, then stands up to our enemies for us.

The devil still hunts you, but you are secure in Christ, and your victory is a done deal, now and in the future.

God, You have forgiven my past and secured my present and future through Jesus. You are my shield against the enemy.

TODAY'S HOPE AND
TOMORROW'S BRIGHT FUTURE

*This is what the LORD Almighty says: "I will save my people
from the countries of the east and the west. I will bring
them back to live in Jerusalem; they will be my people, and
I will be faithful and righteous to them as their God."*
ZECHARIAH 8:7–8 NIV

Zechariah's prophecy looks ahead to the cross but also to the kingdom of Christ, and ultimately, to the New Jerusalem, where God's people will serve and love Him and each other faithfully, without restraint, full of joy and peace, satisfied in the deepest part of our being.

It sounds impossible, doesn't it? A coming day when we will repay God's relentless love with our full devotion. We won't strive to do what's right; we'll just do it. No more fear undergirding our thoughts and actions, loving God for who He is, untainted by our personal agendas. It will be everything our hearts want now but struggle to do. Crazy, right? There's so much to overcome—the world, our selfishness, all the suffering.

It will happen, though. Nothing is impossible for God. Because Jesus came and paid for our sins, then sent His Spirit to guide and keep us until He returns, we live in hope, and we see glimpses of the heaven that earth will become.

....

*Lord Jesus, come soon. Until You do, I know You will
keep making all things new, including my heart.*

IN THE END, WE WIN

"They will go to war against the Lamb but the Lamb will defeat them, proof that he is Lord over all lords, King over all kings, and those with him will be the called, chosen, and faithful."

REVELATION 17:14 MSG

The end-times world John describes makes our current era look like a picnic. All the things we fear now will happen then in spades, and it will look hopeless. But God will come through, like He does, upping the odds against success so there will be no mistake that He is the one who saves, delivers, redeems, and restores.

Since God will conquer against the ultimate stacked deck, He can certainly strengthen and encourage us today. Jesus called all the hard things we're experiencing these days "birth pangs"—spasms of suffering that point to the great day of the Lord when He will no longer restrain His wrath and righteous judgment.

Until then, we live in the certainty that He is with us and for us, working all things together for good because He has called us and saved us so we will never be apart from Him, now and when the end comes. Neither life nor death can separate us from His love. We will stand with Him in the end as beloved overcomers.

Father God, King of kings and Lord of lords, You are victorious now and forever, and in the end, I will stand at Your side.

JUSTICE IS COMING

"O Heaven, celebrate! And join in, saints, apostles, and prophets! God has judged her; every wrong you suffered from her has been judged."
REVELATION 18:20 MSG

We love justice. All the movies and stories we love best hit right because the good guys win and the bad guys get what's coming to them. We know that, as Christians, we shouldn't be rejoicing when a particularly nasty villain falls off a cliff—Jesus never gave up on us and He doesn't permit us to give up on others.

Is it wrong to take satisfaction in the demise of someone who has shown no interest in God or love or redemption? Maybe not (movies aside!), but as Revelation 18 makes clear, justice is coming against a system and its people who hate God and oppose everything that matters to Him—and we are to rejoice when it falls.

In these days of grace and kingdom-building, we are still to seek justice, help those in need, and be God's salt and light to a hurting world. One day, God will avenge the wrongs done to His great name and the injuries His people have suffered at the world's hands. His faithfulness, holiness, and righteousness are always worth celebrating, now and in the future.

. . . .

Just and righteous God, in the face of injustice, I will still seek Your good will and praise Your name, because You're going to come out on top and all Your people will rejoice.

JESUS IS COMING BACK

I saw Heaven open wide—and oh! a white horse
and its Rider. The Rider, named Faithful and True,
judges and makes war in pure righteousness.

REVELATION 19:11 MSG

The year is winding down, a time both to reflect and to look ahead, a time to give thanks and to offer God your hopes. You're off to a good start today, seeking God.

As you do that, take a moment to think about Revelation 19. Jesus is coming back. That's not a wild hope but a certainty—and when He does, the world will know Him for who He is: Faithful and True, the just Judge, King of kings and Lord of lords, the Word of God whose speech obliterates His enemies. He is bringing justice and righteousness and will rule the world with a firm grip. When Jesus returns, your accuser and his minions will be destroyed. The world system will fail and fall for good, and the divine work of making things new will go global. It's okay to get stoked!

Whatever awaits you today and in the days ahead is in His hands. The great God and Creator of all gave His life for you, and He will protect you, provide for you, and finish the good work He began in you.

Lord Jesus, I can't wait till You come back and make
all things right. Let me live today with You in the
center of my thoughts, words, and deeds.

REST EASY—YOU'RE HIS

They shall be Mine, says the Lord of hosts, in that day
when I publicly recognize and openly declare them to be
My jewels (My special possession, My peculiar treasure).
MALACHI 3:17 AMPC

Whatever matters most to you effectively owns you—family, career, lifestyle, political or ideological identity. If that's not God, you will be let down and left high and dry. To be God's possession is to be treasured, set apart by Him and for Him—adopted as His son, co-heir of Christ's glory, bearer of His light and truth, doer of good works that He has planned just for you. To be a Christian is to be special to God because you have identified with Him through His Son, Jesus Christ.

God has determined your value, dying to make you His own. First Peter 2:9 (NIV) details your purpose: "You are a chosen people... God's special possession, that you may declare the praises of him who called you out of darkness into his wonderful light." Everything you suffer now, according to Romans 8:18 (NIV), isn't "worth comparing with the glory that will be revealed in [you]." The world treats you like a lump of coal, but God shapes you into a diamond. What you mean to God can't be measured nor taken away.

God, I take heart knowing that You have
chosen me, called me, and made me Yours.
I offer everything I have and am for Your glory.

CONTRIBUTORS

Quentin Guy writes from the high desert of New Mexico, to encourage and equip people to know and serve God. He currently works in publishing for Calvary Church and has cowritten such books as *Weird and Gross Bible Stuff* and *The 2:52 Boys Bible*, both of which are stuck in future classic status. A former middle school teacher, he serves with his wife as marriage prep mentors and trusts God that his children will survive their teenage years. Quentin's devotions appear in March, August, and December.

Paul Muckley is a long-time editor who, under the pseudonym Paul Kent, has also written several books including *Know Your Bible, Oswald Chambers: A Life in Pictures,* and *Playing with Purpose: Baseball Devotions.* He and his family live in Ohio's Amish Country. Paul's devotions appear in April, July, and October.

Tracy M. Sumner is a freelance author, writer, and editor in Beaverton, Oregon. An avid outdoorsman, he enjoys fly-fishing on world-class Oregon waters. Tracy's devotions appear in January, May, and September.

Glenn A. Hascall is an accomplished writer with credits in more than 130 books. He is a broadcast veteran and voice actor and is actively involved in audio drama. Glenn's devotions appear in February, June, and November.

READ THROUGH THE BIBLE
IN A YEAR PLAN

1-Jan	Gen. 1-2	Matt. 1	Ps. 1
2-Jan	Gen. 3-4	Matt. 2	Ps. 2
3-Jan	Gen. 5-7	Matt. 3	Ps. 3
4-Jan	Gen. 8-10	Matt. 4	Ps. 4
5-Jan	Gen. 11-13	Matt. 5:1-20	Ps. 5
6-Jan	Gen. 14-16	Matt. 5:21-48	Ps. 6
7-Jan	Gen. 17-18	Matt. 6:1-18	Ps. 7
8-Jan	Gen. 19-20	Matt. 6:19-34	Ps. 8
9-Jan	Gen. 21-23	Matt. 7:1-11	Ps. 9:1-8
10-Jan	Gen. 24	Matt. 7:12-29	Ps. 9:9-20
11-Jan	Gen. 25-26	Matt. 8:1-17	Ps. 10:1-11
12-Jan	Gen. 27:1-28:9	Matt. 8:18-34	Ps. 10:12-18
13-Jan	Gen. 28:10-29:35	Matt. 9	Ps. 11
14-Jan	Gen. 30:1-31:21	Matt. 10:1-15	Ps. 12
15-Jan	Gen. 31:22-32:21	Matt. 10:16-36	Ps. 13
16-Jan	Gen. 32:22-34:31	Matt. 10:37-11:6	Ps. 14
17-Jan	Gen. 35-36	Matt. 11:7-24	Ps. 15
18-Jan	Gen. 37-38	Matt. 11:25-30	Ps. 16
19-Jan	Gen. 39-40	Matt. 12:1-29	Ps. 17
20-Jan	Gen. 41	Matt. 12:30-50	Ps. 18:1-15
21-Jan	Gen. 42-43	Matt. 13:1-9	Ps. 18:16-29
22-Jan	Gen. 44-45	Matt. 13:10-23	Ps. 18:30-50
23-Jan	Gen. 46:1-47:26	Matt. 13:24-43	Ps. 19
24-Jan	Gen. 47:27-49:28	Matt. 13:44-58	Ps. 20
25-Jan	Gen. 49:29-Exod. 1:22	Matt. 14	Ps. 21
26-Jan	Exod. 2-3	Matt. 15:1-28	Ps. 22:1-21
27-Jan	Exod. 4:1-5:21	Matt. 15:29-16:12	Ps. 22:22-31
28-Jan	Exod. 5:22-7:24	Matt. 16:13-28	Ps. 23
29-Jan	Exod. 7:25-9:35	Matt. 17:1-9	Ps. 24
30-Jan	Exod. 10-11	Matt. 17:10-27	Ps. 25
31-Jan	Exod. 12	Matt. 18:1-20	Ps. 26
1-Feb	Exod. 13-14	Matt. 18:21-35	Ps. 27
2-Feb	Exod. 15-16	Matt. 19:1-15	Ps. 28
3-Feb	Exod. 17-19	Matt. 19:16-30	Ps. 29
4-Feb	Exod. 20-21	Matt. 20:1-19	Ps. 30
5-Feb	Exod. 22-23	Matt. 20:20-34	Ps. 31:1-8
6-Feb	Exod. 24-25	Matt. 21:1-27	Ps. 31:9-18
7-Feb	Exod 26-27	Matt. 21:28-46	Ps. 31:19-24
8-Feb	Exod. 28	Matt. 22	Ps. 32
9-Feb	Exod. 29	Matt. 23:1-36	Ps. 33:1-12
10-Feb	Exod. 30-31	Matt. 23:37-24:28	Ps. 33:13-22
11-Feb	Exod. 32-33	Matt. 24:29-51	Ps. 34:1-7
12-Feb	Exod. 34:1-35:29	Matt. 25:1-13	Ps. 34:8-22
13-Feb	Exod. 35:30-37:29	Matt. 25:14-30	Ps. 35:1-8
14-Feb	Exod. 38-39	Matt. 25:31-46	Ps. 35:9-17
15-Feb	Exod. 40	Matt. 26:1-35	Ps. 35:18-28
16-Feb	Lev. 1-3	Matt. 26:36-68	Ps. 36:1-6
17-Feb	Lev. 4:1-5:13	Matt. 26:69-27:26	Ps. 36:7-12
18-Feb	Lev. 5:14 -7:21	Matt. 27:27-50	Ps. 37:1-6
19-Feb	Lev. 7:22-8:36	Matt. 27:51-66	Ps. 37:7-26
20-Feb	Lev. 9-10	Matt. 28	Ps. 37:27-40
21-Feb	Lev. 11-12	Mark 1:1-28	Ps. 38
22-Feb	Lev. 13	Mark 1:29-39	Ps. 39
23-Feb	Lev. 14	Mark 1:40-2:12	Ps. 40:1-8
24-Feb	Lev. 15	Mark 2:13-3:35	Ps. 40:9-17
25-Feb	Lev. 16-17	Mark 4:1-20	Ps. 41:1-4
26-Feb	Lev. 18-19	Mark 4:21-41	Ps. 41:5-13

27-Feb	Lev. 20	Mark 5	Ps. 42-43
28-Feb	Lev. 21-22	Mark 6:1-13	Ps. 44
1-Mar	Lev. 23-24	Mark 6:14-29	Ps. 45:1-5
2-Mar	Lev. 25	Mark 6:30-56	Ps. 45:6-12
3-Mar	Lev. 26	Mark 7	Ps. 45:13-17
4-Mar	Lev. 27	Mark 8	Ps. 46
5-Mar	Num. 1-2	Mark 9:1-13	Ps. 47
6-Mar	Num. 3	Mark 9:14-50	Ps. 48:1-8
7-Mar	Num. 4	Mark 10:1-34	Ps. 48:9-14
8-Mar	Num. 5:1-6:21	Mark 10:35-52	Ps. 49:1-9
9-Mar	Num. 6:22-7:47	Mark 11	Ps. 49:10-20
10-Mar	Num. 7:48-8:4	Mark 12:1-27	Ps. 50:1-15
11-Mar	Num. 8:5-9:23	Mark 12:28-44	Ps. 50:16-23
12-Mar	Num. 10-11	Mark 13:1-8	Ps. 51:1-9
13-Mar	Num. 12-13	Mark 13:9-37	Ps. 51:10-19
14-Mar	Num. 14	Mark 14:1-31	Ps. 52
15-Mar	Num. 15	Mark 14:32-72	Ps. 53
16-Mar	Num. 16	Mark 15:1-32	Ps. 54
17-Mar	Num. 17-18	Mark 15:33-47	Ps. 55
18-Mar	Num. 19-20	Mark 16	Ps. 56:1-7
19-Mar	Num. 21:1-22:20	Luke 1:1-25	Ps. 56:8-13
20-Mar	Num. 22:21-23:30	Luke 1:26-56	Ps. 57
21-Mar	Num. 24-25	Luke 1:57-2:20	Ps. 58
22-Mar	Num. 26:1-27:11	Luke 2:21-38	Ps. 59:1-8
23-Mar	Num. 27:12-29:11	Luke 2:39-52	Ps. 59:9-17
24-Mar	Num. 29:12-30:16	Luke 3	Ps. 60:1-5
25-Mar	Num. 31	Luke 4	Ps. 60:6-12
26-Mar	Num. 32-33	Luke 5:1-16	Ps. 61
27-Mar	Num. 34-36	Luke 5:17-32	Ps. 62:1-6
28-Mar	Deut. 1:1-2:25	Luke 5:33-6:11	Ps. 62:7-12
29-Mar	Deut. 2:26-4:14	Luke 6:12-35	Ps. 63:1-5
30-Mar	Deut. 4:15-5:22	Luke 6:36-49	Ps. 63:6-11
31-Mar	Deut. 5:23-7:26	Luke 7:1-17	Ps. 64:1-5
1-Apr	Deut. 8-9	Luke 7:18-35	Ps. 64:6-10
2-Apr	Deut. 10-11	Luke 7:36-8:3	Ps. 65:1-8
3-Apr	Deut. 12-13	Luke 8:4-21	Ps. 65:9-13
4-Apr	Deut. 14:1-16:8	Luke 8:22-39	Ps. 66:1-7
5-Apr	Deut. 16:9-18:22	Luke 8:40-56	Ps. 66:8-15
6-Apr	Deut. 19:1-21:9	Luke 9:1-22	Ps. 66:16-20
7-Apr	Deut. 21:10-23:8	Luke 9:23-42	Ps. 67
8-Apr	Deut. 23:9-25:19	Luke 9:43-62	Ps. 68:1-6
9-Apr	Deut. 26:1-28:14	Luke 10:1-20	Ps. 68:7-14
10-Apr	Deut. 28:15-68	Luke 10:21-37	Ps. 68:15-19
11-Apr	Deut. 29-30	Luke 10:38-11:23	Ps. 68:20-27
12-Apr	Deut. 31:1-32:22	Luke 11:24-36	Ps. 68:28-35
13-Apr	Deut. 32:23-33:29	Luke 11:37-54	Ps. 69:1-9
14-Apr	Deut. 34-Josh. 2	Luke 12:1-15	Ps. 69:10-17
15-Apr	Josh. 3:1-5:12	Luke 12:16-40	Ps. 69:18-28
16-Apr	Josh. 5:13-7:26	Luke 12:41-48	Ps. 69:29-36
17-Apr	Josh. 8-9	Luke 12:49-59	Ps. 70
18-Apr	Josh. 10:1-11:15	Luke 13:1-21	Ps. 71:1-6
19-Apr	Josh. 11:16-13:33	Luke 13:22-35	Ps. 71:7-16
20-Apr	Josh. 14-16	Luke 14:1-15	Ps. 71:17-21
21-Apr	Josh. 17:1-19:16	Luke 14:16-35	Ps. 71:22-24
22-Apr	Josh. 19:17-21:42	Luke 15:1-10	Ps. 72:1-11
23-Apr	Josh. 21:43-22:34	Luke 15:11-32	Ps. 72:12-20
24-Apr	Josh. 23-24	Luke 16:1-18	Ps. 73:1-9
25-Apr	Judg. 1-2	Luke 16:19-17:10	Ps. 73:10-20
26-Apr	Judg. 3-4	Luke 17:11-37	Ps. 73:21-28
27-Apr	Judg. 5:1-6:24	Luke 18:1-17	Ps. 74:1-3
28-Apr	Judg. 6:25-7:25	Luke 18:18-43	Ps. 74:4-11
29-Apr	Judg. 8:1-9:23	Luke 19:1-28	Ps. 74:12-17

30-Apr	Judg. 9:24-10:18	Luke 19:29-48	Ps. 74:18-23
1-May	Judg. 11:1-12:7	Luke 20:1-26	Ps. 75:1-7
2-May	Judg. 12:8-14:20	Luke 20:27-47	Ps. 75:8-10
3-May	Judg. 15-16	Luke 21:1-19	Ps. 76:1-7
4-May	Judg. 17-18	Luke 21:20-22:6	Ps. 76:8-12
5-May	Judg. 19:1-20:23	Luke 22:7-30	Ps. 77:1-11
6-May	Judg. 20:24-21:25	Luke 22:31-54	Ps. 77:12-20
7-May	Ruth 1-2	Luke 22:55-23:25	Ps. 78:1-4
8-May	Ruth 3-4	Luke 23:26-24:12	Ps. 78:5-8
9-May	1 Sam. 1:1-2:21	Luke 24:13-53	Ps. 78:9-16
10-May	1 Sam. 2:22-4:22	John 1:1-28	Ps. 78:17-24
11-May	1 Sam. 5-7	John 1:29-51	Ps. 78:25-33
12-May	1 Sam. 8:1-9:26	John 2	Ps. 78:34-41
13-May	1 Sam. 9:27-11:15	John 3:1-22	Ps. 78:42-55
14-May	1 Sam. 12-13	John 3:23-4:10	Ps. 78:56-66
15-May	1 Sam. 14	John 4:11-38	Ps. 78:67-72
16-May	1 Sam. 15-16	John 4:39-54	Ps. 79:1-7
17-May	1 Sam. 17	John 5:1-24	Ps. 79:8-13
18-May	1 Sam. 18-19	John 5:25-47	Ps. 80:1-7
19-May	1 Sam. 20-21	John 6:1-21	Ps. 80:8-19
20-May	1 Sam. 22-23	John 6:22-42	Ps. 81:1-10
21-May	1 Sam. 24:1-25:31	John 6:43-71	Ps. 81:11-16
22-May	1 Sam. 25:32-27:12	John 7:1-24	Ps. 82
23-May	1 Sam. 28-29	John 7:25-8:11	Ps. 83
24-May	1 Sam. 30-31	John 8:12-47	Ps. 84:1-4
25-May	2 Sam. 1-2	John 8:48-9:12	Ps. 84:5-12
26-May	2 Sam. 3-4	John 9:13-34	Ps. 85:1-7
27-May	2 Sam. 5:1-7:17	John 9:35-10:10	Ps. 85:8-13
28-May	2 Sam. 7:18-10:19	John 10:11-30	Ps. 86:1-10
29-May	2 Sam. 11:1-12:25	John 10:31-11:16	Ps. 86:11-17
30-May	2 Sam. 12:26-13:39	John 11:17-54	Ps. 87
31-May	2 Sam. 14:1-15:12	John 11:55-12:19	Ps. 88:1-9
1-Jun	2 Sam. 15:13-16:23	John 12:20-43	Ps. 88:10-18
2-Jun	2 Sam. 17:1-18:18	John 12:44-13:20	Ps. 89:1-6
3-Jun	2 Sam. 18:19-19:39	John 13:21-38	Ps. 89:7-13
4-Jun	2 Sam. 19:40-21:22	John 14:1-17	Ps. 89:14-18
5-Jun	2 Sam. 22:1-23:7	John 14:18-15:27	Ps. 89:19-29
6-Jun	2 Sam. 23:8-24:25	John 16:1-22	Ps. 89:30-37
7-Jun	1 Kings 1	John 16:23-17:5	Ps. 89:38-52
8-Jun	1 Kings 2	John 17:6-26	Ps. 90:1-12
9-Jun	1 Kings 3-4	John 18:1-27	Ps. 90:13-17
10-Jun	1 Kings 5-6	John 18:28-19:5	Ps. 91:1-10
11-Jun	1 Kings 7	John 19:6-25a	Ps. 91:11-16
12-Jun	1 Kings 8:1-53	John 19:25b-42	Ps. 92:1-9
13-Jun	1 Kings 8:54-10:13	John 20:1-18	Ps. 92:10-15
14-Jun	1 Kings 10:14-11:43	John 20:19-31	Ps. 93
15-Jun	1 Kings 12:1-13:10	John 21	Ps. 94:1-11
16-Jun	1 Kings 13:11-14:31	Acts 1:1-11	Ps. 94:12-23
17-Jun	1 Kings 15:1-16:20	Acts 1:12-26	Ps. 95
18-Jun	1 Kings 16:21-18:19	Acts 2:1-21	Ps. 96:1-8
19-Jun	1 Kings 18:20-19:21	Acts 2:22-41	Ps. 96:9-13
20-Jun	1 Kings 20	Acts 2:42-3:26	Ps. 97:1-6
21-Jun	1 Kings 21:1-22:28	Acts 4:1-22	Ps. 97:7-12
22-Jun	1 Kings 22:29- 2 Kings 1:18	Acts 4:23-5:11	Ps. 98
23-Jun	2 Kings 2-3	Acts 5:12-28	Ps. 99
24-Jun	2 Kings 4	Acts 5:29-6:15	Ps. 100
25-Jun	2 Kings 5:1-6:23	Acts 7:1-16	Ps. 101
26-Jun	2 Kings 6:24-8:15	Acts 7:17-36	Ps. 102:1-7
27-Jun	2 Kings 8:16-9:37	Acts 7:37-53	Ps. 102:8-17
28-Jun	2 Kings 10-11	Acts 7:54-8:8	Ps. 102:18-28
29-Jun	2 Kings 12-13	Acts 8:9-40	Ps. 103:1-9

30-Jun	2 Kings 14-15	Acts 9:1-16	Ps. 103:10-14
1-Jul	2 Kings 16-17	Acts 9:17-31	Ps. 103:15-22
2-Jul	2 Kings 18:1-19:7	Acts 9:32-10:16	Ps. 104:1-9
3-Jul	2 Kings 19:8-20:21	Acts 10:17-33	Ps. 104:10-23
4-Jul	2 Kings 21:1-22:20	Acts 10:34-11:18	Ps. 104: 24-30
5-Jul	2 Kings 23	Acts 11:19-12:17	Ps. 104:31-35
6-Jul	2 Kings 24-25	Acts 12:18-13:13	Ps. 105:1-7
7-Jul	1 Chron. 1-2	Acts 13:14-43	Ps. 105:8-15
8-Jul	1 Chron. 3:1-5:10	Acts 13:44-14:10	Ps. 105:16-28
9-Jul	1 Chron. 5:11-6:81	Acts 14:11-28	Ps. 105:29-36
10-Jul	1 Chron. 7:1-9:9	Acts 15:1-18	Ps. 105:37-45
11-Jul	1 Chron. 9:10-11:9	Acts 15:19-41	Ps. 106:1-12
12-Jul	1 Chron. 11:10-12:40	Acts 16:1-15	Ps. 106:13-27
13-Jul	1 Chron. 13-15	Acts 16:16-40	Ps. 106:28-33
14-Jul	1 Chron. 16-17	Acts 17:1-14	Ps. 106:34-43
15-Jul	1 Chron. 18-20	Acts 17:15-34	Ps. 106:44-48
16-Jul	1 Chron. 21-22	Acts 18:1-23	Ps. 107:1-9
17-Jul	1 Chron. 23-25	Acts 18:24-19:10	Ps. 107:10-16
18-Jul	1 Chron. 26-27	Acts 19:11-22	Ps. 107:17-32
19-Jul	1 Chron. 28-29	Acts 19:23-41	Ps. 107:33-38
20-Jul	2 Chron. 1-3	Acts 20:1-16	Ps. 107:39-43
21-Jul	2 Chron. 4:1-6:11	Acts 20:17-38	Ps. 108
22-Jul	2 Chron. 6:12-7:10	Acts 21:1-14	Ps. 109:1-20
23-Jul	2 Chron. 7:11-9:28	Acts 21:15-32	Ps. 109:21-31
24-Jul	2 Chron. 9:29-12:16	Acts 21:33-22:16	Ps. 110:1-3
25-Jul	2 Chron. 13-15	Acts 22:17-23:11	Ps. 110:4-7
26-Jul	2 Chron. 16-17	Acts 23:12-24:21	Ps. 111
27-Jul	2 Chron. 18-19	Acts 24:22-25:12	Ps. 112
28-Jul	2 Chron. 20-21	Acts 25:13-27	Ps. 113
29-Jul	2 Chron. 22-23	Acts 26	Ps. 114
30-Jul	2 Chron. 24:1-25:16	Acts 27:1-20	Ps. 115:1-10
31-Jul	2 Chron. 25:17-27:9	Acts 27:21-28:6	Ps. 115:11-18
1-Aug	2 Chron. 28:1-29:19	Acts 28:7-31	Ps. 116:1-5
2-Aug	2 Chron. 29:20-30:27	Rom. 1:1-17	Ps. 116:6-19
3-Aug	2 Chron. 31-32	Rom. 1:18-32	Ps. 117
4-Aug	2 Chron. 33:1-34:7	Rom. 2	Ps. 118:1-18
5-Aug	2 Chron. 34:8-35:19	Rom. 3:1-26	Ps. 118:19-23
6-Aug	2 Chron. 35:20-36:23	Rom. 3:27-4:25	Ps. 118:24-29
7-Aug	Ezra 1-3	Rom. 5	Ps. 119:1-8
8-Aug	Ezra 4-5	Rom. 6:1-7:6	Ps. 119:9-16
9-Aug	Ezra 6:1-7:26	Rom. 7:7-25	Ps. 119:17-32
10-Aug	Ezra 7:27-9:4	Rom. 8:1-27	Ps. 119:33-40
11-Aug	Ezra 9:5-10:44	Rom. 8:28-39	Ps. 119:41-64
12-Aug	Neh. 1:1-3:16	Rom. 9:1-18	Ps. 119:65-72
13-Aug	Neh. 3:17-5:13	Rom. 9:19-33	Ps. 119:73-80
14-Aug	Neh. 5:14-7:73	Rom. 10:1-13	Ps. 119:81-88
15-Aug	Neh. 8:1-9:5	Rom. 10:14-11:24	Ps. 119:89-104
16-Aug	Neh. 9:6-10:27	Rom. 11:25-12:8	Ps. 119:105-120
17-Aug	Neh. 10:28-12:26	Rom. 12:9-13:7	Ps. 119:121-128
18-Aug	Neh. 12:27-13:31	Rom. 13:8-14:12	Ps. 119:129-136
19-Aug	Esther 1:1-2:18	Rom. 14:13-15:13	Ps. 119:137-152
20-Aug	Esther 2:19-5:14	Rom. 15:14-21	Ps. 119:153-168
21-Aug	Esther. 6-8	Rom. 15:22-33	Ps. 119:169-176
22-Aug	Esther 9-10	Rom. 16	Ps. 120-122
23-Aug	Job 1-3	1 Cor. 1:1-25	Ps. 123
24-Aug	Job 4-6	1 Cor. 1:26-2:16	Ps. 124-125
25-Aug	Job 7-9	1 Cor. 3	Ps. 126-127
26-Aug	Job 10-13	1 Cor. 4:1-13	Ps. 128-129
27-Aug	Job 14-16	1 Cor. 4:14-5:13	Ps. 130
28-Aug	Job 17-20	1 Cor. 6	Ps. 131
29-Aug	Job 21-23	1 Cor. 7:1-16	Ps. 132
30-Aug	Job 24-27	1 Cor. 7:17-40	Ps. 133-134

31-Aug	Job 28-30	1 Cor. 8	Ps. 135
1-Sep	Job 31-33	1 Cor. 9:1-18	Ps. 136:1-9
2-Sep	Job 34-36	1 Cor. 9:19-10:13	Ps. 136:10-26
3-Sep	Job 37-39	1 Cor. 10:14-11:1	Ps. 137
4-Sep	Job 40-42	1 Cor. 11:2-34	Ps. 138
5-Sep	Eccles. 1:1-3:15	1 Cor. 12:1-26	Ps. 139:1-6
6-Sep	Eccles. 3:16-6:12	1 Cor. 12:27-13:13	Ps. 139:7-18
7-Sep	Eccles. 7:1-9:12	1 Cor. 14:1-22	Ps. 139:19-24
8-Sep	Eccles. 9:13-12:14	1 Cor. 14:23-15:11	Ps. 140:1-8
9-Sep	SS 1-4	1 Cor. 15:12-34	Ps. 140:9-13
10-Sep	SS 5-8	1 Cor. 15:35-58	Ps. 141
11-Sep	Isa. 1-2	1 Cor. 16	Ps. 142
12-Sep	Isa. 3-5	2 Cor. 1:1-11	Ps. 143:1-6
13-Sep	Isa. 6-8	2 Cor. 1:12-2:4	Ps. 143:7-12
14-Sep	Isa. 9-10	2 Cor. 2:5-17	Ps. 144
15-Sep	Isa. 11-13	2 Cor. 3	Ps. 145
16-Sep	Isa. 14-16	2 Cor. 4	Ps. 146
17-Sep	Isa. 17-19	2 Cor. 5	Ps. 147:1-11
18-Sep	Isa. 20-23	2 Cor. 6	Ps. 147:12-20
19-Sep	Isa. 24:1-26:19	2 Cor. 7	Ps. 148
20-Sep	Isa. 26:20-28:29	2 Cor. 8	Ps. 149-150
21-Sep	Isa. 29-30	2 Cor. 9	Prov. 1:1-9
22-Sep	Isa. 31-33	2 Cor. 10	Prov. 1:10-22
23-Sep	Isa. 34-36	2 Cor. 11	Prov. 1:23-26
24-Sep	Isa. 37-38	2 Cor. 12:1-10	Prov. 1:27-33
25-Sep	Isa. 39-40	2 Cor. 12:11-13:14	Prov. 2:1-15
26-Sep	Isa. 41-42	Gal. 1	Prov. 2:16-22
27-Sep	Isa. 43:1-44:20	Gal. 2	Prov. 3:1-12
28-Sep	Isa. 44:21-46:13	Gal. 3:1-18	Prov. 3:13-26
29-Sep	Isa. 47:1-49:13	Gal 3:19-29	Prov. 3:27-35
30-Sep	Isa. 49:14-51:23	Gal 4:1-11	Prov. 4:1-19
1-Oct	Isa. 52-54	Gal. 4:12-31	Prov. 4:20-27
2-Oct	Isa. 55-57	Gal. 5	Prov. 5:1-14
3-Oct	Isa. 58-59	Gal. 6	Prov. 5:15-23
4-Oct	Isa. 60-62	Eph. 1	Prov. 6:1-5
5-Oct	Isa. 63:1-65:16	Eph. 2	Prov. 6:6-19
6-Oct	Isa. 65:17-66:24	Eph. 3:1-4:16	Prov. 6:20-26
7-Oct	Jer. 1-2	Eph. 4:17-32	Prov. 6:27-35
8-Oct	Jer. 3:1-4:22	Eph. 5	Prov. 7:1-5
9-Oct	Jer. 4:23-5:31	Eph. 6	Prov. 7:6-27
10-Oct	Jer. 6:1-7:26	Phil. 1:1-26	Prov. 8:1-11
11-Oct	Jer. 7:26-9:16	Phil. 1:27-2:18	Prov. 8:12-21
12-Oct	Jer. 9:17-11:17	Phil 2:19-30	Prov. 8:22-36
13-Oct	Jer. 11:18-13:27	Phil. 3	Prov. 9:1-6
14-Oct	Jer. 14-15	Phil. 4	Prov. 9:7-18
15-Oct	Jer. 16-17	Col. 1:1-23	Prov. 10:1-5
16-Oct	Jer. 18:1-20:6	Col. 1:24-2:15	Prov. 10:6-14
17-Oct	Jer. 20:7-22:19	Col. 2:16-3:4	Prov. 10:15-26
18-Oct	Jer. 22:20-23:40	Col. 3:5-4:1	Prov. 10:27-32
19-Oct	Jer. 24-25	Col. 4:2-18	Prov. 11:1-11
20-Oct	Jer. 26-27	1 Thes. 1:1-2:8	Prov. 11:12-21
21-Oct	Jer. 28-29	1 Thes. 2:9-3:13	Prov. 11:22-26
22-Oct	Jer. 30:1-31:22	1 Thes. 4:1-5:11	Prov. 11:27-31
23-Oct	Jer. 31:23-32:35	1 Thes. 5:12-28	Prov. 12:1-14
24-Oct	Jer. 32:36-34:7	2 Thes. 1-2	Prov. 12:15-20
25-Oct	Jer. 34:8-36:10	2 Thes. 3	Prov. 12:21-28
26-Oct	Jer. 36:11-38:13	1 Tim. 1:1-17	Prov. 13:1-4
27-Oct	Jer. 38:14-40:6	1 Tim. 1:18-3:13	Prov. 13:5-13
28-Oct	Jer. 40:7-42:22	1 Tim. 3:14-4:10	Prov. 13:14-21
29-Oct	Jer. 43-44	1 Tim. 4:11-5:16	Prov. 13:22-25
30-Oct	Jer. 45-47	1 Tim. 5:17-6:21	Prov. 14:1-6
31-Oct	Jer. 48:1-49:6	2 Tim. 1	Prov. 14:7-22

1-Nov	Jer. 49:7-50:16	2 Tim. 2	Prov. 14:23-27
2-Nov	Jer. 50:17-51:14	2 Tim. 3	Prov. 14:28-35
3-Nov	Jer. 51:15-64	2 Tim. 4	Prov. 15:1-9
4-Nov	Jer. 52-Lam. 1	Ti. 1:1-9	Prov. 15:10-17
5-Nov	Lam. 2:1-3:38	Ti. 1:10-2:15	Prov. 15:18-26
6-Nov	Lam. 3:39-5:22	Ti. 3	Prov. 15:27-33
7-Nov	Ezek. 1:1-3:21	Philemon 1	Prov. 16:1-9
8-Nov	Ezek. 3:22-5:17	Heb. 1:1-2:4	Prov. 16:10-21
9-Nov	Ezek. 6-7	Heb. 2:5-18	Prov. 16:22-33
10-Nov	Ezek. 8-10	Heb. 3:1-4:3	Prov. 17:1-5
11-Nov	Ezek. 11-12	Heb. 4:4-5:10	Prov. 17:6-12
12-Nov	Ezek. 13-14	Heb. 5:11-6:20	Prov. 17:13-22
13-Nov	Ezek. 15:1-16:43	Heb. 7:1-28	Prov. 17:23-28
14-Nov	Ezek. 16:44-17:24	Heb. 8:1-9:10	Prov. 18:1-7
15-Nov	Ezek. 18-19	Heb. 9:11-28	Prov. 18:8-17
16-Nov	Ezek. 20	Heb. 10:1-25	Prov. 18:18-24
17-Nov	Ezek. 21-22	Heb. 10:26-39	Prov. 19:1-8
18-Nov	Ezek. 23	Heb. 11:1-31	Prov. 19:9-14
19-Nov	Ezek. 24-26	Heb. 11:32-40	Prov. 19:15-21
20-Nov	Ezek. 27-28	Heb. 12:1-13	Prov. 19:22-29
21-Nov	Ezek. 29-30	Heb. 12:14-29	Prov. 20:1-18
22-Nov	Ezek. 31-32	Heb. 13	Prov. 20:19-24
23-Nov	Ezek. 33:1-34:10	Jas. 1	Prov. 20:25-30
24-Nov	Ezek. 34:11-36:15	Jas. 2	Prov. 21:1-8
25-Nov	Ezek. 36:16-37:28	Jas. 3	Prov. 21:9-18
26-Nov	Ezek. 38-39	Jas. 4:1-5:6	Prov. 21:19-24
27-Nov	Ezek. 40	Jas. 5:7-20	Prov. 21:25-31
28-Nov	Ezek. 41:1-43:12	1 Pet. 1:1-12	Prov. 22:1-9
29-Nov	Ezek. 43:13-44:31	1 Pet. 1:13-2:3	Prov. 22:10-23
30-Nov	Ezek. 45-46	1 Pet. 2:4-17	Prov. 22:24-29
1-Dec	Ezek. 47-48	1 Pet. 2:18-3:7	Prov. 23:1-9
2-Dec	Dan. 1:1-2:23	1 Pet. 3:8-4:19	Prov. 23:10-16
3-Dec	Dan. 2:24-3:30	1 Pet. 5	Prov. 23:17-25
4-Dec	Dan. 4	2 Pet. 1	Prov. 23:26-35
5-Dec	Dan. 5	2 Pet. 2	Prov. 24:1-18
6-Dec	Dan. 6:1-7:14	2 Pet. 3	Prov. 24:19-27
7-Dec	Dan. 7:15-8:27	1 John 1:1-2:17	Prov. 24:28-34
8-Dec	Dan. 9-10	1 John 2:18-29	Prov. 25:1-12
9-Dec	Dan. 11-12	1 John 3:1-12	Prov. 25:13-17
10-Dec	Hos. 1-3	1 John 3:13-4:16	Prov. 25:18-28
11-Dec	Hos. 4-6	1 John 4:17-5:21	Prov. 26:1-16
12-Dec	Hos. 7-10	2 John	Prov. 26:17-21
13-Dec	Hos. 11-14	3 John	Prov. 26:22-27:9
14-Dec	Joel 1:1-2:17	Jude	Prov. 27:10-17
15-Dec	Joel 2:18-3:21	Rev. 1:1-2:11	Prov. 27:18-27
16-Dec	Amos 1:1-4:5	Rev. 2:12-29	Prov. 28:1-8
17-Dec	Amos 4:6-6:14	Rev. 3	Prov. 28:9-16
18-Dec	Amos 7-9	Rev. 4:1-5:5	Prov. 28:17-24
19-Dec	Obad-Jonah	Rev. 5:6-14	Prov. 28:25-28
20-Dec	Mic. 1:1-4:5	Rev. 6:1-7:8	Prov. 29:1-8
21-Dec	Mic. 4:6-7:20	Rev. 7:9-8:13	Prov. 29:9-14
22-Dec	Nah. 1-3	Rev. 9-10	Prov. 29:15-23
23-Dec	Hab. 1-3	Rev. 11	Prov. 29:24-27
24-Dec	Zeph. 1-3	Rev. 12	Prov. 30:1-6
25-Dec	Hag. 1-2	Rev. 13:1-14:13	Prov. 30:7-16
26-Dec	Zech. 1-4	Rev. 14:14-16:3	Prov. 30:17-20
27-Dec	Zech. 5-8	Rev. 16:4-21	Prov. 30:21-28
28-Dec	Zech. 9-11	Rev. 17:1-18:8	Prov. 30:29-33
29-Dec	Zech. 12-14	Rev. 18:9-24	Prov. 31:1-9
30-Dec	Mal. 1-2	Rev. 19-20	Prov. 31:10-17
31-Dec	Mal. 3-4	Rev. 21-22	Prov. 31:18-31

SCRIPTURE INDEX

OLD TESTAMENT

NEW TESTAMENT